Risking Grace

Loving Our Gay Family and Friends Like Jesus

~A Father's Story~

Dave Jackson

CASTLE
ROCK
CREATIVE

Evanston, Illinois 60202

Published in Evanston, Illinois. Castle Rock Creative.

Unless otherwise indicated, Scripture quotations are taken from The Holy Bible, New International Version®. NIV®. Copyright © 1973, 1978, 1984, 2011 by International Bible Society. Used by permission of Zondervan Publishing House. All rights reserved.

Scripture quotations marked NKJV are from the New King James Version®. Copyright © 1982 by Thomas Nelson. Used by permission. All rights reserved.

Scripture quotations marked NLT are from Holy Bible, New Living Translation. © 1996. Used by permission of Tyndale House Publishers, Inc., Wheaton, Illinois 60189. All rights reserved.

Scripture quotations marked GNB are from the Good News Bible © 1994 published by the Bible Societies/HarperCollins Publishers Ltd UK, Good News Bible© American Bible Society 1966, 1971, 1976, 1992. Used with permission.

Scripture quotations marked NET (New English Translation) are taken from the NET Bible® copyright ©1996-2016 by Biblical Studies Press, L.L.C. All rights reserved.

"Unity (Jesus Help Us Live in Peace)," Words & Music by M. Gerald Derstine (J.D. Martin), © 1971, 2003. Used by permission.

ISBN: 978-1-939445-01-8
eISBN: 978-1-939445-02-5

Cover Design: Dave Jackson
Cover photo: Li Kim Goh, iStock

Printed in the United States of America

For a complete listing of
books by Dave and Neta Jackson visit
www.daveneta.com
www.riskinggrace.com
www.trailblazerbooks.com

For our beloved
daughter and daughter-in-law

CONTENTS

Foreword

WHEN DAVE JACKSON APPROACHED ME to write the Foreword for *Risking Grace*, I was sure he had the wrong person. For sixteen years I co-hosted a talk show on the Moody Radio Network. That's certainly not the profile of someone who might be interested in having their name attached to a book like this.

I grew up in a system and culture that was, as a friend of mine says, addicted to certainty. I was a Baptist minister's daughter who went to a conservative Christian high school and a more conservative Christian college. As a woman in that culture, I was regularly asked to believe what I was told and not to question. I did that for about forty years and then my marriage fell apart. Life moved from certain to uncertain and even to unstable. As I began thinking for myself, with the help of the Holy Spirit, something significant happened. I began to see the pain and hurt in the world. I began to feel the pain and hurt in my own life. And my view of God began to expand. I went from certainty about everything to a willingness to accept that not all things are black and white. I had to learn about grace. Grace for others and even grace for myself.

A couple of years before leaving my radio gig, my co-host was hosting the program alone with the topic focused on how to build bridges to the homosexual community. Evangelicals hadn't exactly been doing a great job of that, and we wanted to move the dialog forward. I knew this program topic was risky for us, yet important. We opened the phone lines and my co-host asked, "If you are gay and listening, give us a call." All available lines lit up. I was surprised at the number of gay listeners who regularly listened and also financially supported the radio network. But what deeply troubled me was the volume of email we received from people who were incensed that we would put these homosexual callers on the air.

Our team got pretty beat up because of that program. I was deeply saddened at how Christians acted toward other Christians. Equally unsettling is how those claiming Christ act toward those outside of the faith.

I have to be honest; I haven't settled my own views on this topic. What Dave talks about in *Risking Grace* is compelling. I believe this book is important reading for all who claim to know Christ. *Risking Grace* challenged me in countless ways and I will be re-reading it.

There will always be points of disagreement among Christians. At the very least, can we extend more grace and mercy to those we disagree with? A friend gave me this thought that I've been chewing on for months: "God is great and the limits of his mercy have not been set."

Dave has been thoughtful and thorough in his approach to this complex issue. As he challenged me to think more deeply, I was forced to ask myself whether or not I was willing to "risk grace" at the expense of the "certainty of being right" so many of us are unwilling to abandon. I believe God wants us to be all about *Risking Grace!*

—Anita Lustrea, author and producer
of *Faith Connections* podcasts,
former co-host of Moody Radio's *Midday Connection*

Introduction

Why I'm writing this book

As the nurse placed the towel-wrapped bundle in my arms and said, "It's a girl!" tears streamed down my cheeks while the doctor finished caring for Neta.

Leah,[1] long awaited and already deeply loved, had finally arrived. Six years earlier, when our son was born, I had no idea what I was getting into, and when we went home and he lay squalling on the middle of our bed, I blurted, "What have we done?" But this time, we were ready and oh so eager! And a girl—how blessed we were!

I was fiercely protective of her, which kicked in big time twenty-five years later when she told us she was gay. The news triggered a tumble of emotions, but the biggest was my fear of the pain that lay before her, and I had no idea how to protect her.

Much of that pain has come from the church and the attitudes of well-meaning Christians who hoped to dissuade her from what they believed was a bad decision—like the woman who said, "I'd rather find my son at the bottom of a pool than have him tell me he's gay!"

Think about that for a minute.

If a mother could say that about her own son, how could Leah hear anything other than that this woman thought she'd be better off dead too?

Most of us cringed when we heard the late Fred Phelps and the Westboro Baptist Church chanting, "God hates fags." But I began hearing comments that were far more "polite" and "acceptable" in evangelical circles through my daughter's ears. Some were person-

---

1. The names of all individuals have been changed except for people who have expressed their views publicly by speaking, publishing, or heading organizations.

3

al jabs, others were stated as aloof, theological "truths" that could not be compromised even though they rejected and condemned gay people. I used to think "Love the sinner, and hate the sin" articulated a compassionate but accurate balance that gay people ought to welcome—"Oh, how nice. They love me." But like most gay people, Leah believes her orientation is as immutable as her skin color, so hatred of her orientation is inevitably hatred of her.

And when in a Christian bookstore I saw the title, Can You Be Gay and Christian?[2] I tried to imagine alternate questions: "Can you be a white male and Christian?" "Can you be overweight and Christian?" Or ". . . divorced and Christian?"

As devastated as we were over Leah's announcement, Neta and I began to realize how ineffective and damaging the evangelical church had become in relating to gay people—a far more serious gap than exists with any other demographic. Most troubling was a frequent distortion of the basic gospel message that we are "saved by grace through faith" alone by effectively adding a "works" requirement for gay people.

In the middle of all this, we still had the typical questions: Have gay people chosen to be gay? Could they change if they were seriously committed to the Lord? What does it mean if they don't change? Are they likely to encourage straight people—especially the young and impressionable—to become gay? Are they likely to molest children? Are they mounting a culture war against biblical truth? And one of the most haunting questions: What have I, as a parent, done to cause this?

Our journey was a lonely one, but I don't want that to be the case for you. And that is why I'm writing this book.

Where I'm coming from

Maybe we share a similar spiritual history with you. My wife and I were both raised in conservative, Bible-believing churches,

---

2. Michael L. Brown, *Can You Be Gay and Christian? Responding with Love and Truth to Questions About Homosexuality* (Lake Mary, FL: Frontline, an imprint of Charisma House, 2014). Brown says, "If you say [you are] a practicing homosexual . . . and following Jesus at the same time, I say, no. According to the scriptures, the two are mutually incompatible" (https://www.youtube.com/watch?v=-3Mtgj5R2Qk).

decided to follow Jesus at an early age, trained at Multnomah University (then called Multnomah School of the Bible), Judson University, and Wheaton College. We worked for years as editors for prominent evangelical publishers and have written more books than we care to count for most of the other major evangelical publishers.

We believe "All Scripture is given by inspiration of God, and is profitable for doctrine, for reproof, for correction, for instruction in righteousness" (2 Timothy 3:16, NKJV). But because of our family's personal journey, we realized we needed to look more closely at the subject of same-sex attraction than we previously had. We were already aware that not every Scripture supposedly dealing with the subject was as simple as we'd once thought. And we knew reexamining a long-held *interpretation* was not the same as questioning the Source anymore now than when the church reexamined the widespread interpretation that the Bible taught the earth was the center of the universe or justified slavery. We were desperate to search the Scriptures with other believers who took the Bible as seriously as we did.

For a long time, we felt alone. There seemed to be only two camps: "traditionalists" who weren't about to reconsider any interpretation and "liberals" who dismissed passages they didn't like as though God had not inspired the whole Bible. Instead, we wanted to be like the Bereans, who "were of more noble character . . . for they received the message with great eagerness and examined the Scriptures every day to see if what Paul said was true" (Acts 17:11).

I don't discount anyone's personal story. If someone reported with reasonable evidence that God changed him or her from gay to straight, I'd celebrate the miracle. We have a miracle-working God, who raises the dead. But in all my years, I have not met one "ex-gay" person whose same-sex orientation has genuinely changed. So, though I initially suggested "reparative therapy" to my daughter, I could not promise it as a panacea.

The Apostle Paul pleaded with the Lord three times to remove his "thorn in the flesh," but God said, "My grace is sufficient for you" (2 Corinthians 12:9). Many gay people have prayed longer and harder than Paul did (whatever his "thorn" may have been) only to receive a similar answer: "My grace is sufficient."

So how can we facilitate that all-sufficient grace? What does it look like?

I still have many questions, and the answers I've come to may not be final, which leaves me feeling vulnerable and also in great need of God's grace myself. It would be easier to just keep quiet, love my daughter, and avoid the public discourse . . . but the stakes are too high. As I watched what happened to her and numerous other LGBT people, I knew there was something terribly wrong with how we have applied the gospel to gay people, particularly the church's own children who gave their hearts to Jesus, grew up in the faith, learned the Word, dedicated themselves to service, and in many cases, prayed and agonized *for years* that God would change their same-sex orientation . . . only to have our churches virtually disown them when they "came out." Not all evangelical churches behave that way, but the attitudes prevail, attitudes I once helped disseminate . . . but I'll explain that later.

Language

People have a right to be known by terms they choose. And while "gay" as I use it, is not a precise term, it's generally accepted as a generic term among most of the LGBTQ[3] community. Unless otherwise noted, my use of "gay" indicates a person's orientation (i.e., same-sex attracted), not necessarily the person's sexual behavior. For instance, the fact that I am straight (opposite-sex attracted) doesn't mean I am sexually involved with or lusting after all women. So, if a friend or family member comes out and says they are gay, I don't presume they are sleeping with someone.

There are some gay people who are sex-crazed, follow the party circuit, flaunt their bodies, "hook up," pursue serial sexual partners, use drugs, or participate in orgies, and try to lure other people into the same behavior. This is what many of us thought of as the "homosexual lifestyle," and we characterized all gay people with that

---

3. The acronym LGBTQ stands for: L=lesbian, G=gay men, B=bisexual, T=transgender, Q=questioning (or sometimes queer). This book does not address bisexual or transgender issues.

stereotype. *But such behavior is just as prevalent among straight people.* Do we call that the "heterosexual lifestyle"? Would we like others to presume those are our standards? So I try to avoid the term "homosexual lifestyle." It's useless, presumptive, and often hurtful.

I struggled with what terms to use in identifying various viewpoints concerning same-sex orientation and finally settled on these three:

- **Traditional**—Believes the Bible unequivocally condemns homosexuality, both the act and the inclination. Same-sex orientation is thought to result from trauma or deprivation combined with the individual's choices. Therefore, it can be "repaired" through healing therapy that includes sincere repentance, persistent faith and discipline, and counseling.
- **Neo-traditional**—Acknowledges genuine orientation change is rare and, therefore, should not be prescribed as normative. Also acknowledges that *temptation* to sin is not in itself sin. Therefore, gay people should be welcomed and supported in the church *provided* they commit themselves to living a celibate life (avoiding physical homosexual relations). "Falls" are sin, but genuine repentance restores.
- **Inclusive**—Accepts that God made some people with same-sex orientation. Therefore, we need to accept gay people on the same basis we accept straight people. Furthermore, the church can support the fulfillment of that orientation in committed relationships when the courtship and marriage conform to the same standards of sexual faithfulness expected of straight believers. But an "inclusive" church also respects and supports gay people called to remain celibate.[4]

---

4. I wanted descriptive, nonpejorative terms. Twenty years ago most evangelicals were "traditionalists." Today, many are becoming "neo-traditionalists." Justin Lee of the Gay Christian Network uses the commendably neutral "Side A" and "Side B" terminology. (Side A people accept the possibility of same-sex marriage while Side B feels celibacy is required for gay Christians.) The common term "affirming" accurately describes approval of Side A, but I wanted to go further by using "inclusive" to describe active support for both Side A and Side B as I explain more fully in Chapter 16. According to my terminology, the Gay Christian Network is inclusive.

An invitation

Perhaps you, like I, have wondered why God gave *us* loved ones who are gay. Life would be so much simpler if they were straight. But maybe it's not about us, but about our loved ones and the multitude of gay people who have been confused and hurt by the church. Maybe God chose *us* because he knew we loved them enough to care, to listen, to change, and to risk extending his grace. Not that we are anything special, but as the Apostle James reminds us, "The cries of the [oppressed] have reached the ears of the Lord Almighty" (5:4), and he does send deliverance.

Maybe God has called you to join with others in bringing that deliverance through gentle correction to a church that's gone tragically awry.

If so, then in this book you will find a safe place to own the questions that arise as you walk alongside your gay son or daughter or friend or neighbor whom you love, a safe place to agree or disagree with various perspectives and interpretations as together we seek God's heart. Please join me and the many others who are risking grace.

Chapter 1
The Phone Call

Be near me, Lord Jesus, I ask Thee to stay
Close by me forever, and love me, I pray;
Bless all the dear children in Thy tender care,
And fit us for Heaven to live with Thee there.

"Away in a Manger"
William J. Kirkpatrick, 1895, verse 3

MY MOM DIED ON NOVEMBER 3, 2000, one day before she would have turned eighty-seven. It was also my daughter's twenty-fifth birthday. Leah thought of her grandmother as her "birthday buddy," even though their birthdays were one day apart. The last months—years, actually—had been rough as the scourge of Alzheimer's took Mom as we knew her even while her body lingered. She and Dad lived in southern California while we lived in Chicago, which meant lots of grueling trips and a perpetual sense of helplessness over how to assist them.

That may have been a lesson God was trying to teach me and my wife, Neta, in preparation for a challenge much greater and longer than my mother's decline.

It came by phone two weeks before Christmas and before we'd finished grieving Mom's passing. We took the call in the living room, Neta on one extension and I on the other, as Leah tearfully read a letter to us saying her marriage of nearly six years to Robert was ending. My male fix-it mind quickly grasped for the give-it-more-time straw, the counseling straw, and the faith-in-God's-healing straw, anything . . .

Until she added, "I . . . I can't continue in a heterosexual relationship."

Neta stammered, "What are you trying to say?"

I was more blunt. "Are you saying you're gay?"

More tears. A pause. Then . . . "Yes."

Time froze. At that moment, we would have given anything to turn back the clock, to un-hear what she'd just said. But the word rang in our ears like a gunshot.

Leah tried to soften our shock by assuring us she still considered Robert her best friend and they wanted to parent our almost five-year-old granddaughter together and had agreed to work everything out amicably. But I was hardly hearing her. I sucked air like a drowning man and sobbed with my hand over the receiver, hoping she couldn't hear. I didn't want to make this all about me because I was fearful for her, her future, her relationship with God, even her salvation if she didn't repent.

But I felt helpless, and in that sense, it became about me and what I believed regarding the spiritual implications of her decision . . . or what I thought was a decision. Certainly she had decided to end the marriage, which was painful enough, but if she had made a choice about her sexual orientation, the wrong choice, that seemed even more dangerous, a choice that would destroy everything. We loved her and didn't want that to happen, but what could we do? How could I fix it?

Once we'd hung up, I let it go, wailing without restraint, so loudly Neta couldn't stay in the room. When I finally quit weeping, she said she had to get out of the house, needed to go for a walk, even though darkness had fallen. I couldn't let her go alone, so we walked in silence through the frozen streets of a Chicago winter until we were numb, not from the cold, just numb.

Neta later described her feelings that night as "all my worst fears rolled into one broadside—the breakup of my daughter's marriage, my granddaughter growing up without her parents together, not having that model to shape her life . . . and something I never feared, something so remote, my daughter, my own precious daughter, who I thought I knew, saying she was gay."

For us both, it cut through the heart of some of our most precious foundations in life, gifts of God: commitment in marriage, the gift of family life, kids growing up with both their parents, women and men in healthy relationships with one another—"In the image of God he created them; male and female God created them" (Genesis 1:27). How would our granddaughter ever come to a balanced view of men and women, marriage, and God's plan for a happy family?

When we finally returned to the house—it no longer felt like *home*—Neta turned out the Christmas tree lights, the icicle lights on the porch, all the window candles. The Christmas cheer was gone. Why pretend? Then she turned off all the rest of the lights in the house. Indeed, it seemed all the light had gone out of our lives.

We didn't sleep that night. In fact, we couldn't even stay in bed. Instead, we sat in the dark living room, each of us alone with our private thoughts and feelings, until Neta fell to the floor and cried and cried.

The next day, our son called. Leah had told him about her situation earlier, and he helped Neta and me to begin talking to one another. Finally, we prayed and broke the ice of our pain.

* * * *

Thirteen years before the phone call from our daughter, I'd coauthored a book titled *Overcoming Homosexuality* with Ed Hurst, who claimed ten years of experience in helping people change their homosexual orientation through a ministry then associated with Exodus International. At the time, I knew next to nothing about homosexuality, but Neta and I had begun our own writing business by offering our services to Christian publishers to coauthor books with expert resource people—people who had an important message but needed the help of a writer. Working on many of those books had been like graduate courses in new subjects. This project was no exception. I became thoroughly familiar with the traditional Christian interpretations of Scripture on homosexuality and the theories popular at that time about its causes and supposed cures.

11

However, homosexuality was such a touchy subject, I made sure Neta's name appeared with mine on the cover even though I did most of the research and the initial writing. I didn't want any readers to get the wrong idea about *my* orientation.

Ed said when he became a Christian in 1974, he'd never heard of anyone overcoming homosexuality. "This disturbed me greatly," he said. "My other sins—drinking, smoking, taking drugs, lying, etc.—were all things I *did*, but homosexuality was different; it described who I was. No other facet of my life equaled homosexuality in prominence. It had been with me for as long as I could remember."[1] But at the time of writing the book, Ed claimed to have been "out of the lifestyle," as he put it, for twelve years.

I took that claim at face value insofar as he no longer frequented gay bars, pursued lovers, or identified with the gay community. But Ed still exhibited many of the stereotypic trappings in his flamboyant dress and effeminate speech and gestures (characteristics that don't in themselves make one gay). Nevertheless, he was honest enough to admit that he still had same-sex attractions. But he believed no one was born gay and wrote, "Homosexuality is a learned condition and can therefore be unlearned."[2] The causes, he thought, arose from some combination of the individual's own choices, the environment, and how the person chose to respond to his or her environment. By environment, Ed focused on the family experience and put a lot of stock in the opinions of Gerard Van Den Aardweg, Leanne Payne, and Elizabeth Moberly. Moberly, in particular, suggested the most common environmental issue was a broken relationship with a parent at a young age and the child's response to "defensive detachment."[3] Van Den Aardweg and Payne added self-pity and identity conflicts as common responses. All in all, everyone shared in the guilt.

---

1. Ed Hurst with Dave and Neta Jackson, *Overcoming Homosexuality* (Elgin, IL: David C. Cook Publishing Co., 1987), 7.
2. Ibid., 102.
3. At The Colossian Forum's "Christian Faith and Human Sexuality" colloquium in Grand Rapids, MI, on August 14, 2014, I spoke privately with Elizabeth Moberly's brother, Walter, and asked him if Elizabeth had changed her views on the origins of homosexuality over the past thirty years. He said, "I don't know that she has, but she no longer wants to have anything to do with the subject." Walter Moberly is Professor of Theology and Biblical Interpretation at Durham University.

In our case, those theories meant Neta and I must have failed to provide the kind of parenting—the love, support, protection, closeness, and moral instruction—that would protect Leah, and in response to our deficiencies, she had made choices that entangled her in homosexuality. In essence, we represented the same question the disciples put to Jesus about the blind man: "Who sinned, this man or his parents, that he was born blind?" (John 9:2). At the time, of course, we were so overwhelmed with our daughter's news that we heard nothing of Jesus' exonerating answer: "Neither this man nor his parents sinned, but this happened so that the work of God might be displayed in his life. As long as it is day, we must do the work of him who sent me."

But the day after Leah's phone call, neither Neta nor I could work. In fact, it took a long time before the work of God was displayed in our lives. We were exhausted from the stress and a night without sleep and could do no more than busy ourselves shopping for groceries and running mundane errands. I thought I was getting sick, but I didn't, and somehow the day passed.

At some point, it dawned on me that Leah must be hurting too. She'd been crying through most of the phone call as she'd read her letter to us, maybe because she knew she was causing us pain, but she had to be going through a great deal of pain and disappointment herself. And Robert must be devastated too.

We liked—loved—Robert. He'd been like the boy next door all through junior high and high school, Leah's best friend in our church's youth group. They got married at nineteen and our granddaughter was born just over a year later. But during the summer before Leah's call, we had noticed they were struggling. It had been tempting to get involved, jump in with answers even though we didn't know the questions, but they hadn't asked for our help, and now we knew we'd have only complicated things. Still, couldn't we have done something?

Maybe. I don't know. But there was one thing I could do now. I picked up the phone and called my daughter. "Leah, I want you to know that we love you . . . no matter what."

* * * *

13

The next day, Neta wrote the following in her prayer journal:

> O God, what do we do now? I don't believe it for a minute! I don't believe Leah is gay. SATAN IS A LIAR!!! He has found a vulnerable, weak, wounded part in Leah's spirit and is deceiving her.
>
> I AM ANGRY! Angry at our culture, our times, our society, even certain movements that fan sexual confusion and say, "homosexuality is really okay!"
>
> Satan, beware! I am not going to let you have my daughter without a *fight!*"

When we shared our situation with our small group from church, one of the members suggested Leah might be under a "spirit of homosexuality." Years before, our group had included two women who later came out as gay (though they were not involved with each other). At times they had cared for Leah when she was little. Nothing inappropriate ever happened, but could they have somehow "infected" her with a "spirit of homosexuality"? Whatever that meant. We were desperate.

I grasped at other straws. Maybe it was Robert's fault. Certainly if he'd been the husband he should have been, Leah couldn't have come to this conclusion. But that's not what Ed Hurst's book said or the "experts" he'd cited. The responsibility—no, the guilt—pointed closer to home.

And it piled higher and higher, but without any specific focus. For several years Neta and I had worked as the editors of Marriage and Family Products for a major Christian publisher. We edited books and articles by several of the most respected authors in the field. We knew what a good Christian marriage and family life looked like. And while we weren't perfect, we knew we had one, and there were people from our church in our home *all the time* who could attest to that fact. But . . . we must've failed somewhere. Maybe I should've read Leah more stories when she was little. Or maybe Neta should've worked harder to resolve the standoffs she and Leah got into when she was nine years old. But we'd just held the course and trusted the stage would pass, and it had. In fact, our family life was far more pleasant than a lot of families who raised whole tribes of straight kids. Leah went through normal teenage struggles, but she hadn't exhibited unusual "self-pity," "identity conflict," or "defensive detachment." But supposedly those were the roots of homosexuality Ed Hurst and other theorists had identified as negative responses to a "hurtful" environment.

Where had we gone wrong?

Chapter 2
What Went Wrong?

I know not why God's wondrous grace
To me He hath made known,
Nor why, unworthy, Christ in love
Redeemed me for His own.

But I know whom I have believed,
And am persuaded that He is able
To keep that which I've committed
Unto Him against that day.

"I Know Whom I Have Believed"
Daniel W. Whittle, 1883, verse 1, refrain

A S WE TRIED TO SEARCH for what might have gone wrong, we recalled one time when Leah was about thirteen years old. She told her mom she wondered if she was gay. At the time, we were speakers at a Baptist family camp in the Colorado Rockies, and the younger teens had had their own sessions talking about growing up and the Christian life. "Oh, honey, you don't need to worry about that," Neta reassured her. "When I was your age, I had crushes on several women in Pioneer Girls, women I admired. I sought their attention and wanted to be like them. Sorting out that stuff is a normal part of adolescent adjustment. You'll be fine."

That was the end of it, or so we thought. What we didn't realize was that as she progressed through puberty, her unbidden romantic feelings for girls terrified her. She valiantly tried to notice boys. We took comfort in the fact that she wasn't boy crazy and were happy with the low-key nature of her friendship with Robert. Up through their junior year in high school, they didn't "date" because she thought it would ruin their friendship.

And she exhibited extraordinary moral strength to resist peer pressure in other regards. For instance, on her thirteenth birthday, she had a sleepover in our basement with a bunch of her girlfriends. About one in the morning, Neta went down to check on the party, knowing the girls might not get *any* sleep if she didn't "pull the plug" at some point. To her surprise, Leah was the only person in the sleeping bags spread out on the floor.

"Where's everyone else?" Neta asked.

"Um, they went to get something to eat."

"But I just came through the kitchen, and there's no one upstairs."

Leah hesitated and looked sheepish. "They . . . they said they were going to the 7-Eleven."

What? These were thirteen-year-olds, and it was after midnight! In a panic, Neta ran upstairs and woke me. "The girls are gone!" We grilled Leah with a few more questions, and it turned out the girls had actually climbed out the basement window. But we praised Leah for having sense enough not to do such a foolish thing. By now it was 1:30 A.M. I jumped in the car and went after them. They were not at the 7-Eleven. "But I remember them," said the clerk. "They were here about twenty minutes ago." He had no idea where they'd gone.

Worried now, I cruised the streets for the next half hour without any luck. When I got home, the girls still hadn't returned. Our neighborhood wasn't particularly dangerous, but we do live in an urban area, and walking the streets was no place for young girls at that time in the morning. With no sign of our daughter's friends, we finally called the police and then each of their parents. What else could we do?

By the time the girls returned around 2:30 A.M., they found their parents and a police officer standing in our living room. Naturally upset, the parents took their daughters home. We felt badly for Leah, her birthday sleepover ruined.

As we talked to Leah later, it had not been the fear of our wrath that kept her home. Oh, she knew she'd have been in trouble if she got caught, but she also knew it was a dumb thing to do and had the guts to say no.

* * * *

During Leah's teen years, there were minor rebellions, and we put our foot down when necessary, but things seemed to be working out normally. Leah mostly hung out with her teen group. For a short time, she dated a guy five years older, and that concerned us, but it didn't last. Then in her senior year, she began going with Robert in a more serious fashion.

Twice during her teen years, Leah went on short-term mission trips to El Salvador with our church. The Gospel permeated our family and church life, and from an early age, Leah loved and followed Jesus, but our church did not push *young* children to formalize their commitment to Christ lest it be a rote response to adult pressure. But following her graduation from high school, she said she wanted to be baptized.

What greater joy could parents experience!

At her baptism in August, we wrote her this affirmation:

As you make this public declaration that, "I have decided to follow Jesus," we realize you are moving away from our spiritual care and more fully into God's care and the care of his people, the church. That's fantastic! We want to hold you with open arms and open hands.

It is also our prayer that the symbolism of baptism—of dying to yourself, of being raised to new life in Christ—will grow in meaning and blessing to you as you confront new situations and challenges in the months and years ahead.

You have accepted the gift of salvation.
You are God's beloved daughter.
You belong to him.
He will never, ever forsake you.

We love you and just want to take this occasion to tell you so.

All our love,
Mom & Dad

Though she'd been accepted at three Christian colleges, Leah wanted to take a gap year and go on a mission project to Central America. But during the extended training period for this longer mission, she developed insomnia—serious insomnia, as in not being able to sleep for many nights in a row. After a couple of weeks, she was so physically exhausted that she came home. It was a huge discouragement for her and shook her self-confidence, but she moved on and enrolled in college. Looking back later, we wondered if, underneath it all, she was struggling with her sexual orientation, but that was never mentioned, perhaps not even something she realized.

In fact, she began spending more and more time with Robert, and before she completed college, they announced their engagement to be married . . . soon. They were a little young, but they were both committed Christians, seemed mature and level-headed, planned to finish college after the wedding, and went through pre-marital counseling. It was a joyous event celebrated by our whole church—two of our own, joining their lives in holy matrimony.

A little over a year later, we welcomed the arrival of our beautiful granddaughter, Emma. And that fall, we helped them load their belongings into a truck as this little family headed off to finish their schooling at a Christian college in another state.

Neta and I visited them as often as possible, and in the summer after Leah's graduation (she graduated a year before Robert), they returned to the Chicago area to house-sit for an acquaintance. It was great to have them close and wonderful to see more of our granddaughter, but that was when we first sensed there was tension between Leah and Robert. But what could we do?

We really didn't do anything but pray for them.

In October, after they'd gone back to school so Robert could finish his senior year, Neta wrote in her prayer journal, "O God, I'm so frightened. Something is wrong with Leah and Robert—I feel it in my bones. I'm uneasy . . . ." But whatever tension she sensed was vague and undefined and seemed to blow over.

It was that November when my eight-seven-year-old mother died. With the trips out to California to see her during her last days, and then again for the funeral, our attention was not focused on Leah and Robert and little Emma. Thankfully, Leah and our son were both able to go with us out to the funeral, and the time we spent just talking together as a family about their grandmother and many other good family memories was one of great joy occasioned by my mom's passing. Leah's struggles with Robert—if they still existed—cast no cloud over our long family talks together.

But just over a month later, we got the phone call.

Less than a week after Leah's phone call, Robert and little Emma flew back to Chicago for the Christmas holidays because his parents also lived in town. Leah couldn't come until later because of her work schedule. We picked up daddy and daughter at the airport, and it caused Neta to wonder . . .

Oh, God! Does Emma know her parents are about to split up? She is so full of life and joy—and now her life is about to shatter. I know Leah and Robert will try to parent her the best they can under the circumstances, but the truth is, the best gift parents can give their child is their own secure love for one another. Oh, God, she's only four!

Over the holidays, Robert met with us to explain a little about what had happened. He avoided sharing things that were Leah's to tell, and he didn't dump on her. He simply reported that over the last year, after she'd shared her feelings with him about her orientation, they had begun counseling with the hope of saving their marriage. They talked a lot over the summer—when we had sensed the tension—and he had hoped they could work it out. But with the start of school again, they realized whatever progress they'd made in relating to one another, it hadn't changed Leah's conviction that she couldn't continue the pretense of a heterosexual relationship.

After talking with Robert, Neta and I experienced a measure of release from the pain that had gripped us like a vice. Somehow my terror was replaced by compassion for my daughter.

Maybe when Leah got here, we could talk. Maybe in sharing God's Word and what I thought I knew about homosexuality, she would reconsider.

* * * *

After Robert graduated, they both moved back to Illinois and settled in the same town so they could cooperate in parenting Emma. We were grateful for their closer proximity to us.

The near normality of our visits over the next spring and summer were cut short by the shock of the 9-11 attacks. Again, our world seemed to be falling apart, and so was everyone else's. And we felt helpless. In October my father died, just short of a year after Mom had passed. Later that month, Leah came home for a visit . . . and brought a friend with her, Jane. We, of course, wondered whether the young woman represented a "relationship" Leah was embarking on, but then, bringing friends home for dinner or visits was routine with our kids, and Leah had lots of friends.

Many visits continued during the following year (2002), including several weeklong stays with us by Emma. When we were with Leah, we occasionally discussed her "decision" with her, hoping we could convince her to change. We even suggested she explore Exodus International as an organization that could "help" her. But she said, "Dad, I read a lot of the testimonials, and I can't identify with those people. Some of them came from abusive backgrounds, some have sexual addictions, and most were into really destructive sexual lifestyles—but that's just not me."

Okay. Good point. But we also felt her stance was unbiblical, so it worried us as to what it meant spiritually for her. In response to that, she wrote the following:

> I hold only three absolutes, it seems. And for the first two, I would die standing on my convictions. First, my spirit holds the truth that I was created by and am deeply loved

by Yahweh. This I can never be shaken from since it came upon me so very young and it cannot even be successfully explained through human utterance. Second, I am sure that Jesus Christ walked among us as God's son in human form, lived by example and suffered in our place. I know this simply and only because I hold a personal faith that it is true. And third, I am aware that I may know very little of what else there is to know. I say that just because I think it's stupid not to admit it.[1]

That should have been enough for us. But at least we sensed God telling us everything we knew to say had been said already, and we should just focus on praying for her and loving her. *And don't burn any bridges.*

The following Christmas, Leah, Emma, and Jane arrived for the holidays. Jane, it turned out, had moved to the same town where Leah lived because they had, in fact, developed a serious friendship. They lived in separate apartments, but it still felt like one more nail in the coffin, and the possibility of turning back seemed more and more remote. We had no idea whether they were physically intimate and were afraid to ask. But we presumed that's what gay people did, so should we allow them to share a bedroom "under our roof" over holidays?

Graciously, they didn't even protest the separate arrangements we made for them.

And then the day came when Leah and Jane rented a three-bedroom house *together*, a more significant step in their relationship. But when we went to visit, and they showed us separate bedrooms, we again grasped at that detail like a life ring in the ocean. Maybe, just maybe . . .

For some time, we'd been fasting every Monday, praying that Leah would "change." Why weren't our prayers being answered? Gradually we became convicted that we needed to stop telling God what we wanted him to do and trust our daughter fully into

---

1. Personal letter, November 24, 2002.

his care. Our prayer changed to: "Lord, work out *your* purpose in Leah's life, whatever it might be."

As the months went by, and Leah and Jane's relationship grew—in spite of our hopes that they were "just friends"—we couldn't help liking Jane and noticing that she had a distinctly positive influence on Leah. Together they were building a mutual and orderly family, complimenting one another in ways that made them stronger, more stable, and happier. And Emma seemed to be doing surprisingly well living with her mom while spending special times with her dad who lived only a few blocks away. All of them attended the same church, a church where we knew and respected the pastors.

In April of 2004, Leah and Jane called to eagerly invite us to come see the new house they had purchased together. Again, there were three bedrooms, but this time one was for Emma, one was a guestroom, and that meant the third one was for Leah and Jane. My heart sank—not just because the place needed a lot of work, but also because buying a house together felt like one more major step that would be hard to reverse.

Still, for birthdays, holidays, and any other excuse, we kept in touch, visiting in their home and inviting them to come for a weekend or keeping Emma over an extended vacation whenever we could. We were beginning to accept that "this is our family" and Jane is part of it. We also knew that Jane's mom, especially, was extremely upset with their relationship and wouldn't let Leah or Emma come visit when Jane went home to visit her parents. Because we had come to know and even love Jane as a person as well as someone significant in Leah's life, we didn't want her to experience more rejection from us. Neta said she felt God telling her to love Jane like another daughter.

We didn't have answers for the issues being debated in society and the church, but as a family, we felt our calling was clear: just love them, keep in relationship, and don't burn any bridges. And hope for no more surprises.

And then we got the invitation.

Illinois had not yet approved same-sex marriages, but in September of 2006, Leah and Jane decided to celebrate their relationship with a wedding in a friend's backyard. Knowing our basic belief about same-sex relationships, they didn't expect us to attend, and we had no intention of going either. But gradually I began to feel we needed to be there. It was obviously an extremely important occasion for our daughter, and choosing to stay away would have conveyed far more rejection than the mere fact that we didn't agree. After all, they already knew we didn't agree. And I didn't want the only people in attendance to be those who agreed while we, as some of the closest family, stayed away. But to me, it felt like the end of any hopes that Leah would change her direction. Jane's parents didn't even attend. In fact, they had nearly cut off relating to her.

The two pastors from their own church held differing perspectives on gay relationships. One affirmed them in theory while the other did not. They had "agreed to disagree," and therefore Leah and Jane asked a different minister friend to conduct their ceremony.

Leah maintained her trust in Jesus, but I could tell their strain with church was increasing. Where would it all lead? My heart ached as I recalled scriptures like, "If anyone, then, knows the good they ought to do and doesn't do it, it is sin for them" (James 4:17). And "If we deliberately keep on sinning after we have received the knowledge of the truth, no sacrifice for sins is left" (Hebrews 10:26).

We needed God's help!

Chapter 3
Is She Safe?

Come, Thou Fount of every blessing,
Tune my heart to sing Thy grace;
Streams of mercy, never ceasing,
Call for songs of loudest praise.
Teach me some melodious sonnet,
Sung by flaming tongues above.
Praise the mount! I'm fixed upon it,
Mount of Thy redeeming love.

"Come, Thou Fount of Every Blessing"
Robert Robinson, 1758, verse 1

A S A TESTIMONY TO THEIR ENDURING FAITH and their focus on Jesus' grace, Leah and Jane had a soloist sing the above hymn at their wedding celebration, but I was unable to take any comfort in it. The dissonance in my own mind was too loud.

As mentioned previously, years earlier I'd immersed myself in the traditional theories and research necessary to help Ed Hurst write his book, *Overcoming Homosexuality*. And though I knew there was some biblical and logical weakness in the traditional perspective, I basically bought into it because it reinforced who I was and what I'd been taught all my life. All I could think about was that my daughter needed to change or she was going to destroy her life.

Additionally, my opinion was loaded with a history of disappointment and betrayal by five significant Christian leaders I'd personally known who'd destroyed their ministries by their alleged homosexual activity. One had even died of AIDS back before retroviral drugs became effective and available.

Four of these people were married, and apparently all five had engaged in broad deception and unfaithfulness and the betrayal of people who trusted them. For those reasons alone—if the accusations were true—loss of their ministries and damage to their reputations were inevitable.

A couple of these people appeared—as the facts came out—to have been pedophiles, consumed by lust for power, domination, and control, and not interested in a relationship with an adult of the same sex.[1] But at the time, I was ignorant of the clear and very important distinction between gay people and pedophiles, and so the anecdotal reports merely reinforced my homosexual stereotypes. However, in the years since, one question will not let me go: What might have been the outcome for those who were gay—*and not pedophiles*—had they been given the legitimate option of an approved and supported same-sex marriage? What might have happened to them if that had been a choice from the time they were adolescents? Might they have found peace and a productive place in society?

When Paul said, "it is better to marry than to burn with passion" (1 Corinthians 7:9), he used an apt figure of speech. Fire in a controlled environment can cook our food, heat our homes, and power our vehicles, but without a legitimate "container," it can create immense destruction. All of society benefits from the institution of marriage among straight people because it encourages responsibility and openness and love and permanence. (Imagine the chaos without it.) I rightly felt betrayed by the damage wrought by those five leaders, but some of my gay friends have reminded me that marriage equality as it's been approved in our country encour-

---

1. "Empirical research does *not* show that gay or bisexual men are any more likely than heterosexual men to molest children. This is not to argue that homosexual and bisexual men never molest children. But there is no scientific basis for asserting that they are more likely than heterosexual men to do so. . . . Many child molesters cannot be characterized as having an adult sexual orientation at all; they are fixated on children." Gregory Herek, "Facts about Homosexuality and Child Molestation," http://psychology.ucdavis.edu/faculty_sites/rainbow/html/facts_molestation.html.

ages the same kind of stability and responsibility that we value for straight people and discourages philandering and deception.

But I wasn't asking such insightful questions when we attended our daughter's wedding. Given my indoctrination while helping write *Overcoming Homosexuality*, what I experienced as betrayal by the above-mentioned leaders, and my emotional aversion to any same-sex attraction—I mean, I couldn't even imagine how anyone could be sexually attracted to someone of the same gender—I was a mess. I could barely sit through Leah and Jane's backyard wedding.

During the ceremony, a five-year-old sitting near us whispered, "Wait a minute, how can two girls get married?" Yeah, that's what I wanted to scream at the top of my lungs to all the guests. I didn't, of course, and I slipped away after the ceremony to go for a long walk and calm down before returning to face people during the reception.

When I got back, Leah and Jane were glowing, and many friends and other relatives were joyous, just as people ought to be when a couple publicly declares their love and life-long commitment to one another. But I was stumbling around, muttering greetings to friends and relatives, and wondering why God hadn't dissolved the relationship long before it got this far.

Taking pictures to record all our family events is Neta's hobby. We have dozens of albums, but neither of us took even one photo that day. I recently had a look at Leah and Jane's wedding book, which they had titled with a quote from the Song of Solomon: "I have found the one whom my soul loves." I didn't remember ever seeing it before, but the last part of the book had served as a guest register, and there was my scrawled entry: "To Leah & Jane. We Love you! Dad." In different colored ink, Neta added, "We're glad we came. Mom." Pretty stark recognition alongside all the other warm entries that wished them well and expressed joy and delight on their happy day. I don't know to what degree Leah and Jane knew of our turmoil. They had dutifully sent us an invitation to their wedding, but they hadn't really expected us to accept. Could they see the dismay on my face? If they did, they bore their disappointment graciously.

In the weeks that followed, Leah and Jane found it harder and harder to feel accepted at their church. Going to church was like donning a cloak of shame, never knowing who was friend or foe. One pastor was more accessible, the other more aloof, but among the congregation, Leah said it was like being the invisible cousin at a family meal. "Often people's interactions seemed so patronizing—you know, 'Love the sinner, hate the sin.' We sensed some people saw us as the enemy while others considered us their ministry project."

"I guess we stayed in church out of a sense of duty," Jane recalls, "as though this was just what it is like if you are gay but want to be in the church. But I got tired of not knowing who really cared about me for who I was."

Cemented by a baby's love

Leah had always been very home and family oriented—family life meant a great deal to her. She and Jane were devoted parents to Emma, but they wanted more children. A year or so later, Jane gave birth to a baby boy they named Jacob, conceived by artificial insemination from a donor. What a happy family they were. Leah adopted Jacob, and they dedicated baby Jacob to God at their church, a celebration we attended along with godparents they chose among long-term friends, promising to support these parents physically and spiritually as they raised this little boy.

There was no way around it—this was our family. There would be no disowning, no denying, no rejection. Jacob was our grandson, as much as Emma and our other grandchildren, and he quickly found his way deep into our hearts . . . as he did in the hearts of Jane's parents. We found joy in that reconciliation to Jane's family, and joy and pride far beyond mere tolerance in the kind of home life they were building—stable, peaceful, well-disciplined, and in every way the kind of family any grandparent would be proud of.

Under attack

But Jacob's dedication in front of the whole church—a public affirmation of their family and a request for other church members to support them—precipitated a major crisis. A special church meeting was called where several families threatened to leave the church if a position wasn't adopted opposing same-sex relationships. Somehow trusting that a congregational process would lead to a peaceful resolution, Leah and Jane attended the meeting and sat there as some people referred to them as "a dark cloud over the church." Then someone stood up and declared, "Satan is tricking everyone. I'll never let them into my house."

That was too much. Leah stood up to speak on her own behalf, only for the whole meeting to deteriorate until a few people were yelling her down from across the room.

The pastors did nothing to defend them, and in fact, in an attempt to bring order to the meeting, the more traditional pastor stood up and read from a church policy paper declaring that the church did not and would not allow anyone in a gay relationship to be teachers or in leadership positions.

"That was the last straw for me," Jane said. "There I was, a full-time teacher of young children in a renowned primary school in the community, and yet my own church wouldn't allow me to teach Sunday school. What did they think I was going to do?"

"There were other gay people in the church," Leah notes, "though we were the only ones out of the closet. But the example of what happened to us gave them fair warning of what was in store for them if they dared reveal themselves."

"A few days after that huge blow-up," said Jane, "we received delivery of a huge bouquet of flowers with a nice card that read, 'You are loved. Thank you for being you.' For quite a while, we thought it had come from someone in the church, which gave us additional hope we might be able to remain in the congregation. But then we discovered that it had come from a visitor who somehow happened to be in that nasty meeting. No one in the church reached out to us with any such sentiments."

In spite of the smash-down Leah and Jane had taken, it was not they but four or five of the most traditional families who chose to leave the church in the weeks that followed. In many ways, that only increased the tension they lived under, feeling blamed for all the trouble—including the loss of income to the church because of the departing givers—and seeing that all the leadership, some of whom had been very hurtful in the meeting, remained in power.

During this time, I knew very little of what was happening to Leah and Jane in their church, but we sensed they were distancing themselves from the congregation, and I couldn't help wondering: What did their situation mean for them spiritually? I needed a word from the Lord.

God speaks

God usually speaks to me through the Bible and sometimes through the words of a pastor or insights from Neta or in the lyrics of a song. Each of those usually represents the "still small voice" of the Holy Spirit that I slowly recognize to be God's word to me as I test it with brothers and sisters or other biblical passages. It was this kind of direction from God we felt had guided us to dial down our efforts to persuade Leah to "change" and just focus on loving her and praying for her. But on occasion, I had heard God speak more directly to me.

The first occurred when I walked in on an armed robbery in progress at a neighbor's home. The assailant swung around to hold a large knife just a few inches from my throat. In that moment, God spoke in a near-audible voice within my head, telling me what to do to subdue the robber, assuring me no one would be hurt. I obeyed, and the outcome was exactly as God had said.

The second time the Lord spoke to me in such a dramatic way occurred during my battle to keep from losing my sight. After five months and five surgeries, during which time the vision in my left eye deteriorated to 20/200—legally blind—God finally said to me in that same clear, near-audible voice, "The nightmare is over." And it was. From that day on, my eye ceased falling apart and began to heal. In spite of my fears, the right eye was never affected, and my vision is now corrected to 20/30 in my left eye and 20/15 in my right eye.

I'm not sure what kind of word from God I was hoping for regarding my concern for our daughter. All I knew how to do was to just keep praying, love as best I knew how, and pray more.

One day, while driving to Home Depot to pick up something for the house, I was listening to WMBI, Moody Radio. I think David Jeremiah was teaching about prayer on his "Turning

Point" program when he related an incident involving the famous nineteenth-century preacher, Charles Spurgeon. One night, a young seminarian was given the privilege of praying for Spurgeon before he preached to a huge crowd. The young man embarked on a flowery prayer so long-winded it ate into Spurgeon's speaking time. Finally, the great preacher stepped up and interrupted. "Son, just call him Father and tell him what you want!"[2]

Those words went straight to my heart. *That's right!* I thought. Just like the old gospel song, "Jesus is on the mainline. Call him up and tell him what you want!"[3]

And that's what I did! Alone in the car, I yelled at the top of my lungs, "Yes, Father, I just want to know, is my daughter safe?" Instantly, and without any musing or calculating on my part, God spoke as clearly and distinctly as any words I have ever heard . . .

"She's under the blood."

I was stunned! Could that be true? And then it struck me. Of course it's true! That's the only way *anyone* can come to Jesus! He had said, "No one comes to the Father except through me" (John 14:6). That great grace is as effective for her as it is for me! It's the only way anyone can approach God. In fact, whether a person appears righteous or not . . . whether they are *right* or not . . . we all must come under the blood. It is one of the most fundamental truths of the Gospel. And our daughter had availed herself of that grace from the hour she first believed. As John 1:12 says, "To all who received him, to those who believed in his name, he gave the right to become children of God."

I pulled to the side of the street and wept as the reality of God's grace flowed over me.

The truth of this message from God is based on God's written Word, the Bible, which is the primary test of any prophetic

---

2. While I could not document the actual event, this comment reflected a theme Spurgeon often emphasized. For instance, in his sermon, "True Prayer—True Power!" (August 12, 1860) he said, "If there is a mercy in your household that you crave, don't go in a round-about way, but be simple and direct in your pleadings with God. When you pray to him, tell him what you want. If you don't have enough money, if you are in poverty, if you are in desperate need, state the case. Don't be shy with God."

3. "Jesus Is on the Mainline," traditional, public domain.

word. And it expressed the very core of the Gospel. But receiving it did more than relieve my anxiety. I accepted God's word to me with joy, even though I didn't understand its implications for how I should regard my daughter. But those words started me on a path of reviewing the foundational principles of the Gospel—well-established among most evangelicals—and how those principles, the good news and the example of Jesus, should inform all our thinking, including how we relate to gay people.

Slowly, our prayer that had first focused on asking God to change Leah, and then, "Lord, work out your purpose in Leah's life, whatever it might be," shifted again. But this time, our prayer was, "Lord, what are you trying to teach *us*?"

PART I

THE GOSPEL FOUNDATION

Chapter 4
Grace and Truth

Neither life nor death shall ever
From the Lord His children sever;
Unto them His grace He showeth,
And their sorrows all He knoweth.

"Children of the Heavenly Father"
Karolina Sandel-Berg, 1858, verse 3

RECENTLY, I HEARD RADIO HOST CHRIS FABRY interview Glenn Stanton, author of *Loving My (LGBT) Neighbor: Being Friends in Grace and Truth*,[1] as a guest on his Moody Radio program.[2] Both Chris and Glenn affirm a neo-traditional point of view on the subject of homosexuality. That is, they don't condemn people with same-sex attractions, but they do claim it is a sin to act on it.[3] During the conversation, Glenn encouraged listeners not to make projects out of their gay acquaintances but just be their friend. Good advice. But when a caller pressed him about when to confront someone with

---

1. Glenn Stanton, *Loving My (LGBT) Neighbor: Being Friends in Grace and Truth* , (Chicago: Moody Publishers, 2014).
2. *Chris Fabry Live* (Chicago, IL: Moody Radio, October 8, 2014).
3. As explained more fully in the introduction, I use "traditional" to refer to the belief that the Bible unequivocally condemns homosexuality, both the act and the inclination, and that homosexuality can and must be overcome. "Neo-traditionalists" acknowledge genuine orientation change is rare and therefore should not be promoted as normative, but same-sex attraction must not be acted upon. "Inclusive" people accept that God made some people with same-sex orientation. Therefore, we need to accept gay people on the same basis we accept straight people, including the possibility of marriage while respecting and supporting any gay people who feel called to remain celibate.

their sin, Glenn responded tongue-in-cheek, "You mean, when do I get to tell them they're wrong?" Then he explained that it's better to let the person bring it up and for *them* to ask you why you believe what you do about homosexuality.

Chris, however, injected, "But what if they get in a car accident tomorrow and go into eternity *wrong*?"

I was startled at the implication. As sensitive and compassionate as Chris is—we greatly respect him and have been interviewed on his program before—his question sadly reflects where many of us evangelicals "slip a theological cog" on the question of homosexuality, treating it as we do no other issue.[4] Several times during the program, both men, speaking from their neo-traditionalist position, affirmed that homosexual relationships were no worse than any other sin and that all of us are *still* sinners. Glenn quoted Paul: "Christ Jesus came into the world to save sinners—of whom I am the worst" (1 Timothy 1:15), pointing out that Paul didn't say he *had been* a sinner (past tense) but that he still counted himself a sinner. Most evangelicals live in this confidence that God's grace through faith in the death of Jesus forgives us of *all* sin—known and unknown, past and present—and therefore, we don't have to constantly fear where we'll spend eternity should we die tomorrow, even if we're *wrong* about something. (And we evangelicals have been wrong about a lot of things over the years—the sin of racism, especially, comes to mind.)

That's grace! And yet we can't seem to trust that a gay Christian will enjoy that same grace. So Chris's question lingers in the back of our minds: "What if they go into eternity wrong?"

That, of course, was the very question that had caused me to cry out to God on behalf of my daughter: "Is she safe?" While God's answer—*she's under the blood*—immediately reassured me because I recognized it as the Gospel truth so obvious in the Scriptures, the experience started me on a quest to discover why and how we as

---

4. I give both men the benefit of the doubt that if challenged, they would have admitted they misspoke in implying that anyone who died with a "wrong view" concerning homosexuality was thereby in danger of damnation. Still, that's the impression our hot debates on the subject often engender in the minds of gay people and the public.

evangelicals had become confused on this matter when it comes to gay people. Even if we grudgingly concede that gay people might be saved, "but only as one escaping through the flames" (1 Corinthians 3:15), we often don't want to accept them as full brothers and sisters even though Romans 15:7 tells us to accept one another just as Christ accepted us. But why, *why* do we feel they are on the very brink of hell and about to drag the rest of us down with them?

The consistent heart of God

In the foreword to Glenn Stanton's book, *Loving My (LGBT) Neighbor*, Jim Daly, the current head of Focus on the Family, wrote, "Glenn's book . . . reminds us that there are some things on which we can't compromise—namely, the teaching of Scripture and *the historical position of the church*" (emphasis added).[5] However, those are not equal authorities. For many of us who are evangelicals, *the Bible* is our final authority and infallible rule for faith and practice. But while it is sobering to challenge the teachings of the church, as an institution, it *is* fallible. After fifteen hundred years of eroding doctrine, the Reformation was overdue, and the "historical position of the church" needed challenging. Galileo risked his life challenging the church's geo-centrism. For centuries, the church supported slavery, segregation, colonialism, the subjugation of women—all supported by proof texts from the Bible . . . the list could go on. Most of these corrections came when people recognized that the fruit of the historical position was bad fruit, revealed by new information or the evident damage wrought by the old policy. But at each juncture, there was huge resistance by those who maintained that we "can't compromise . . . the historical position of the church," which is what is going on right now concerning gay people.

Therefore, though we don't do it lightly, on occasions like this, it is right and good for those of us who really consider the Bible our authority to go back to it and ask whether the "historical position" held by the church is from God or not.

---

5. Glenn Stanton, *Loving My (LGBT) Neighbor: Being Friends in Grace and Truth*, (Chicago: Moody Publishers, 2014), 12.

As a novelist, I'm aware of how critical consistency of character is to a story. For a story to hang together, the actions of each person need to be generated by motives, and those motives must be consistent with the person's character. So the cohesiveness of the gospel story is immediately jeopardized if we say God offers salvation by faith in Jesus Christ alone to all humanity . . . except God changes the rules when it comes to gay people. They must first change something about themselves before they can be saved. If we were looking at a painting or a photograph, we'd say, "Hey, there's something wrong with this picture." But James tells us that God "does not change like shifting shadows" (James 1:17), and the writer of Hebrews reminds us, "Jesus Christ is the same yesterday and today and forever" (Hebrews 13:8). In fact, the book of Hebrews goes to great lengths to demonstrate that all the Old Testament saints were themselves saved by faith just like we New Testament believers are. This is the same point Paul makes in Romans 4.

Writing to the Colossian church, Paul says, "For God was pleased to have all his fullness dwell in [Christ]" (Colossians 1:19) and, "For in Christ all the fullness of the Deity lives in bodily form" (2:9). Whatever we want to know about God, about his character, about how we may approach him, we can discover most clearly in Jesus Christ, who is Emmanuel, "God with us." And John introduces Jesus by saying he came "full of grace and truth" (John 1:17).[6] So God, too, must be full of grace and truth. That's the heart of God.

Grace and truth

When evangelicals get into a discussion about homosexuality, the term "grace and truth" pops up regularly, often presuming "truth" is synonymous with the *Law*. "Yes, there's grace, but first we've got to make sure gay people see the truth and admit they're wrong because they're going against the Law," just as it played out on Chris Fabry's radio program.

But that's not the good news John announced at the beginning of his gospel. Look at the phrase in context: "The *law* was given

---

6. There may be a reason why the Bible always mentions grace first. See also Colossians 1:6 and 2 John 1:3.

through Moses, but *grace and truth* came through Jesus Christ" (John 1:17, NKJV, emphasis added). The contrast was between the Law on one hand and the grace-and-truth-of-Jesus on the other, not grace *versus* truth (Law).

The Greek word, *alētheia*, translated here as "truth," is clearly distinct from the Greek word here for "law," *nomos*, so there's no semantic confusion. The truth associated with Jesus is definitely not the Law of Moses. Later when Jesus said, "I am the way, the truth, and the life" (John 14:6), he did not mean, "I am the way, the *Law*, and the life." But too often we've thought of the grace and truth of Jesus as some kind of a proposition: *If* we keep the Law, then we can get some grace. Instead, John presents "grace and truth" as the *unified* attributes of Jesus, which themselves are in contrast to the Law as it had been calcified and distorted by the Pharisees.

So if the "truth" as used in John 1:17 is not synonymous with the Law, what is the truth that so dramatically distinguishes Jesus? Jesus explained it himself in John 8:31-59 where he was disputing with the Jews who could not accept that he really was from God and therefore should be believed. In the end—almost in exasperation—Jesus blatantly revealed the mystery: "Very truly I tell you . . . before Abraham was born, *I am!*" (v. 58, emphasis added). The crowd went berserk because they knew what he was saying. The name, "I am," is how God identified himself to Moses in Exodus 3:14, so Jesus was claiming to be God. "At this, they picked up stones to stone him, but Jesus hid himself, slipping away from the temple grounds" (v. 59).

That fact is the most profound truth in the New Testament: Jesus is God incarnate! And that gives him the authority to dispense grace. That is why earlier in this dispute with the Jews, Jesus said, "If you hold to my teaching, you are really my disciples. Then you will know the truth, and the truth will set you free. . . . So if the Son sets you free, you will be free indeed" (vv. 32, 36). But we miss the profundity of John's announcement at the beginning of his gospel—that "grace and truth came through Jesus Christ"—when we reduce grace and truth to some kind of a good-cop-bad-cop balancing act between grace and Law. In fact, if we don't believe this amazing truth—that Jesus is God—we can't experience his grace because they both define who he is.

John's introduction continues, "No one has ever seen God, but God the One and Only [begotten], who is at the Father's side, has made him known" (John 1:18). Theologian N.T. Wright says it this strongly: "This is the theme of John's gospel: If you want to know who the true God is, look long and hard at Jesus."[7]

Was John suggesting that the Law as given by Moses didn't represent God and needed abolishing? Not at all! The grace manifested in Jesus had always been present in the Old Testament. Indeed, God's mercy, his kindness, and his faithfulness are lauded throughout the Scriptures. However, we can see through the life and ministry of Jesus that he felt the Law had been misinterpreted and misapplied *without grace* by the Pharisees, and therefore, Jesus was all about getting things straightened out by fulfilling its proper function.

According to Rabbi Moshe ben Maimon (Rambam), one of the greatest medieval Jewish scholars, the Torah (our Old Testament) contains 613 commandments.[8] In Matthew 5:17-19, Jesus commented on these commands:

> Do not think that I have come to abolish the Law or the Prophets; I have not come to abolish them but to fulfill them. I tell you the truth, until heaven and earth disappear, not the smallest letter, not the least stroke of a pen, will by any means disappear from the Law until everything is accomplished. Anyone who breaks one of the least of these commandments and teaches others to do the same will be called least in the kingdom of heaven, but whoever practices and teaches these commands will be called great in the kingdom of heaven.

Was Jesus reinforcing strict adherence just like the Pharisees demanded? Definitely not. If we try to follow the Pharisees' graceless way, Jesus offered this scathing irony: "I tell you that unless your

7. N.T. Wright, *JOHN, N.T. Wright for Everyone Bible Study Guides*, (Downers Grove, IL: IVP Connect, 2009) 13.

8. http://www.jewfaq.org/613.htm.

righteousness surpasses that of the Pharisees and the teachers of the law, you will certainly not enter the kingdom of heaven" (v. 20). Instead, Jesus promised to "fulfill" the Law until every detail was "accomplished," thereby pointing to *how the Law is applied* . . . with the grace he epitomized. Every single command needs to be applied with that same grace. As Paul later explains, "Whoever loves others has fulfilled the law. . . . Therefore love is the fulfillment of the law" (Romans 13:8, 10). Otherwise we—like the Pharisees—are guilty of breaking the commands by distorting their purpose and teaching others to do the same.

Biblical scholars then and now

We usually consider "Pharisee" a pejorative term because of how sternly Jesus rebuked them, but they were the most highly respected biblical scholars of their day. Paul appealed to his training under the great Gamaliel in Acts 22:3 and his status as a Pharisee in Acts 23:6. When deciphering what the law said on an issue, no one (other than Jesus) was better equipped to *get it right*. Unfortunately, Jesus had several serious grievances against the Pharisees, among which were the following:

- Concerning *getting it right*, Jesus said, "You diligently study the Scriptures because you think that by them you possess eternal life. These are the Scriptures that testify about me, yet you refuse to come to me to have life" (John 5:39-40).
- Jesus faulted them for the pride they took in *getting it right*. "The Pharisee stood up and prayed about himself: 'God, I thank you that I am not like other men—robbers, evildoers, adulterers—or even like this tax collector. I fast twice a week and give a tenth of all I get'" (Luke 18:11-12). According to Jesus, the Pharisee was *not* justified no matter how right he was (v. 14). Seeking God's justice is other-focused, while the Pharisees were individualistically driven to make sure they were right, and "to hell" with all those sinners.
- Their demands to *get it right* lacked compassion or help for those who would bear the burden most directly. "And you experts in the law, woe to you, because you load people

down with burdens they can hardly carry, and you your-selves will not lift one finger to help them" (Luke 11:46).

Biblical scholarship has its place as long as it (1) doesn't substi-tute *getting it right* for a relationship with Jesus, (2) isn't employed to prove how righteous the scholars and their followers are, and (3) offers real grace and truth—good news!—to the people it im-pacts most. Unfortunately, some of our most scholarly evangelical works on the subject of homosexuality read as though the writers never left their academic towers to share daily life with gay people on the street or in their neighborhood or in their homes. How dif-ferent this is from the way Jesus taught. He was constantly *with* the people. When he was not commenting on a practical situation right in front of him, he told a parable so that everything he said had a real-world application. As Jesus pointed out, "Wisdom is shown to be right by the lives of those who follow it" (Luke 7:35, NLT), not by increasingly unassailable arguments.

But the scholarly approach is seductive. When a hot topic comes up, *getting it right* according to what the scholars say, also makes us look right. An example can be seen in the ninety-page position paper of scholarly arguments one evangelical denomination gath-ered and titled, "Pastoring LGBT Persons."[9] Less than 10 percent of the document has anything to do with pastoring, and even that isn't about how to love gay people. It's about what boundaries should be placed on them within the church, what they can and cannot do. All the rest of this heavily documented paper (283 foot-notes, 137 bibliographic sources) is devoted to biblical, historical, or clinical scholarship "proving" gay sex is always sinful.

Columnist and commentator David Brooks got it right: "Hu-mility is the awareness that there's a lot you don't know and that a lot of what you think you know is distorted or wrong."[10]

---

9. "Pastoring LGBT Persons," (Stafford, TX: Vineyard USA, 2014), http://vineyardusa.org/site/files/PositionPaper-VineyardUSA-Pastor-ing_LGBT_Persons.pdf.
10. David Brooks, *The Road to Character*, (New York: Random House, 2015), 8, 9.

Requiring from others what we don't even understand

Hypocrisy was another of Jesus' major complaints against the Pharisees. (See Matthew 23.) Objecting to marriage equality is not necessarily hypocritical, but hypocrisy is usually understood to demand a standard of someone else that you don't meet yourself. So it's understandable why many gay people *feel* that it's hypocritical for straight people, who are free to marry, to tell them they cannot marry. That's why I respect Wesley Hill[11] and Christopher Yuan[12], two gay Christians who are themselves celibate and believe the Bible requires that of all gay Christians. But for straight people to convey the same message, we should at the very least personally know the people to whom we deliver it and genuinely empathize with the life-long burden it will place on them. In this regard, Glenn Stanton is one neo-traditional writer who seems to do this well. Even though he is straight, he apparently has many gay friends and claims to respect them.[13]

Beware the "yeast" of the Pharisees

Matthew 16:5-12 records an incident when the disciples forgot to bring bread on one of their outings. Knowing how upset they were over not getting it right, Jesus warned, "Be on your guard against the yeast of the Pharisees and Sadducees." Perhaps the disciples thought he was also scolding them for forgetting the bread. Instead, he was telling them to relax, reminding them of his generous provision of food for the five thousand and the four thousand. Then he said, "'How is it you don't understand that I was not talking to you about bread? But be on your guard against the yeast of the Pharisees and Sadducees.' Then they understood that he was not telling them to guard against the yeast used in bread, but against the teaching of the Pharisees and Sadducees."[14]

---

11. Wesley Hill is the author of *Washed and Waiting: Reflections on Christian Faithfulness and Homosexuality*, (Grand Rapids, MI: Zondervan, 2010).

12. Christopher Yuan is the author of *Out of a Far Country*, (Colorado Springs, CO: WaterBrook Press, 2014).

13. Glenn Stanton, *Loving My (LGBT) Neighbor: Being Friends in Grace and Truth*, (Chicago: Moody Publishers, 2014).

14. If Luke 12:1 refers to the same incident, Luke adds the additional quality of "hypocrisy."

The Pharisaic approach is as insidious as yeast, cropping up and spreading through everything. A rule for this, a rule for that. It's human nature to see our acceptability before God and before one another in terms of doing it right, even for a mistake as small as the disciples' lack of preparation for their trip. Once rule-keeping takes hold, it spreads. As if those 613 rules of the Old Testament weren't enough, we create more for each age and culture: Don't drink, don't dance, don't say certain words, etc. Isn't this exactly what Paul warned against?

> Why, as though you still belonged to [this world], do you submit to its rules: "Do not handle! Do not taste! Do not touch!"? These are all destined to perish with use, because they are based on human commands and teachings. Such regulations indeed have an appearance of wisdom, with their self-imposed worship, their false humility and their harsh treatment of the body, but they lack any value in restraining sensual indulgence (Colossians 2:20-23).

What the disciples were worried about didn't matter. It's our relationship with Jesus that matters. When they arrived at Caesarea Philippi, Jesus redirected their conversation to a relationship with him by asking, "Who do people say I am?" When Peter said, "You are the Christ, the Son of the living God" (Matthew 16:16), Jesus commended him because Peter realized that *who* he was relating to was far more important than the theological speculations of others.

John tells us, "God did not send his Son into the world to condemn the world, but to save the world through him" (John 3:17). Jesus knew his mission for this age—and our mission as well—was not judgment but the deliverance of the grace that has always been in the heart of God. Philip Yancey sums up the whole theme of the Bible as, "God gets his family back."[15] Certainly that describes Jesus' objective during his ministry.

But the Pharisees had no sympathy for Jesus' approach. They were concerned about maintaining power by excluding the mar-

---

15. Philip Yancey, *Vanishing Grace: What Ever Happened to the Good News?* (Grand Rapids, MI: Zondervan, 2014) 49-52.

ginalized, controlling the people, and—as Jesus put it—loading "people down with burdens they can hardly carry" (Luke 11:46). And so they found all kinds of ways to accuse Jesus of breaking the rules . . . as they interpreted them.[16] The commandments as the Pharisees tried to enforce them were so radically different from Jesus' teachings that he could say, "A new command I give you: Love one another" (John 13:34). Actually, the Old Testament does call us to love one another,[17] but the Pharisees had so distorted the law given by Moses that Jesus' command qualified as new and became a major, revolutionary theme throughout the New Testament.

The result was that under the leadership of the biblical scholars of the day (the Pharisees) and the preachers (the teachers of the law), God's grace had been set aside, and God was losing his family.

(Following this and subsequent chapters that deal more with ideas than personal narrative, I include "Collateral Damage" stories to remind us that all our interpretations impact real people.)

Collateral Damage

Justin Lee[18] grew up in a loving Southern Baptist home. His nickname in high school was "God Boy" because he was the kid with a Bible in his backpack, ready to witness to anyone who would listen . . . and some who wouldn't. He was also ready

---

16. Some of the "violations" the Pharisees accused Jesus of included: allowing his disciples to pick and eat grain from a field on the Sabbath (Luke 6:1), healing on the Sabbath (John 5:1-18), being contaminated by touching a leper (Matthew 8:3), being touched by a woman with an issue of blood (Mark 5:25-33), associating with Samaritans who were despised by the Jews (John 4:1-26). And yet in John 15:10, Jesus claimed that he had "obeyed my Father's commands."

17. Leviticus 19:18 says, "Love your neighbor as yourself."

18. His real name.

to comment on Christian issues, including homosexuality. He believed in "loving the sinner and hating the sin."

In his sophomore year, someone put up a poster in the school hallway that said, "It has come to our attention that there are fags and dykes in this school," followed by some suggested violent acts to rid the school of such undesirables. The administration tore down the poster, but half a dozen students created a flier they distributed the next day saying they believed there was nothing wrong with being gay. They were promptly suspended, which ignited a great controversy in the school and community.

Some of Justin's friends asked "God Boy" what he thought about the whole thing. He denounced the hate speech of the poster, but he affirmed his conviction that homosexuality was a sin. As far as he knew, he'd never met a gay person . . . but he did have a secret that he couldn't tell his friends.

When he'd first hit puberty and all his male friends began "noticing" girls, Justin started to find guys attractive—not just curious about who was developing how fast, but "attractive." It terrified him, but he hoped it was just some phase that would pass, so he tried to ignore it and focus on his schoolwork, his faith, and all the things he should do as a Christian. As he got older, those feelings increased. During his waking hours, he resisted thinking about sex at all, but at night he would have dreams about guys, and he had no way to control them. Embarrassment and self-loathing plagued him. What was wrong? What could change him?

He got to the point where he was crying himself to sleep every night praying, "Please, God, don't let me feel this way anymore!" Nevertheless, during this time, he considered himself straight and tried dating girls. But his anguish continued, and he didn't tell anyone about his deep, dark secret. He just kept hoping and praying that he would grow out of it.

At age eighteen, he began to acknowledge to himself that he must be gay. "I sat up late at night, after everyone else had gone to bed," he later wrote, "trying to come to grips with what this word meant for my life. In my softest whisper, paranoid about being overheard by anyone, I tried to muster up enough courage to say to myself those two words: 'I'm gay.'"[19] It took a while, but as horrifying as it was, there was a sense of relief in admitting what he'd been struggling with so hard. Now all he had to do was fix it. So he got involved with "ex-gay" ministries that offered to help people become straight.

Unfortunately, that didn't work for Justin . . . nor did it work for anyone he met in those ministries. He even met many of the national leaders of the movement, people whose public testimony was that they'd left homosexuality. Some had gotten married to the opposite sex and even had children. But when Justin talked to them privately, they confessed that they remained attracted to the same sex and were not attracted to people of the opposite sex in the way straight people are. They continued to struggle with their gay feelings just like Justin did. Some of the marriages were in turmoil. They just didn't admit it publicly.

When Justin asked why they weren't open about their struggles, the answer was, "People in the church don't understand what we go through. If they knew the truth, they would never accept us."

In frustration, Justin determined that if this were a temptation he would have to face every day for the rest of his life, he would do that, but he wasn't going to lie about it. He wasn't going to pretend he'd overcome it. But what was God asking of him? Was he asking him to fight this every day as a temptation and live a celibate life? If so, he would obey. But was it possible he had misinterpreted the Bible? Was there room for him to someday fall in love with someone of the same sex and get married? What was God asking him to do?

So far his struggle with owning his sexual orientation had just been between himself and God. But when he turned to his Christian friends, his family, pastors and folks he respected in the church, the response he got was largely ostracism. Those who cared more personally for him often said, "Well, just don't be gay. Don't be gay!"

Really? Just "don't be gay"?

---

19. Lee, Justin. *TORN: Rescuing the Gospel from the Gays-vs.-Christians Debate* (New York: Jericho Books, 2012) 33.

When Justin began writing about his situation and questions online, he started hearing from dozens and then hundreds and finally thousands of gay Christians in the same situation—men and women who had committed their lives to following Jesus but found no supportive faith community because of their sexual orientation. That finally led him to organize the Gay Christian Network, which supports thousands of gay Christians whether they are, as Justin calls them, "Side A" who accept the possibility of covenanted same-sex marriage) or "Side B" who feel called to celibacy. Though he believes God allows gay people the same privileges of marriage as straight people, Justin has not yet found "the right person" and is living a chaste life until marriage, which to me says a lot about his integrity.

One day my wife, Neta, feeling the tension between hearing God calling us to simply love and accept our family "as is" versus the constant barrage of preaching against the "homosexual agenda" and negative attitudes about gays among fellow Christians, wrote in her prayer journal: "I feel so torn! . . . And then God gave me TORN." She'd seen a review of Justin Lee's book, TORN: Rescuing the Gospel from the Gays-vs.-Christians Debate, which turned out to be one of the most helpful books on our journey because of its reconciling nature and rock solid biblical faith in the gospel of Jesus.

Chapter 5
How God Gets His Family Back

No condemnation now I dread;
Jesus, and all in Him, is mine;
Alive in Him, my living Head,
And clothed in righteousness divine,
Bold I approach th' eternal throne,
And claim the crown, through Christ my own.
Amazing love! How can it be,
That Thou, my God, shouldst die for me?

"And Can It Be?"
Charles Wesley, 1738, verse 6

HOW MIGHT MY DAUGHTER HAVE EXPERIENCED JESUS had she met him during his earthly ministry? Even if he hadn't approved of her gay marriage, how might he have responded? Would she have encountered his wrath? Would he have told her she wasn't welcome to follow him unless she changed? Or would it have been like the woman caught in adultery (John 8:1-11)? Jesus actively *defended* her from those who condemned her. Furthermore, he told her *he* didn't condemn her. How huge is that?

At this point, traditionalists quickly point out that he added one caveat: "Go and sin no more." But he did not say that publicly. None of those eager to condemn the woman were around to hear it. It was a private message, delivered in what might be called that "still small voice" at a time and *in a way* she could receive. If there is sin in someone's life, didn't Jesus say it is the Holy Spirit who brings conviction (John 16:8) and guides the person into all truth (v. 13)? What makes us think that is our responsibility? How different that approach is from shouting gay people's condemnation from the rooftops (or over the airwaves) as practiced by so many who seem more eager to demonstrate why their side is right than to win people to Jesus.

But what about repentance?

Aren't the Gospels full of calls to repentance by John the Baptist, Jesus, and in the writings of the apostles? Yes, but usually they're worded: "Repent, for the kingdom of heaven is near," or "Repent and believe the gospel," or "Repent and be baptized." There are a few instances where the call to repent was over a *specific* sin, such as Simon the Sorcerer's attempt to buy the power of the Holy Spirit (Acts 8:22). However, typically the call involved a much larger recognition that "all our righteous acts [all our efforts to *get it right*] are like filthy rags" (Isaiah 64:6), and therefore we need a Savior, who "is Christ the Lord" (Luke 2:11).

Do gay people need to repent like this? Yes. Do straight people need to repent? Yes, in exactly the same way. This kind of repentance is not the process of identifying specific sins in my life for which I'm sorry, but the more profound recognition that my *righteousness* won't buy me entrance into God's holy presence. That's the turnaround—the change of heart and mind—involved in true repentance. It is the grace and truth of Jesus that makes it possible, and this is how Jesus fulfilled the law. Conversely, it's a perversion of the Gospel to point at a person's particular behavior and say, "Because you do that [and I don't] or are that [and I'm not], you're going to hell."

In *Loving My (LGBT) Neighbor*, Glenn Stanton says, "It is disobedience that sends us to hell. . . . The difference between those going to heaven and those who are not is that some have recognized their disobedience, desired to change it, and then trusted in the only thing that can take our sin away, the grace and sacrificial death of God's Son, Jesus Christ."[1] Stanton went on to explain that while ho-

---

1. Glenn Stanton, *Loving My (LGBT) Neighbor: Being Friends in Grace and Truth,* (Chicago: Moody Publishers, 2014), 65.

mosexuality itself is not a sin, he believes acting on it is disobedience. Would that "disobedience," particularly if the person doesn't repent because he or she doesn't believe it's wrong, send them to hell? We might ask it this way: Is Martin Luther, the great reformer who reminded the church of the centrality of justification by faith, now in hell because he also argued that the Jews' synagogues and schools should be set on fire, their prayer books destroyed, rabbis forbidden to preach, homes burned, and property and money confiscated?[2] What if someone's lifestyle is sinfully greedy, but they don't see anything wrong with it . . . will they go to hell if they don't repent? I have no idea whether Glenn would say Luther's hateful attitudes would send him to hell or whether defenders of greed cannot be Christian, but in a more recent interview, Stanton made it clear: "I don't think you can be gay and a Christian" if the person says, "I support same-sex [marriage]," a position Glenn considers is "[dis]obedient to the sexual ethic that Christ gave us."[3]

After acknowledging he was gay, Justin Lee, the author of *TORN*, said, "If God was calling me to celibacy, I would be celibate, but I needed to be sure. To settle the issue once and for all in my own mind, I had to ignore the half-baked ideas on both sides and go straight to the source—not just a quick perusal of what the Bible had to say, but an honest, prayerful, in-depth study."[4] After reading his whole story and meeting him personally, I believe him. If the Lord required it, he would remain celibate for life, no matter how challenging. However, in the end, Justin concluded God endorses life-long, monogamous marriages and sexual purity before

---

2. Martin Luther, *On the Jews and Their Lies*, 1543. Pastor Wilhelm Rehm from Reutlingen declared publicly that "Hitler would not have been possible without Martin Luther" (Heinonen, Anpassung und Identität 1933-1945 Göttingen 1978, 150). In fact, Hitler himself said, "I do insist on the certainty that . . . Luther, if he could be with us, would give us his blessing" ("Hitler's Speeches," edited by Professor N. H. Baynes (Oxford, 1942), 369).

3. Warren Cole Smith, "Glenn Stanton on loving your LGBT neighbor," World News Group, Nov. 17, 2015. http://www.worldmag.com/2015/11/glenn_stanton_on_loving_your_lgbt_neighbor/page 1. I should point out that Glenn made it clear that he does not believe anyone is condemned for merely having same-sex attractions, only if they believe it is okay to act on them even in a gay marriage.

4. Lee, Justin. *TORN: Rescuing the Gospel from the Gays-vs.-Christians Debate* (New York: Jericho Books, 2012), 169.

marriage—for both straight people and gays. Because he is single, he is not sexually active, but if he were to find the right life-partner and marry him, would he go to hell?

I recall an incident in my childhood church in northern California that provides a prime example of the difference between Glenn Stanton's and Justin Lee's approaches. Someone said Mr. Harper—who'd been nominated to become a deacon—couldn't possibly be a Christian because he smoked. And smoking, as our pastor taught, was a sin because it harmed the body, and our bodies were the temple of the Holy Spirit, deserving reverence and care. Bible verses were offered in support of this position, and of course, subsequent decades have proved the medical wisdom of that view. But at the time, it was mostly a religious position, which Mr. Harper rejected and "disobeyed" because he'd grown up as a Southern Baptist in the south where many sincere Christians made their living raising tobacco, so he had no personal conviction against smoking. I cannot recall whether his "disobedience" sent him to an early grave, but I seriously doubt it sent him to hell. That's just not the Gospel Jesus taught, but that is the way so many are framing the issue of marriage equality today: Disobey their interpretation of the Scriptures, and you are disobeying God, which is sin, and if unrepented, permanently separates us from God.

Consider the example Jesus offered of the Pharisee and publican (tax collector) who went to the temple to pray (Luke 18:9-14). The Pharisee listed the *specific* sins he avoided as well as the holy acts he performed. He did not think he needed God's mercy, so God essentially dismissed him. The publican, on the other hand, approached God in an attitude of repentance, not for the time he cheated someone or broke the Sabbath or any other specific sin, significant as they might have been. He simply approached God with a profound sense of needing God's mercy because of being a sinner, characterized by having lived his life apart from God. Because of that *attitude* of repentance—not merely tweaking a couple of faults—he "went home justified before God."

Gay Christians would affirm that they are sinners in need of salvation just like you and me. But they are not sinners because they are different than you and me.

Relationship is paramount

In his book, *A Praying Life*, Paul E. Miller reminds us of the Canaanite woman who hounded Jesus to heal her daughter from demon possession (Matthew 15:21-28). At first Jesus seemed to ignore her, and then he put her off with, "I was sent only to the lost sheep of Israel." When the woman knelt before him and persisted, he replied, "It is not right to take the children's bread and toss it to their dogs." But she would not give up. "Yes, Lord," she said, "but even the dogs eat the crumbs that fall from their masters' table." Then Jesus answered, "Woman, you have great faith! Your request is granted."

Jesus' apparent standoffishness on this occasion always embarrassed me. Why would he treat her that way? But Miller offers an important insight:

> If Jesus were a magic prayer machine he'd have healed this woman's daughter instantly. . . . [But] if the miracle comes too quickly, there is no room for discovery, for relationship. With both this woman and us, Jesus is engaged in a divine romance, wooing us to himself. The waiting that is the essence of faith provides the context for relationship.[5]

As I mentioned previously, I too had to learn this lesson in 2005 when I underwent five surgeries in an attempt to save the vision in my left eye while I pled with God for months to heal me. God cared about my eye and my anguish, but I finally learned he was far more interested in renewing and deepening my relationship with him. I came to value his presence far more than my eyesight, and now, in retrospect, I would never have forgone that painful experience if I'd been left with my old, much shallower relationship with God.[6]

---

5. Paul E. Miller, *A Praying Life*, (Colorado Springs, CO: NavPress, 2009), 190-91.

6. For the full story of this experience, especially the spiritual lessons God was teaching me, go to: "'I was blind, but now I see . . .' Reflections on losing my sight," Dave Jackson, August 2005, http://www.daveneta.com/support-pages/dave-eye.html.

From the day he created Adam and Eve, God has been more concerned about his relationship with us than anything else—and that includes our being right, which I think is often surprisingly low on his list of priorities because, like the Pharisee praying in the temple, being right is such a pride stimulant.

What about deliberate sin?

Some evangelicals say grace is canceled if someone sins deliberately and tries to justify it. Certainly deliberate sin and attempting to justify it is a grave matter, but most gay Christians who affirm marriage equality aren't deliberately living in or justifying sin of which the Holy Spirit has convicted *them*. They simply believe covenant marriage for people born with same-sex orientation is accepted by God in the same way it is for people born with a heterosexual orientation. But suppose they *are* wrong. Suppose, as Paul says in 1 Timothy 1:13, they are acting "in ignorance"? Perhaps that's why Paul added in verse 16, "I was shown mercy so that in me, the worst of sinners, Christ Jesus might display his unlimited patience as an example for those who would believe on him and receive eternal life."

Patience! Can't we extend Jesus' patience, confident that the Holy Spirit will convict a gay person *if and when* he chooses? If my daughter had done what I thought she should do ("fix this problem" through reparative therapy), she would have been responding only to my conviction, not to the Lord, who had a different agenda for her. Other people's opinions of what is right and wrong—whether correct or not—is very different from being convicted yourself. James concludes a passage in which he pleads for us to submit *ourselves* to God while warning against judging other people when he said, "To him who knows to do good and does not do it, to *him* it is sin" (James 4:17, NKJV, emphasis added).

I am old enough ("in the Lord" and otherwise) to realize I've had to change my mind and behavior on several matters over the years, things I once believed were right or wrong but had to repent of later. Having had this happen in the past, I will undoubtedly die with imperfect, sinful attitudes or actions or while still defending my own pet "wrong views," perhaps even on the subject of this book. But I still depend on God's grace. So why would we deny that same grace to gay Christians? Why should we presume their salvation would be canceled if their views are wrong?

The center of our faith

You may have noticed I've introduced each chapter of this book with verses from classic hymns, primarily emphasizing God's "marvelous, infinite, matchless grace, freely bestowed to all who believe."[7] These hymns declare, in poetic variation, that the requirement for salvation is not good works, not the avoidance of sin, or even right beliefs about various behaviors. The "right to become children of God" is simply available—in the words of John 1:12—"To all who received him, to those who believed in his name." We know this to be true. We base our own lives on it. We have taught it in a remarkably generous way because it rightly represents the Gospel of Jesus Christ.

And yet, having written extensively on people of faith who lived throughout Christian history, I can attest to how easily disputes arose in which one group denied the brotherhood of others over various issues—Methodists, Presbyterians, Baptists, Congregationalists, Anabaptists, Lutherans, Catholics. "They can't possibly be true believers if they believe *that!*" And none of the issues even touched on such core beliefs as are represented in the Apostles' Creed.

Nevertheless, salvation by faith alone isn't a new teaching or a modern, watered down interpretation. I am not proposing some aberrant doctrine. That's why I selected hymns, each over one hundred years old, to introduce each chapter. Hymns beloved and affirmed for ages because they reflect the church's consensus around the theme, "[Our] hope is built on nothing less than Jesus' blood and righteousness."[8]

I do not mean to imply that the old hymns have nothing to say about sin, discipleship, and total surrender. Those and many other themes are richly prevalent, but it all begins with, "Just as

---

7. "Grace Greater Than Our Sin," Julia H. Johnston, 1911, verse 4.
8. "The Solid Rock," Edward Mote, 1834, verse 1.

I am, without one plea, / But that Thy Blood was shed for me, / And that thou bidst me come to Thee, / O Lamb of God, I come. I come."[9]

And yet, when it comes to gay people, we slip a cog and can't quite affirm that their hope and peace requires "Nothing but the blood of Jesus."[10] We want to add a little something more, but something that for them is huge, like working on becoming "ex-gay" or at the very least, committing to a lifetime of celibacy and agreeing that marriage equality is sinful.

Let's get it biblically straight and be clear as we consider many of the other hard questions in the remainder of this book and as we relate to our gay family and friends: No one is *saved* by changing their sexual orientation, living celibate, or renouncing marriage equality as wrong. Likewise, no one is lost for owning his or her same-sex attraction, choosing to enter a gay marriage, or even advocating its legitimacy. "For it is by grace you have been saved, through faith—and this not from yourselves, it is the gift of God—not by works, so that no one can boast" (Ephesians 2:8-9).

Collateral Damage

When I learned a college classmate from my years at Multnomah School of the Bible—fifty years ago—was gay and had nearly lost his faith, I tracked him down by email just to let him know I cared. Kenneth had been a top scholar, prominent in student government, a superb musician who planned to serve on the mission field after further study. For years before, and throughout Bible school, he'd successfully hidden his gay orientation. Now, by merely reaching out to him without condemnation, he responded,

---

9. "Just As I Am," Charlotte Elliot, 1835, verses 1, 5.
10. "Nothing But the Blood of Jesus," Robert Lowry, 1876, verse 4.

"What a wonderful surprise! I cried with joy! I'm so happy to hear from you, especially in this vein," and he shared some of his story.

When Kenneth transferred to Wheaton College, he almost committed suicide from the debilitating fear of being "found out." Finally, he talked to his psych professor, who referred him to counseling but was honest enough to tell him, "The prognosis of change is not good." Nevertheless, my friend was highly motivated to get a miracle if need be. He wanted to live as normal a life as possible—get married, have children and a wife's companionship. But as the counseling proceeded and no change ensued, he slowly came to terms with his orientation . . . without abandoning his dreams of family life. There were, after all, reports of gay/straight marriages sometimes working.

After confessing his orientation to his best female friend in college, they agreed to get married. They had a family while he pursued a PhD at Yale Divinity School, but the marriage ultimately failed, and though he initially feared losing contact with his three daughters, his wife agreed to visitation. With relief, he resigned himself to whatever other consequences he might face and began to come out, ending the decades of pretending in all his church circles and leadership positions. Unfortunately, his ex-wife reneged on the visitation agreement, and years of painful acrimony and legal battles ensued. Many of the arguments involved her (and her family's) evangelical condemnations and their fear he would corrupt their girls.

By this time, my friend had found a partner who was, as he put it, "perfect for me, very loving, glad I had kids." But the fights with his ex took their toll, and after nine years, even that relationship collapsed.

He wrote to me: "The way God saved me and brought me out of the closet, allowing me to 'come out to myself,' i.e., accept myself as gay and good—keeping me from suicide and from despair over the rejection/disowning I experienced from my parents and my evangelical 'home'—was, more than anything else, by my thorough knowledge of and loyalty to Scripture!" But the wounds are deep. "I'm a recovering fundy, as you can imagine, barely a theist, though there must be a God to have brought me alive to this point!"

Chapter 6
What Can Separate Gay People from the Love of God?

The soul that on Jesus has leaned for repose,
I will not, I will not desert to its foes;
That soul, though all hell should endeavor to shake,
I'll never, no never, no never forsake.

"How Firm a Foundation"
John Rippon, 1787, verse 4

W E VISITED LEAH AND JANE RECENTLY to celebrate Jacob's seventh birthday. What a delightful young man he's becoming. But I felt that familiar pang as we prepared to depart for home. Not over their family situation, which we've not only accepted but appreciate for its many strengths as both Leah and Jane have matured individually and as a couple over the years. But even though we had planned to attend church Sunday morning, things got busy and we never made it. On one hand, completely understandable, as they had just arrived home from a long trip only a few hours before we arrived, and I'm not one who feels church can never be missed. However, Leah and Jane have also confided that the "affirming" church to which they switched has not proved to be the life-giving community of faith they would like. So, they go when they can, but . . .

I'm sorry about that because I believe the Body of Christ is important for our spiritual growth and health. We may complain about a lot of things concerning our church experience, but in the end, it should be where we are regularly drawn into worship, enjoy support through fellowship, and receive instruction and encouragement for our life with God.

Thousands of gay men and women grew up in the church—our evangelical churches—where they gave their hearts to Jesus, were baptized, and still want to follow and serve him. But in our determination to "stand firm on homosexuality," we have caused many to lose heart. *Shame* is the predominant message they experience for being who they are and what they cannot change, causing "home," whether it is their family home or the church, to no longer be a place they feel welcomed or affirmed. Thankfully, many remain committed to Jesus, as is evidenced by the Gay Christian Network with over 40,000 members.[1] Some find a place of support in an affirming church or with an informal group of fellow believers. But when that doesn't happen, faith itself can fade.

Romans 8:35-39 assures us that *nothing* can "separate us from the love of God that is in Christ Jesus our Lord." Because of Jesus, God always extends his grace toward us, through all our trials, hardships, and the fog of life. Nothing shuts off God's love. But we can become so discouraged and so hurt that we lose heart and our faith wavers until we may fall away from that vital, daily connection with Jesus and his body. In that sense, any of us can suffer *feeling* separated from the love of God. And certainly those who have never established a relationship with Christ can be driven away by bad experiences with Christians and the church.

One day, as Jesus was teaching, he stressed how serious this is:

> If anyone should cause one of these little ones to lose his faith in me, it would be better for that person to have a large millstone tied round his neck and be drowned in the deep sea. How terrible for the world that there are things

---

1. While membership is open to straight people like ourselves, the vast majority are LGBT folks. The GCN's statement of faith proclaims, "Jesus Christ is God incarnate, the sinless Son of God, who was crucified for our sins and rose again on the third day" and affirms "the Bible is Holy Scripture, divinely inspired and authoritative, and not merely a human work."

that make people lose their faith! Such things will always happen—but how terrible for the one who causes them! (Matthew 18:6-7, GNB).

Some translations say, "If anyone causes one of these little ones . . . *to sin,*" which conjures up the idea of tempting a child to smoke the first cigarette, but that's not the intent of Jesus' message. Of course, cigarettes can kill you, but Jesus was speaking of something far more serious. The Greek word, *ptaió,* is better translated as to cause to stumble or fall away or, as the *Good News Bible* says, "cause . . . to lose his faith in me." Nothing is worse than causing someone to lose faith in Jesus.

And yet, according to the Pew Research Center, 73 percent of LGBT people find evangelical churches unfriendly.[2] By God's grace, some gay people still overcome those barriers and find Jesus, and some who are already in the church hang in there in spite of their environment. But if seven out of ten people who walked into my home found it unfriendly, I would be alarmed. Something would need to change. However, when our churches get that kind of a review, we tend to blame the visitor: They just don't want to hear the Gospel or follow Jesus or meet God. And yet . . . why did they come through the door in the first place? Church isn't supposed to be a show or a place of entertainment. People come there to meet God. So we can't absolve ourselves by saying, "We're just telling it like it is, and if gay people won't accept the truth, that's on them." We at least have to ask whether something *we* are saying or doing is shaming gay people and thereby separating them from the love of God.

Let's take a look at what kind of thing drives people away from Jesus.

Delivering ourselves from "evil"

Victor and Maria are members of a conservative church where Victor serves as a deacon. Their daughter, Michelle, is gay, and

2. "A Survey of LGBT Americans, Attitudes, Experiences and Values in Changing Times," Pew Research Center, June 13, 2013. http://www.pew-socialtrends.org/2013/06/13/a-survey-of-lgbt-americans/.

their relationship with her has been tenuous at best for several years. Michelle no longer espouses any belief in God, but recently she reached out to her parents saying she would like to come visit them . . . and bring her partner for them to meet.

Maria was excited. After so long, she just wanted to see her daughter. But Victor foresaw the conundrum: If they invited them, Michelle and her partner would expect to sleep in the same bedroom. He couldn't have that happening in his home, not under his roof, not when he was such a prominent leader in the church.

I knew how they felt. We'd faced the same question. The only difference being we'd not been so estranged from Leah, and she and Jane had been more tolerant of us when we said, "Here's the bedding for the couch. You guys choose who sleeps there and who gets the guest room." That went on for a while even though we began to realize our "stand" wasn't changing anything and wasn't necessary for them or anyone else to know our convictions at the time. All it was doing was making our home an awkward place for them to visit.

Soon after their wedding, we moved to a new house and during their first visit to us there, it seemed the right time to accept the situation. We didn't say anything; just helped them both carry their luggage up to the guest room as we would any other couple.

It's a hard question. Like many parents, we had told ourselves we had a right to require compliance with our personal values in our own home, and at the time I didn't approve of their marriage any more than I had their cohabitation. Yet, the fact was, they were a couple, had made a public commitment (which now has become legal) and nothing I could have done would have changed that.

But as I've looked more closely at the Scriptures, I think Jesus gave some guidance for us in this kind of a dilemma. First of all, I cannot think of any situation where Jesus said, "You have to change your behavior before I'll relate to you." Second, I cannot recall any time when he was the least bit concerned whether his reputation, his influence as a teacher, or his ability to lead others might be damaged by his association with outcasts. In fact, he acknowledged, "The Son of Man came eating and drinking, and you say, 'Here is a glutton and a drunkard, a friend of tax collectors and sinners'" (Luke 7:34). Luke follows this with the story of the woman who poured perfume on Jesus' feet and wiped them with her hair and tears while Simon the Pharisee observed, assuming Jesus did not know he was being touched by a sinner (presumably a prostitute) in this most intimate act of devotion (vv. 36-50).

For generations, many of us were taught a code of conduct based on the way the 1611 King James Version (and the 1582 Catholic Douay Bible) translated 1 Thessalonians 5:22: "Abstain from all *appearance* of evil" (emphasis added). This is the only time the King James Version translates the Greek word, *eidos*, as "appearance."[3] Newer and better translations render *eidos* in this verse as "kind," "form," or "sort" of evil, emphasizing that actual evil is to be avoided, not what someone else thinks or perceives as wrongdoing. Given the code of conduct built around that old translation, many Christians (even pastors) would avoid ever being seen entering a bar lest someone think they were going there to get drunk. And as children, we were taught not to use playing cards because someone might *think* we were gambling (though Rook or Uno was allowed), along with a myriad of other prohibitions onlookers might misunderstand, including not associating with the "wrong people." The tragedy of this approach is how quickly and widely it spread so that we ended up living contrary to Jesus' example. It even tempted us to take pride in abstentions of no moral consequence so as to be people pleasers rather than God pleasers.

But we cannot "deliver ourselves from evil" either by worrying about what people will think of us or over the possibility they will presume we approve of what those around us are doing.

Nagging people with our convictions

How we convey our convictions about homosexuality may have far more to do with whether people are attracted to or driven away

---

3. In 2 Corinthians 5:7, *eidos* is translated by most versions as "sight"— "For we live by faith, not by sight." However, the broader context of 1 Thessalonians 5:22 makes it clear Paul was warning against actual evil, not benign behaviors some busy-body might see you doing and gossip that it is wrong.

from Jesus than by *what* we actually believe. Some gay people will have come to their own convictions about what God approves of and may choose to fellowship with more like-minded brothers and sisters. But if they come to the typical evangelical church, the thing that makes us *seem* unfriendly has more to do with our compulsion to tell people they are wrong . . . again and again. Believe me, you won't be the first or the last to point out the relevant Scriptures or the church's position, and yet, each person they meet somehow feels compelled to say it again.

Not long ago, I was listening to a message on Colossians 3 by a pastor of a church that claims to "radically welcome" gay people while still holding a neo-traditional position on the subject of homosexuality. Verse 5 of Colossians 3 mentions "sexual immorality" along with other sins:

> Put to death, therefore, whatever belongs to your earthly nature: sexual immorality, impurity, lust, evil desires and greed, which is idolatry. Because of these, the wrath of God is coming.

Whether the term "sexual immorality" includes same-sex relationships is a question in itself, but that was by no means the point of his message. However, when the pastor explained that Paul was talking about "sexual lust of all sorts and its gratification outside of God's given context of marriage . . ." he added the descriptive qualifier, "which is *between a man and a woman.*" In so doing, he announced in a kind of shorthand that gay marriage is sinful without taking the time to deal with that claim in a serious and compassionate manner. I don't know why he felt it was necessary to do so. Perhaps it had become routine for him, a quick litmus test to prove his orthodoxy, or possibly he wanted to capture a "teachable moment" to instruct unsure listeners. But buzz phrases seldom persuade anyone.

I've begun to hear the phrase, "marriage is between one man and one woman," through my daughter's ears and realize how easily it must come across as constant shaming, a reminder that "God doesn't accept your marriage, and *we don't accept it either.*" How could she understand it as anything other than that?

And this question isn't as hypothetical as it may seem, even for the church mentioned above. One mother began bringing her junior high son to that church because of the dynamic youth group—until the boy kept hearing the youth leader characterize gay marriage as sinful. The mom's sister-in-law (the boy's aunt) is in a gay marriage, raising children who are the boy's cousins, and the mother decided she didn't want her son continually hearing the family structure of their closest relatives being berated. So she took her son and dropped out.

Crusading against homosexuality

Some people think they are witnessing against sin when they point their finger at homosexuality as a sign of our culture's moral decay. But it's a little different than preaching against anger, lying, lust, cheating, gossip, gluttony, unfaithfulness, greed, etc. Who identifies themselves by those behaviors, even if they are honest enough to confess doing them? And yet most gay people have come to the point of acknowledging that they are, in fact, gay, which is far more than admitting it as something they do. And they know that no matter how much they want to change or seek the Lord's help, they can't stop being gay. They just are, along with the natural desire to, at some point, fulfill that aspect of themselves . . . just as most straight people desire to get married some day.

So when you assail someone's orientation, you are doing far more than telling the person to control their anger or wait for sex until marriage or don't devote yourself to accumulating more stuff. Whether you are right or wrong in your views regarding homosexuality, at least ask yourself whether your comments are likely to drive someone away from Jesus or invite them to him.

In the spring of 2015, Indiana passed the Religious Freedom Restoration Act that allowed individuals or corporations to cite religious beliefs as a defense when sued by a private party. The typical example was to protect a bakery owner from a lawsuit if he or she, for religious reasons, refused to cater a gay wedding. Without getting into the pros and cons of the case, simply think of the impact on gay people. Proponents of the law were as eager as anyone to use the media, claiming the law would defend the

Christian perspective and represent biblical values. It defined us to the world and drew a line in the sand—"us" against "them." I can't imagine such a crusade causing even one gay person to want to come to Jesus.

If you find it hard to see how political crusading can drive gay people away from Jesus, imagine a different scenario. Imagine you are in the military, returning from combat after losing a leg in battle (a condition that forever defines you). You end up attending a traditional "peace church"[4] where Sunday after Sunday the pastor or someone else makes impromptu references to the immorality of war and the unbiblical views of those who participate. Would you stay?

Presuming gay people "struggle with homosexuality"

In a similar vein, you've undoubtedly heard of books and ministries and churches dedicated to helping people who "struggle with homosexuality." To our straight ears, that sounds like a compassionate endeavor, but think about it. First of all, not all gay people struggle with their orientation. Many have come to terms with it as the way they were created and only struggle with how others treat them. But more significantly, when was the last time you heard of helping people who "struggle with *heterosexuality*"? Certainly straight people are as tempted to fornicate, commit adultery, and view pornography. But those are actions—sins—for which a person can repent and from which the person can abstain, with God's help, especially because God has provided a way of dealing with our sexual desires—a committed relationship in marriage.

However, when Christians presume gay people struggle with homosexuality, gay people hear this as an expectation that they *should* struggle against or resist *who they are* because there is no acceptable way for their sexuality to find fulfillment. In fact, there is no acceptable way for them to even dream of having the kind of loving, committed relationship exemplified by marriage. This

---

4. I value peace and abhor war and have a great deal of respect for peace churches. But perhaps out of fear that their convictions will dissolve, some peace churches harp on the theme as though that will convince those who disagree when the issue is so complex and challenging that no one's mind will be changed apart from a careful consideration of the subject from all sides.

understanding is reinforced by the fact that you rarely hear a neo-traditionalist encourage gay people to embrace their orientation. That's because they can't conceive of an acceptable way to do it.

An environment can become so unfriendly that it drives gay people away when we say or do things that imply something is fundamentally wrong or unacceptable about who a person is, something the person cannot change or, at least, something the person sees no hope of changing. On one hand, neo-traditionalists would say, "Oh, we're not demanding a gay person becomes straight. We're just saying it's wrong to act on their orientation." But what is heard is that you are demanding them to be celibate for life—which is a lot more than just "no sex," but no family life, no children, no partner to go through life. Celibacy is a high calling, but—except for occasional splinter sects like the Shakers—the church has never allowed it to be a demand for the laity, and the vow of celibacy that the Catholic religious make requires a clear sense of calling and extended testing. We're all called to remain chaste *until* marriage and faithful within marriage, but forcing celibacy on people is simply contrary to the way God made us . . . except for those he has specifically called and gifted for that discipline. "But," say some Christians, "aren't we all called to 'Come and die,' total surrender, 'Is your all on the altar of sacrifice laid?'"

Yes, and there are things in our lives that can hinder our relationship with God, but that doesn't mean *I* have the authority to tell *you* what *specific* thing God wants you to lay on the altar. Only Jesus could look into the heart of the rich young ruler and say, "You still lack one thing. Sell everything you have and give to the poor, and you will have treasure in heaven. Then come, follow me" (Luke 18:22). Some Christian groups have tried to require even this or similar proofs of total surrender for everyone, but only Jesus sees the heart.

I'm not big into politically correct speech, but we need to realize that some of the things we say end up conveying underlying messages that are so unfriendly they drive gay people away from a relationship with Christ. Unfortunately, we can hear these and other off-putting comments every day on Christian radio and television, which are our most public portrayals of Jesus to the world.

How relationship *invites* people to Jesus

As with racial divides, nothing is more healing than personal relationships. It may have been easy for the pastor I mentioned earlier in this chapter to use Colossians 3 as an occasion to remind everyone that he thinks marriage is only "between one man and one woman." However, I can't imagine if he had a personal relationship with a gay couple that he'd feel compelled to remind them that their relationship was invalid every time he sat down to a meal with them. The deeper we know people, the more sensitive we become.

After engaging the Samaritan woman in conversation at the well outside the village of Sychar, Jesus offered her "living water" (John 4:1-38). She quickly took him up on it, but Jesus said, "Go, call your husband and come back." Why did he bring up her marital status when he already knew she had gone through five husbands and was living with someone to whom she wasn't married? To the woman, it proved he was a prophet, but it also brought her out of the closet without laying down any conditions for their relationship. She was undoubtedly used to rejection. You don't go through five husbands in a small town without everyone knowing . . . and despising you. But Jesus didn't reject her. He didn't say, "Come to a place of holiness regarding your marital status, and then I'll give you living water." His unconditional love led not only to her salvation but "Many of the Samaritans from that town believed in [Jesus] because of the woman's testimony, 'He told me everything I ever did.'" Interestingly, there is no record of Jesus even returning to the subject of her marital status—marry the guy she was with, go back to husband number five, four . . . number one? Her relationship with Jesus was what mattered. Apparently, Jesus trusted the Holy Spirit to work out the details of the woman's life in God's own time.

Recently, I spent time with Pastor Bill Shereos of the First Free church in the Andersonville neighborhood on Chicago's north side. Though his church takes a neo-traditional position, I'd heard they have a substantial ministry to the many gay people around them. I wanted to hear how it was going and especially learn their response to gay couples. Bill doesn't claim to have all the answers (that in itself was refreshing!), but he and his congregation are deeply involved with gay men and women. And open and regular relationships usually result in two-way transformations. In their congregation they talk about the questions and have learned enough about the painful points of difference that it's highly unlikely any church meeting at First Free could deteriorate into shouting cruel remarks at the gay people in the room as happened in my daughter's church. In fact, Bill is deeply disturbed by anything that requires anyone to "sit at the back of the bus," as he put it. He admitted how deeply painful—even wrong—it felt to him to have to tell a woman (privately) who had recently come to the church and was eagerly wanting to serve that she couldn't take a certain ministry position in the church because she had a same-sex partner.

Regarding another situation, he described how the church members rallied around a gay man when his partner died, in just the same way they've done for opposite-sex couples divided by death—visiting him, attending the funeral, bringing meals and cards of condolence to him, offering to help.

Even though Bill and his denomination don't affirm gay marriage, he believes it's loving to ask a gay person how his or her partner is doing, to show interest in their families, their jobs or careers. Why? Because for that human being, whom God loves, the relationship with his or her partner is one of the most important human relationships in life, and to love someone is to genuinely care about what or who they care about . . . whether or not you agree with their choices or decisions.

Bill would be the first to admit he and his congregation haven't worked through all the details of how to respond to married gay couples, but with the legalization of gay marriage by the Supreme Court, they realize this is a question they cannot ignore.

Later in his ministry, Jesus again returned to the topic of things we do that separate people from the love of God. This time he did not focus on the vulnerable "children" in our own church family whom we might cause to lose faith in him. Instead, he spoke of those outside the kingdom who would like to come in, but whom we hold at a distance. "Woe to you, teachers of the law and Pharisees, you hypocrites! You shut the kingdom of heaven in men's faces. You yourselves do not enter, nor will you let those enter who are trying to" (Matthew 23:13).

Brothers and sisters, driving people away from Jesus, whether they are "family" or seekers, is a very serious offense. How many gay people are we driving away from Jesus and the church by treating them as worse sinners than all the rest of us?

Collateral Damage

As the family and youth pastor for a church of fourteen hundred people, Esther Gilmore had numerous individuals and families come to her seeking wisdom for how to respond to same-sex attraction. But when her son, Roger, came out as gay, the price of honesty broke the church's "relational bank" for the Gilmores and many others.

I met Esther at the 2016 Gay Christian Network conference in Houston where I sat across the table from her at the parents' dinner. I had noticed her son in the lobby of Hilton as well as in the Convention Center. I could see by the way people responded to him that he was a dynamic leader, and I wanted to hear their family's story.

Nearly eighteen years earlier, shortly after Esther joined the pastoral staff of their church, two young women came to her. Both of them were talented musicians and on the praise team. One was even the daughter of one of the other pastors. They'd grown up in the church. It was their home, even when they'd been away at college together. But they were same-sex attracted . . . and to each other. They had tried everything to overcome their attraction, including marriage to a man for one of them, hoping that would end it all, but it didn't, and the marriage was a disaster.

"At the time," Esther recalls, "I didn't know anything more about homosexuality than what I'd been told—simply that it was wrong. But they'd come to me for help, and all I could think to do was take it to the other pastors and elders, hoping to walk through it all to a redemptive resolution."

However, the leadership had very little personal relationship with the women—other than the one pastor to his daughter—and so once they were involved, it became an issue that had to be dealt with regardless of the people it might affect. Sadly, the process went south, and the consequences drove both women out of the church. Esther lost contact with one of the women, but she managed to remain close to the pastor's daughter and has been challenged through the years by her faith as well as her wisdom. "Even though the outcome was sad, I consider her a gift to me from the Lord to have had the privilege of walking alongside her through that hard process. Seeing the fruit in her life has discipled and taught me."

Since then, there've been several other people who have come to Esther for counsel about same-sex attraction. But with the sting of what happened the first time she brought such a personal matter to the leadership, she hesitated to engage them on it again.

Esther and her husband, Greg, had recognized early on that there was something different about their eldest son. Roger was unusually articulate, expressive, passionate, and full of joy—all desirable qualities. He excelled in all the arts and was an A-student, never in trouble. What's not to like? And yet . . . there was something different about him. She and Greg talked about it occasionally, but it wasn't until Roger was in junior high and high school that they noticed among his many friends—who always seemed to gather at their house—far more were girls than guys. And yet he didn't seem to chase after any of them like he wanted a girlfriend. Maybe that was why they felt so comfortable around him.

"There was also a sense we had," says Esther, "that he was dealing with something that he wasn't letting us in on. Of course, kids have their moods and struggles, so we weren't hyper worried, but it did cross our minds that it might be homosexuality. Greg and I didn't want to put that on him, of course, so we just prayed about it."

But by the time Roger turned seventeen, their concern was sufficient that Esther talked to her lesbian friend who had left their church so many years before. "You need to ask him what's going on," her friend said. "Don't forget, I'm a pastor's kid too, and I know what it's like. You've gotta open that door and give him permission to walk through it if he chooses."

For the next couple of months Esther and Greg considered her advice and prayed about it until one day they sat down with Roger and said, "We don't know what's going on, but if this has anything to do with same-sex attraction or anything like that, we want you to know that it's safe to come out."

Esther recalls that he appeared not only relieved but was incredibly gracious and honest and brave in how he responded. "Mom and Dad, I want you to know that I've been on my knees for four years about this. And at one point God and I made a pact that I would keep my orientation to myself until I'd gone away to college because I didn't want to jeopardize your ministry or even my own ministry here in the church."

Roger was very involved in the church as a youth worship leader and in many other ways. He deeply loved the church, but he was also acutely aware of how dangerous it was for him to come out, even though she'd never told him about what had happened with the pastors and the elder board. But he was glad to talk to his family about it. He knew they had several gay friends, so he wasn't afraid of how they might respond, but he was just trying to avoid a big crisis in the church.

Esther and Greg were unsure whether remaining closeted for those reasons was good for Roger or even for them. It's not desirable for anyone to live with something in their life that always poses the threat of blowing up. So, as a family, they prayed together for another couple of months until they all came to unity that it was time to go to the church leadership. Esther hoped that because they were all *her* colleagues and because Roger was so high profile as a youth leader in the church that those relationships would transform the conversation. After all, Roger and their younger son had been born there and grew up in the church. Everybody liked him. Certainly that would make a difference. In fact, Esther began to feel that perhaps God had chosen their family to have a gay son for just such a time as this, to help the church come to a new understanding that would enable it to receive other gay people rather than force them to hide or leave.

They began by sharing with the senior pastor and the executive pastor. From the beginning, the senior pastor had a very negative response. He wanted to know what Esther and Greg had done wrong in their parenting to produce this. He asked if and when they had confronted Roger with the "truth" about his salvation. He was convinced that Roger's orientation was his own sinful choice for which he needed to repent. Over the next year as conversations continued, he did soften somewhat on that point to admit that it might be something a person was born with, but he never budged on his claim that it threatened one's salvation.

The executive pastor appeared to be somewhat more understanding.

The next step was to take the situation to the elders' board, where more surprises erupted. One elder became so apoplectic he couldn't even stand to listen to their story. But it also came out that one of the elders had a gay daughter. Esther agreed that while the leadership was discussing the subject, she would not share it with her own staff of ten people or the multitude of volunteers who worked with her. Nevertheless, suddenly more and more families and individuals began to come out of the woodwork—over a dozen in the next few months.

Esther realized that if God was entrusting her with this situation, she needed help, beginning with studying the Scriptures more intensely. She could no longer espouse or contend with the pat, traditional answers. She started reading and soon began to understand some of the theology and history of how the church had claimed more clarity on this issue than biblical honesty merited. Her studies didn't answer all her questions, but the most compelling piece to her was how God revealed himself in the person of Jesus Christ. There was no denying the contrast between Jesus' ministry and how the church traditionally had been behaving toward marginalized people, particularly gay people.

71

The further she got into her personal studies, the more she wanted to talk it through with her colleagues. But it was so hard to engage them because everyone was so afraid of the implications, all they wanted to do was espouse their positions. So when she heard about the Gay Christian Network, she decided to go their conference. There she would meet people. In fact, their whole family attended the 2015 conference . . . along with the executive pastor of their church and the elder with a gay daughter.

Maybe this would be the breakthrough.

It was amazing to Esther to see hundreds of gay Christians of all ages gathered in the name of the Lord, worshiping with the same praise songs familiar back home, hearing powerful messages from Jesus that urged forgiveness and love toward their persecutors. Roger, of course, fit in quickly. And Esther and Greg learned a lot in the workshops about what gay Christians were saying and how they were navigating their faith and orientation. To them it was a confirmation that the Holy Spirit was truly present in hundreds of these gay Christians. Of course, some were obviously still searching, doubting even, perhaps still reeling from the wounds they had received from the church. But the Holy Spirit was at the conference. It seemed undeniable to her.

But not undeniable to everyone!

Back at their church, when she gathered with the pastors and elders, the executive pastor gave a very different report. To him, it was appalling for all these gay people to claim to be Christian. Unthinkable. He had no idea that was going on all across the country. It was something to be denounced rather than affirmed.

The senior pastor took his cue from the executive's report. Simply to talk about this subject was like inviting the "Serpent" into the room. He felt like they were engaging Satan in conversation as demonstrated by all the families that had started asking questions about homosexuality. It was time to bring clarity!

The solution was to bring in a man from the outside who had been a reparative therapy counselor within the Exodus ex-gay movement. His task was to train the staff about gay people.

"For me the training was brutal," says Esther. "The way he talked about gay people and the way he talked about their families was so disparaging, it left me trembling. And as far as gay Christians were concerned, he didn't believe they were authentic and painted them in alarmist, fear-filled terms as a conspiracy intent on subverting the church. The whole event polarized the staff. People were either repelled by what he had to say or were cheering him on."

In the end, the leadership decided to clarify the church's doctrine relative to LGBT people. Based on 1 Corinthians 6:9-10—"Do you not know that wrongdoers will not inherit the kingdom of God? Do not be deceived: Neither the sexually immoral . . . nor men who have sex with men . . . will inherit the kingdom of God"—they declared homosexuality a salvation issue.

"I think it was at that point that they actually decided to fire me," Esther says. "It was presented to the congregation as a separation by mutual agreement, but I had to go along if I wanted references for another job. But really, they fired me because it was too dangerous to continue the conversation." The pain has been great, and the loss of their church family has been costly. More tragic, however, are the gay people and their families who left and others from the area who may never darken the doors of that large church because they know it's not safe.

In the end, what Roger had feared most, happened. But according to Esther, the amazing thing is, his faith has never been stronger. And neither has the faith of their family. Still, she's uncertain about her sense that God had positioned her in this church and Roger in their family for such a time as this. But just because it didn't turn out well, doesn't mean God didn't give that church a chance to make some changes, and God may not be finished with them yet, either.

Chapter 7
Did God Create Gay People?

Trust in Him, ye saints, forever,
He is faithful, changing never;
Neither force nor guile can sever
Those He loves from Him.

"Praise the Savior, Ye Who Know Him"
Thomas Kelly, 1806, verse 3

COMING AS I HAD FROM A TRADITIONALIST PERSPECTIVE, I had never seriously raised the question of whether God could be responsible for anyone's same-sex attraction. In helping Ed Hurst write his book, *Overcoming Homosexuality*, I had not only absorbed his theories, but I had read many of the theoreticians and theologians of the day on which he based his ideas. In summary, they maintained homosexuality was the result of inadequate parenting, sexual abuse or enticement by others, and/or the gay person's own sinful choices.

Therefore, reversing a person's same-sex attraction was a reasonable expectation if he or she genuinely repented, completely surrendered to God, submitted to protracted counseling, prayed for divine healing, and faithfully practiced disciplines designed to change life patterns and resist temptation. In various forms, this remains the goal of so-called reparative therapy. Traditional interpretations and applications of the "prohibitive passages" we will look at in Part II of this book provided ample motivation (often in the form of guilt and shame) for trying to overcome homosexuality. And certainly, if homosexuality were such an abominable sin,

74

God couldn't have had anything to do with creating someone gay since James 1:13 tells us "God cannot be tempted by evil, nor does he tempt anyone."

Is anyone born gay?

In December 2014, a large billboard over I-95 in downtown Richmond, Virginia, proclaimed, "Nobody is born gay." The sign appears to portray photos of two identical twins, one gay and one straight. The sponsor, PFOX (Parents and Friends of Ex-Gays and Gays), said twins research shows nobody is born gay. Of course, the billboard incensed many gay people because they felt it amounted to a public condemnation of their family of origin, of themselves, or both.

PFOX bases its claim that nobody is born gay on the conclusions of Dr. Neil Whitehead from eight studies of identical twins in Australia, the U.S., and Scandinavia. Whitehead postulated that if homosexuality had a genetic origin, and one twin was gay, then 100 percent of the time, both identical twins would be gay. Instead, he found, "If an identical twin has same-sex attraction, the chances the co-twin has it [was] only about 11 percent for men and 14 percent for women." Therefore, he concluded same-sex attraction had to come from "non-shared factors."[1]

In spite of having mapped the human genome, a specific genetic cause for homosexuality has not been established, and traditionalists often point this out as a *fait accompli*, discussion over. But the opposite is equally true—genetics and other in utero influences have *not* been ruled out, either.[2] For instance, one might think if one identical twin were left-handed, the other one would be so as well. But that's not the case about 21 percent of the time. Researchers suggest that a combination of genetic *and* environmental factors such as stress during birth, hormone levels

---

1. Mark Ellis, "Identical twin studies prove homosexuality is not genetic," http://www.hollanddavis.com/?p=3647.
2. More recent research suggests that epigenetics rather than specific DNA markers may influence sexual orientation. These would be epi-marks or androgen signaling that switch parts of the genome on and off at strategic times during the fetus's development. http://www.jstor.org/stable/10.1086/668167.

during pregnancy, or position in the womb could have some impact on hand preference.[3]

While identical twins come from the same fertilized egg and have very *similar* DNA, they are not necessarily identical in every respect. In the case of identical twins, both babies develop in the womb from a single cell, which throughout life may divide into over 37 trillion cells,[4] the DNA being copied for each one. The process of copying the DNA is incredibly good but not perfect. Most deviations have no obvious effect. But genetic variations can develop prior to birth. In fact, even serious genetically-based anomalies, such as Down syndrome, have been known to afflict one identical twin and not the other.[5] Furthermore, the environment within the womb can be different for each twin. Identical twins can share a placenta or have separate placentas, share their amniotic sac or have separate sacs,[6] making possible differing hormonal influences. These nonshared factors, which can occur before birth, can result in differences between supposedly "identical" twins. In fact, those differences are sufficiently apparent at birth that most mothers can tell their identical twins apart within a very short time. They even have different fingerprints.

Therefore, since it *is* possible for nonshared factors to occur in the womb, PFOX's claim on their website that "because identical twins are always genetically identical, homosexuality cannot be genetically dictated. [Thus] no one is born gay"[7] is a logical fallacy.

Nevertheless, PFOX continues to assert that "'Gay' is a self-chosen identity," perhaps because it is foundational to their offer to help gay people "out of homosexuality" and to encourage parents

---

3. "Do identical twins always have the same hand preference?" Twin Registry, http://uwtwinregistry.org/do-identical-twins-always-have-the-same-hand-preference/.

4. Rose Eveleth, "There are 37.2 Trillion Cells in Your Body," Smithsonian.com, October 24, 2013, http://www.smithsonianmag.com/smart-news/there-are-372-trillion-cells-in-your-body-4941473/?no-ist.

5. Melissa Healy, "Identical twins, one case of Down syndrome: a genetic mystery," *La Times*, April 16, 2014. http://www.latimes.com/science/sciencenow/la-sci-sn-twins-down-syndrome-genetics-20140416-story.html.

6. World TTTS Awareness. http://www.worldtttsawarenessday.org/mono_placenta.php.

7. "PFOX Billboard Makes the News," http://www.pfox.org/pfox-billboard-makes-news/.

that they do not have to "affirm their child's self-proclaimed gay identity in order to prove their love."

To bolster its program, PFOX claims to offer the testimonies of "thousands of individuals [who] have made the decision to leave the homosexual life and will attest to the fact that change is possible."[8] Okay. We can accept people's stories if their lives appear to back them up. But if testimonials are to be believed, why not also accept the testimonies of those gay people who are convinced gay is the way God made them? Many sincerely declare they did not come from a dysfunctional home, never made any decision to become gay, but "discovered" they were same-sex attracted with an intensity that convinced them they were born that way.

As mentioned earlier, when we first encouraged our daughter to seek "help" from an ex-gay ministry, she couldn't relate to the testimonies she found posted on their websites. Many of those people sounded to her like sexual addicts or sufferers of severely dysfunctional relationships. Of course they needed healing! But those stories didn't represent her experience or that of many other gay people.[9]

Whether PFOX has helped some people or not, many gay people see the agency's motive as self-serving. Their program is a business, and billboards help promote business. In fact, their billboard had an integrity problem that increases skepticism for every organization like theirs. To create the billboard, PFOX used the images, *not of identical twins, as it appears*—one formally attired on the left and the other casually dressed on the right side—but two stock photos of the *same* professional model. Two photos of just one man positioned to *look* like twins. His name is Kyle Roux. He does happen to be gay, but he's *not* a twin, and definitely

---

8. Ibid., PFOX.

9. Ruth Lipschultz, a licensed clinical social worker and personal friend of ours, pointed out that it isn't just Leah's history that doesn't fit that profile. Those factors don't characterize the majority of gay people, either. "In fact," she says, "dysfunction, trauma, family problems are equally present in the families of origin for both gay and straight people. If those factors *caused* people to become gay, a *much* larger percentage of the population would be gay."

not happy that his old stock photos were used in this deceitful fashion.[10]

Is it the result of original sin?

A pastor friend of mine whose daughter also happens to be in a gay marriage, which caused him no small measure of consternation, reminded me that in addition to the traditional view claiming no one is born gay, there is another way of looking at same-sex attraction that acknowledges a person may be born with that characteristic, but he still attributes it to sin. Advocates of this view might admit that same-sex attraction isn't necessarily the parents' fault or the result of the individual's choices. They may even accept that genetic, hormonal, or environmental factors—for which no one is to blame—may play a role in triggering same-sex attraction. Nevertheless, they speculate it is sinful in the sense that it is the result of *original sin*—the fallen nature we all inherit from Adam and Eve's disobedience—and therefore it should never be excused or accommodated. They may think such an explanation is less personal and less condemning since we all must live under the consequences of original sin, but it denies that God might have *made* anyone gay.

Proponents of the original sin view claim if someone has a propensity toward lust or what appears to be a biological predisposition to addictions, we don't console them by saying, "That's okay. That's just the way God made you." No, we all "groan" under various weaknesses visited upon us by the fall, waiting with eager expectation to "be liberated from its bondage to decay and brought into the glorious freedom of the children of God" (Romans 8:21). If part of that bondage is that some people suffer with same-sex attraction, this viewpoint says, then the "prohibitive" passages still define boundaries beyond which there is no legitimate passage.

---

10. David Ferguson, "'Twin' from 'Nobody's born gay' billboard: I am gay and I'm not a twin," *Raw Story*, Dec. 12, 2014. http://www.rawstory. com/rs/2014/12/twin-from-nobodys-born-gay-billboard-i-am-gay-and-im-not-a-twin/.

God doesn't make mistakes

However, for his own reasons, God has created people with a wide variety of characteristics. Some of these we consider normal variations (racial characteristics, height, body shape, etc.) while we label the less common ones "anomalies." Some variations make life hard, even physically painful. Some result in social or psychological challenges or ostracism. But I had never thought about the parallel between sexually-related physical anomalies—about which I knew very little—and sexually-related psychological variations.

The more common sexually-related physical variations (often called secondary sex characteristics) include large or small breasts, narrow or wide hips, more or less body fat, smooth or hairy arms and legs, a clean upper lip or the beginnings of a mustache for women. Men can have a heavy beard or a smooth face, broad or narrow shoulders, hairy body or smooth skin, bald or a full head of hair, a deep or a thin voice. But some anomalies, though rare, are far more significant and not so secondary.

"Intersex" is a general term used for a variety of conditions in which a person is born with a reproductive or sexual anatomy that doesn't seem to fit the typical definitions of female or male. For example, a person might be born appearing to be female on the outside, but having mostly male-typical anatomy on the inside. Or a person may be born with genitals that seem to be in-between the usual male and female types—for example, a girl may be born with a noticeably large clitoris or lacking a vaginal opening, or a boy may be born with a notably small penis or with a scrotum that is divided so that it has formed more like labia. Or a person may be born with mosaic genetics so that some of her cells have XX chromosomes and some of them have XY.[11]

---

11. "What is intersex? Interesex Society of North America, 2008. http://www.isna.org/faq/what_is_intersex.

If there can be physical variations—ranging from common to rare—related to one's sexuality and often affected by prenatal hormones, why are we so surprised to find psychological variations regarding how people perceive themselves (gender identity) or respond in terms of attraction (orientation)? And why would we be so quick to label those variations sinful or the result of sin or even a mistake by God?

It's problematic to start declaring *any* innate characteristic of a person to be the result of the fall rather than how God created the person. God is sovereign, and he doesn't make mistakes. You're not a mistake, I'm not a mistake, and neither are our gay family and friends. Consider the story of Moses' encounter with God in the burning bush. When God commissioned him to confront Pharaoh, Moses offered many objections, finally saying, "O Lord, I have never been eloquent . . . I am slow of speech and tongue" (Exodus 4:10). Surprisingly, God did not dispute this. Instead, he responded (with some pique), "Who gave man his mouth? Who makes him deaf or mute? Who gives him sight or makes him blind? Is it not I, the Lord?" If God willingly took responsibility for those characteristics without blaming them on the fall, who are we to suggest someone's sexual orientation is a mistake? And even if being gay is in some convoluted way the result of original sin, that doesn't make it sinful in and of itself. We are better off affirming, "The Lord is righteous in all his ways and faithful in all he does" (Psalm 145:17).

The problem of sin is that *every* good thing about us can be misused. That *misuse*, rather than the quality itself, is the more direct legacy of original sin. In fact, it is the very definition of our sin nature. Gay people, just like straight people, need to confess that we are all sinners in need of a savior. We all need to resist lust, resist abusing our sexual attractions, refuse to misuse other people, and remain absolutely faithful in marriage. We are all called to control, discipline, mature, and use with wisdom and love every aspect of how God created us. Sanctification is the process of doing that as the Holy Spirit sets us apart to be conformed to the image of Christ as expressed in the many and varied members of his body. Our sanctification happens as we become more and more the unique member of Christ's body God made us to be, which will not look like or function like all the other members.

Spectrums of God-given differences

In trying to appreciate how complex and differently God made each one of us, I have found it helpful to recognize that various aspects of our sexuality fall on spectrums. The following observations aren't presented as scientific studies but as relatively self-evident variables we sometimes overlook.

Envision our sexuality on an X-Y graph. The Y, or the vertical axis, would indicate sexual drive. Some people register low—barely interested—while others are highly interested. Although the intensity of a person's interest in sex may change over their lifespan—with it being highest in late puberty—the person with a strong sex drive might have a lot more trouble with lust than the person with a very low sex drive. But does that mean the more highly-sexed person is the product of original sin? Does it mean the person who seldom thinks about sex more perfectly represents God's "good" creation? Not if the survival of the species is important. Whether high or low, a person's sex drive is a fundamental characteristic that God created as *good*. And though someone with a relatively low sex drive might be able to live a celibate life with relative ease, they should be careful not to presume someone with a high sex drive can manage the same.

The X, or the horizontal axis, denotes whether one is opposite-sex attracted (on the left end) or same-sex attracted (on the right end).[12] If you are on the left end of the X-axis (strongly heterosexual), it may be nearly impossible for you to imagine how anyone could be gay. But perhaps it is just as unthinkable for a strongly

---

12. Someone falling in the middle of the scale would be bisexual or physically attracted to people of either sex. Alfred Kinsey, Wardell Pomeroy, and others published *Sexual Behavior in the Human Male* (1948) and *Sexual Behavior in the Human Female* (1953) in which they used a similar scale. Kinsey explained, "Males do not represent two discrete populations, heterosexual and homosexual. The world is not to be divided into sheep and goats. . . . The living world is a continuum in each and every one of its aspects." (*Male*, p. 639).

gay person to imagine becoming straight. "It just ain't gonna happen" without a bona fide miracle.

Years ago, Leah had tried to explain this to me, but at the time, I couldn't take it in when she wrote . . .

> I understand that if a person believes homosexuality to be a sin, trying to be heterosexual would be part of his/her goal. But what a frustrating, sad task. Can you imagine if you believed that to honor God you needed to live in rejection of *your* sexuality (which makes it possible for you to be completely in love with your one TRUE mate— Dave & Neta) that is natural for you? So it is there that I see frustration, self-loathing, and anguish in these people [people attempting the "ex-gay" therapy I'd encouraged her to try].[13]

It finally took Justin Lee's book, *TORN*,[14] for me to understand what my daughter had clearly said years before. He didn't reference a scale, but as he told his story of agonizing in prayer night after night to change his orientation, I suddenly realized he was hoping for something as impossible for him as it would be for me to develop a sexual interest in men. Why had I expected my daughter to attempt such an unnatural change?

Having envisioned human sexual attraction on a spectrum from straight to gay, I'm not by any means suggesting half of the population falls somewhere toward the straight side while the other half are scattered along the gay end of the spectrum. This spectrum is only to help us understand the range of *orientation*. In reality, over 95 percent of the population falls toward the left or straight end of that spectrum.[15] This fact becomes particularly im-

---

13. Personal letter, November 24, 2002.

14. Lee, Justin. *TORN: Rescuing the Gospel from the Gays-vs.-Christians Debate* (New York: Jericho Books, 2012).

15. The Williams Institute at UCLA School of Law, a sexual orientation law think tank, released a study in April 2011 which says, "Drawing on information from four recent national and two state-level population-based surveys, the analyses suggest that there are more than 8 million adults in the US who are lesbian, gay, or bisexual, comprising 3.5 percent of the adult

portant in the next chapter as we discuss marriage, and especially why Jesus seemed to only speak of marriage between one man and one woman.

But there's one other variable we need to keep in mind: the need for intimacy. Some people are relative loners. They seem to get along just fine without deep friendships while other people thrive best in a relationship that reflects the "becoming one" of a good marriage. But that need is not always or primarily sexual. Even the young person who is initially attracted to the "hot babe" or "hot guy" hopefully matures to seek a permanent relationship based on far more than just physical attraction. Whether it comes with maturity or is intrinsic to a person's personality, some of us— straight or gay—are drawn into relationships more by the need for intimacy than for sex.

Can God change someone?

In 2013, after 37 years of operation as the umbrella organization over 250 "ex-gay" ministries in the United States and Canada, Exodus International's leader, Alan Chambers, speaking for the seven-member board, disbanded the organization, having found very little evidence of genuine orientation change. Recently he said, "Regardless of a person's opinions on sexual morality, efforts to change someone's primary sexual orientation are dangerous and always unsuccessful."[16]

Nevertheless, we worship a miracle-working God who parted the Red Sea, fed a whole nation for forty years in the wilderness, raised people from the dead, and whom I believe will raise all believers from the dead at the last day. So there is no question in my mind that God *could* work a miracle to change a person's sexual orientation. However, holding out that possibility as the *expected*

population." http://williamsinstitute.law.ucla.edu/research/census-lgbt-demographics-studies/how-many-people-are-lesbian-gay-bisexual-and-transgender/#sthash.clQ60FoJ.dpuf.

16. Alan Chambers, "President Obama is right to try to end ex-gay therapy for minors," *The Washington Post*, April 9, 2015, http://www.washingtonpost.com/national/religion/alan-chambers-president-obama-is-right-to-try-to-end-ex-gay-therapy-for-minors-commentary/2015/04/09/3e5fd6f6-def7-11e4-b6d7-b9bc8acf16f7_story.html.

result of a person's complete surrender or sufficient faith is as cruel as promising a bereaved parent that God will resurrect their dead child . . . if they just have enough faith.

First of all, many sincere gay Christians have tried valiantly for years to change their orientation through prayer, discipline, and therapy without success. Their stories are valid and deserve to be respected. Second, it tells the gay person—and everyone else who hears of your expectations—that you don't accept your gay family member or friend just as they are, and you don't think God does, either. Third, God's not a vending machine triggered by the sincerity or quantity of our faith. He has good reasons for sometimes not doing what we ask, and his reasons include his desire to bless us.

For instance, I originally asked God to "fix" my daughter, to change her orientation, to make the problem go away. But if God had answered that prayer, or if he had not given me a daughter who was gay, I might not have come to love and appreciate gay people personally as I have or had the rich occasion to review God's Word regarding his "marvelous, infinite, matchless grace, freely bestowed on all who believe."[17]

The role of choice

As I noted earlier, many traditionalists claim our sexual orientation is a choice, and therefore gay people can choose to "repent and change." I think there is ample evidence to show this is not true. If it were true that there is a point in time when we choose our orientation, why can't more straight people point to the time when they "chose" to be straight? That's just not the way we grow up.

But that doesn't mean choice never plays any role in the complex matrix of our sexual disposition. Our socialization—what happened to us as we grew up, how we chose to respond to it, and other choices—do affect us sexually and in every other aspect of our personality. Certainly childhood sexual abuse can have a horrendous impact on a person. Pornography can warp normal human response. And sexual addictions are as real as substance addictions. But these traumas afflict gay and straight people alike.

---

17. Julia H. Johnston, "Grace Greater Than Our Sin," 1911, verse 4.

Outside input and personal choice can have positive effects too. What a child is taught and how he chooses to apply it can erect remarkably effective barriers to incest even for a straight teenage boy who has a sister so attractive he wouldn't be able to keep his eyes off her if she were part of another family. He can—apart from any genetic or hormonal or prenatal factors—learn to see and treat his sister as . . . well, simply as his sister. But this is more like the kind of choices a person makes to wait for sex until marriage and to remain faithful in marriage. Such choices can impact and help control an individual's behavior, but they don't attempt to change his or her orientation.

The old counsel to adolescents conflicted over same-sex attraction was, "Don't worry about it. You'll grow out of it." And most did, especially those who could not discern between real attraction and mere curiosity or even brief experimentation. Choice may have played some role for some teens, but not for everyone. For many, there were no conscious points of choice, no history of abuse, no seduction by someone else, no experimentation, no willful fanaticizing. They simply became inexplicably attracted to people of their same sex and never grew out of it, just as the majority became inexplicably attracted to people of the opposite sex and never grew out of it.

Does this prove God made some people gay? Not necessarily, but it certainly raises some serious cautions about declaring any fundamental characteristic of a person *not* part of God's creation.

In the end, I'm not sure how important it is to determine precisely whether same-sex attraction comes from nature, nurture, or choice for any specific person. Counseling, even when it has helped people sort out their past and make positive choices for their future, has not proved effective in changing sexual orientation no matter what its origin. Our real goal remains the same—love our gay family and friends like Jesus.

Collateral Damage

A Mother's Story

Gary was born a charmer. He loved people, and as a toddler was unusually expressive, lavishing sweet compliments on those around him, like the day he sighed and told me, "I just love God for making *you*, Mom."

But I did notice that as a preschooler, when the kids played dress up, he always put on girl clothes. I replaced the clothes in the play drawer with men's clothes, but Gary never found them much fun.

In second grade, he began displaying some behavioral problems, vacillating between his sweet, charming self and a touchy, angry side that mystified me. By eighth grade he was on student council and had huge responsibilities in planning the eighth grade dance. Not long before the dance, I went to see a school musical and happened to sit behind a group of girls who were complaining that there weren't going to be enough boys at the dance. Not knowing who I was, they named a few guys; then one added, "And Gary. But he's a girl." They all giggled, but the comment stabbed my heart.

The thing was, girls really liked him and considered him one of their best friends. But it was no encouragement to me when one of their moms gushed to me, "I just *love* Gary! He is the only guy I can trust to hang out with Darlene at our house, even in her bedroom, and I don't have a thing to worry about." She meant he was honorable and trustworthy. But she had no idea he simply was not attracted to Darlene the way other guys were.

Throughout high school Gary had girlfriends and dates, but he also had guy friendships that seemed unusually exclusive, often ending up in painful misunderstanding. But I took comfort in the disparaging gay jokes he often told—certainly that proved he wasn't interested in guys. Besides, he was outrageously busy, involved in every drama, musical, chorus, county chorus, district chorus, swimming, cross country, student council, and long mission trips in the summers. At the end of his junior year, he found a new group of friends that were crazy about Jesus, and he spent lots of time with them at youth worship services and youth conferences. They formed a worship band that was really good, as well as a pop band. In his senior year he chose a ministry-oriented Bible college as the next step in his education.

What I didn't know was that he'd been fighting a desperate battle against same-sex attraction, crying out to the Lord every night that God would deliver him from his "problem."

During Easter break of his first year at college, he finally confessed to my husband and me what he was struggling with. But he assured us he believed it was sin, he wasn't acting on it, and was getting help. Later he explained that he'd always hoped the mission trips, conferences, and Bible college would "fix" him. And, in fact, as soon as the administration found out about his orientation, they put him into their Exodus–type therapy program and kept him there his entire time in college, even though during Easter break of his second year he had a complete emotional breakdown.

While he was home, he admitted to his beloved high school girlfriend that he loved her but not the way she wanted him to, and he was not sure he ever could. She was completely heartbroken. He cried almost all the time. No one in our home area, except our pastor and us, knew the cause of his breakdown and depression. He had been chosen for a youth pastor internship in Louisiana for that summer, so we blindly assumed that this was Satan's way of trying to destroy him. We prayed, cried, begged God, called help lines on TBN, called a friend's suggested prayer warrior in Tennessee . . . who asked if we could send her ten dollars, since praying for people over the phone was her only income.

Saying goodbye to him as he left for Louisiana was heart wrenching. He was crying as he got into his car. He said, "Mom, this is the hardest thing I have ever done." I made him promise to call me several times on the five-hour trip. He did, trying not to worry me. But he told us later that he kept thinking on the whole trip how easy it would be to just drive into a tree, and nobody would need to know what his struggle had been.

When he arrived in Louisiana, he was in such a mess he confessed to the pastor what he was dealing with. They had a visiting pastor who prayed over Gary.

Somehow Gary made it through that summer assignment and even his final year at college. His giftings were strong in spite of his struggle. Whenever he led worship, people wept. He also sang in the gospel choir at the school. I remember going to one of their concerts. He had the lead solo in a very powerful Brooklyn Tabernacle Choir song. Afterward the man behind me asked if he was my son. I said yes. He said, "Some people have talent, some people have anointing. Most people don't have both, but your son does."

After graduation he moved back to our home area, became involved in music ministry, successful employment, and a very active social life, but he constantly battled hopelessness and depression over his inability to overcome his same-sex attraction. After three years I noticed changes that scared me. He seemed less transparent, more argumentative, more careless, and he was making plans to move to California to start a business with a cousin who was in the same line of work.

A week before he left, I finally got a chance to talk with him alone and ask him what was going on. He looked at me and said, "I don't think you want to know." And then he told me about waking up on his birthday and deciding he wasn't going to fight it anymore. He did not want to eventually marry someone and have a family, only to admit at midlife that he was still attracted to men and end up breaking hearts. So he'd actually already struck up a close friendship with a guy, but moving to California was messing that up. He was an emotional mess.

And so was I. That week as I helped him pack, we had deep, heart-wrenching conversations. I cried buckets of tears, and so did he. We pretty much had this little circle of three who really knew what was going on—my husband, Gary, and I. I couldn't find the courage to tell our other children, not even the daughter in Florida whom he was going to join.

And then he left. He kind of went off the deep end at first— away from the watchful eye of Bible college, church, and relatives. My husband and I felt like prisoners of a horrible secret. We had no idea what to do. I felt furious at God for not answering the cries of our hearts, of Gary's heart.

Eventually people from church heard from friends of Gary and came to us. They were not accusatory in any way. But one couple said they felt homosexuality was a demon that jumps onto people and could go from person to person. They said my husband and I should pray together every morning for Gary to be set free from that demon. So we did—every morning for two years. They also said we should not talk with Gary about the same-sex attraction because hearing his struggles might tear down our faith. So we stayed in touch with him, but pretty much acted like the homosexuality did not exist.

I came across a book from James Dobson's ministry that said once a person gets into the "gay lifestyle," they seldom come back. I certainly didn't want to hear that, but the book also said for those who do come back, the love of their family is the biggest contributing factor. I'm actually glad I read that, because I determined that I would keep loving Gary, no matter what.

About two years later he came home for a wedding, and when I took him to the airport afterward he told me he had been going to a gay-friendly church. He mentioned their involvement in missions for those suffering from HIV/AIDS in African countries. There had been a person at the church who was a missionary there, and his story really stirred Gary's compassionate heart. He said he hoped he could do something like that someday. Then he looked across the front seat and with tears in his eyes said, "I'm just glad, Mom, that I still have a heart for ministry."

Something happened to me at that moment. My heavy burden about his homosexuality seemed to fall off my back. That evening I told my husband about it, and even though we did not make a conscious decision to stop praying for Gary's deliverance, we actually never did so again. It was our acceptance of God's sovereignty.

From that time on we discussed his situation more openly with him and found out his friend Bob was actually his boyfriend. We got to know and eventually love Bob. As the years passed, things gradually changed. I've shared our situation with one person at a time as the opportunity arose. Eventually I became less guarded about it on public media. However, there are still friends and relatives with whom the subject of Gary's sexual orientation and "lifestyle" is too difficult to discuss.

Gary and Bob are now engaged and planning to be married. They make a good partnership, and Gary's career is flourishing. He's found some real healing in the church they now attend, but his music ministry and his passion for God seem to have been casualties of "the fight."

So we continue to pray for him, just as we do for all our children—that God's will would be done and his kingdom would come in their lives.

Chapter 8
Marriage: One Man and One Woman

There's a wideness in God's mercy,
Like the wideness of the sea;
There's a kindness in His justice,
Which is more than liberty . . .

But we make His love too narrow
By false limits of our own;
And we magnify His strictness
With a zeal He will not own.

"There's a Wildness in God's Mercy"
Frederick W. Faber, 1854, verses 1 and 11

M Y WIFE HAS A BUTTON THAT SAYS, "I love being married!" Well, me too! When I first saw her in college, I wanted to be married to *that* girl. Some people, even people with good marriages, speak of "the honeymoon being over" as they slip into the routines and sometimes the doldrums of married life. (Our honeymoon was thankfully over when we came out of the mountains where we'd spent a few days in a *very* rustic cabin with an outhouse and two single beds we had to slide together.) Yes, it took us a few years to learn how to communicate our expectations effectively, to not let every molehill become a mountain, to learn the importance of forgiveness, and gain a sense of humor. But our joy and companionship have definitely deepened and increased as the years have gone by. And we still love being married.

Back in the late 1980s when I was helping Ed Hurst write his book, *Overcoming Homosexuality*, describing marriage as only "between one man and one woman," was not common parlance. That's not to say it wasn't society's general presumption; it just wasn't necessary to state it that way. I don't believe it appeared in our book, and scanning some of the research we did at the time, the phrase doesn't seem to have appeared. There had been a few attempts by gay people in committed relationships to have their relationships legally recognized as a marriage, but the primary opposition they faced didn't focus on marriage so much as their homosexuality itself. But all that began to change in the 1990's as gay rights advocates saw marriage as key to establishing basic rights and protections for themselves in society.

In opposition, the Defense of Marriage Act (DOMA), passed by both houses and signed into law by President Clinton in 1996, defined marriage in Section 3 as "only a legal union between one man and one woman." DOMA did not bar individual states from recognizing same-sex married couples, and in 2013, Section 3 was actually ruled unconstitutional by the U.S. Supreme Court, because it barred same-sex couples married in states that allowed it from receiving federal recognition and benefits. Essentially, the court's decision kept the federal government out of the issue. States wouldn't be forced to recognize gay marriage (Section 2), but they wouldn't be penalized under Section 3 (by withholding federal benefits) if they did.

Ever since DOMA's enactment, however, the phrase, "marriage is between one man and one woman" has become not only a political but a religious slogan. Traditional and neo-traditional Christians have claimed it as "*the* Christian position" even though 66 percent of mainline Protestants, 70 percent of Catholics, and even 36 percent of evangelicals say homosexuality should be accepted. In fact, "roughly half (51 percent) of evangelical Protestants in the Millennial generation (born between 1981 and 1996) say homosexuality should be accepted."[1] Obviously, it's not the *only* Christian position or even the most dominant Christian position.

---

1. Caryle Murphy, "Most U.S. Christian groups grow more accepting of homosexuality," Pew Research Center, December 18, 2015. http://www.pewresearch.org/fact-tank/2015/12/18/most-u-s-christian-groups-grow-more-accepting-of-homosexuality/.

"But," some protest, "the kingdom of God is not a democracy. We don't determine truth according to polls." Of course not. But it's not an oligarchy, either. It's the kingdom of *God*, after all.

What is the biblical position?

That depends on how universally one makes the claim concerning one man and one woman. I believe God's *basic design* for marriage is a life-long, monogamous relationship of equality and love between one man and one woman. (I'll explain the basis for my belief later in this chapter.) But the fact that one man and one woman seems to be God's basic design does not eliminate the clear evidence that God on several occasions allowed, blessed, and even endorsed variations. So, it is not the *only* biblically recognized configuration. Certainly not if you think God desires marriage to be a relationship of equality and love. There are several biblical examples where those qualities were missing.

More to the point, the practices of polygamy and concubinary were frequent anomalies for many Old Testament patriarchs without any evidence of God's displeasure—Abraham, Jacob, Gideon, etc. But the lack of any opposition by God doesn't mean he was sleeping on the job. When a moral issue was at stake, he didn't, for instance, hesitate to discipline David for his adultery with Bathsheba and the subsequent murder of her husband. But God never chastised David for having seven named wives as well as concubines. In fact, in 2 Samuel 12:8 where God rebuked David for his adultery with Bathsheba, he reminded him, "I gave your master's house to you, and your master's wives into your arms. And if all this had been too little, I would have given you even more." Some say that while God may have reluctantly permitted polygamy in the Old Testament, he never actually approved of it. But this verse renders that theory false since God actually *gave* David Saul's wives, and he wouldn't have given anyone a gift he considered immoral.

Deuteronomy 17:17 does say the king "must not take *many* wives, or his heart will be led astray" (emphasis added). However, it doesn't seem to be referring to limited polygamy but to the kind of excess represented by David's son Solomon with his seven hundred wives and three hundred concubines (many of them pagan), who "turned his heart after other gods, and his heart was not fully devoted to the Lord his God, as the heart of David his father had been" (I Kings 11:4). The *source* of Solomon's problem wasn't that he deviated from "marriage between one man and one woman," since David did the same on a much smaller scale but was, nevertheless, identified as "fully devoted to the Lord his God." Rather, it was Solomon's excess and the pagan wives he took that caused his problem. After all, it takes only one Jezebel to incite a king to turn from worshiping the true God.[2]

Furthermore, by establishing "levirate marriage" in Deuteronomy 25:5-6, God virtually mandated polygamous relationships in perhaps the majority of instances where levirate marriage might have been invoked. This law said that whenever a married man died without a son, his brother was *obligated* to marry the widow and raise a son in the first brother's stead. In an agrarian and war-ravaged culture where most men married at a young age but were, nevertheless, in danger of disease, famine, accident, and death in battle, occasions for enacting this law would have come up frequently. This was, in fact, the reason Boaz married Ruth. Wealthy, kind, and devout, Boaz was in line to marry thw widow Ruth and give her a son, which he did. One rabbinical legend claims Boaz was the father of sixty children. There's no proof of that in the Scriptures, but given the cultural expectations, it is unlikely this older, prominent landowner would have been single.

The levirate marriage law was sufficiently remembered in Jesus' time that the Pharisees used it to try to trick Jesus by asking whose wife a woman would be in heaven if she had married and outlived seven brothers in succession (Matthew 22:23-33). Whether or not levirate marriage was commonly invoked, it was a law given by God that had a high probability of creating polygamy since, in many cases, the surviving brother would already be married, a condition that did not constitute an exemption from doing his duty.

---

2. 1 Kings 20:7 indicates Ahab may have had other wives, but it was Jezebel who encouraged him to worship Baal and Asherah.

I am by no means advocating polygamy![3] But in these examples, we see that the wideness in God's mercy transcends his "basic design" so as to accommodate the particular needs of individual people and various cultures. More importantly, these variations contradict any claim that the *only* biblical model for marriage God condoned and blessed was between "one man and one woman." Keep that in mind the next time you hear someone make such a claim. It's simply an overstatement.

The case for God's basic design

I said earlier that I believe God's *basic design* for marriage is a life-long, monogamous relationship of equality and love between one man and one woman. My statement includes far more than the male/female element, but let's start there.

Physiology. No one can deny our human anatomy is designed for procreation and requires a man and a woman. It was to a man and a woman God said, "Be fruitful and increase in number; fill the earth and subdue it" (Genesis 1:28). Some gay advocates point out that the procreation assignment has been adequately accomplished with seven billion people on the earth, the vast majority of whom will continue to procreate. True as this might be, it does not cancel the significance of this aspect of marriage. However, in retelling the creation story, Genesis 2:18 reveals God's *far more fundamental* motive for creating marriage: "It is not good for the man to be alone. I will make a helper suitable for him."

While procreation is not possible for some couples, is not chosen by others, and ceases in time to be possible for any couple, companionship and partnership are God's foundational purpose for marriage, and companionship lasts a lifetime. At nearly fifty years of marriage, my wife and I can certainly affirm this truth. And when a couple too old or otherwise unable to have children wants to marry, all of us still delight in celebrating such a mar-

---

3. By New Testament times, 1 Timothy 3:2, 12 and Titus 1:6 required church leaders to be the "husband of one wife." While this stipulation acknowledges polygamy was still sufficiently prevalent to be addressed, God was teaching his people a better way. In Chapter 17 we will see how Jesus' "second commandment" improves our discernment of right from wrong and our disapproval of polygamy.

riage. In fact, most Christians (even most Catholics) believe voluntarily bypassing the procreation option is entirely acceptable.

So while our plumbing says something significant about God's basic design, it doesn't represent the most important aspect of a marriage, and there's nothing in the Bible that instructs us on how that plumbing is to be enjoyed by married couples or that sexual activity is only legitimate when attempting to procreate.

A father and a mother for every child. The 2015 arguments before the U.S. Supreme Court opposing gay marriage were summed up in the words of John Bursch, Special Assistant Attorney General for Michigan: "The State's entire interest springs out of the fact that we want to forever link children with their biological mom and dad when that's possible."[4] And that's a compelling concern for Christians as well. There is a great benefit to every child having a father and a mother, not only for the advantage of together shouldering the load of earning a living along with parenting but also to provide the modeling of both a male and a female—a father and a mother—as the children grow up.

Opponents of marriage equality claim that condoning gay marriage undermines society's expectation for just such homes. But it's a bit of a circular argument when the same people simultaneously object to gay marriage on the basis of gay couples being unable to naturally have children while the children many of them do parent are often the product of failed heterosexual marriages or casual sexual relationships. In this regard, gay couples provide a great social service—one might even say *Christian* service—for children who might otherwise be in the foster care system or, at the very least, living in an overwhelmed single-parent family. Furthermore, having an emotionally healthy and *safe* family environment is the most important requirement for a child's wellbeing.

Nevertheless, I take seriously the need for my grandson to have male role models as he grows up. I wish I could contribute on a daily basis, and I don't abdicate my responsibility to the other adult males in his life—his other grandfather, his uncles, Sunday

---

4. The 2015 United States Supreme Court hearing regarding gay marriage, Washington, D.C., April 28, 2015.

school teachers, grade school teachers, coaches, neighbors, and family friends—important as they are. Yes, "it takes a village," but I'm on the front line . . . and too far away to do right by the job. I've had the same concerns for my college-age granddaughter. Fortunately, her father remains involved in her life. But does all this mean I wish Leah and Jane hadn't had Jacob? I could never say that! They are doing a great job as parents, and he's *my* grandson—a precious child in God's sight.

We evangelicals don't want to encourage abortion, and we claim to sympathize with the burden single parents must shoulder. So why do we get so apoplectic when gay couples—some of them single parents like Leah was—want to embrace something better? And why, when their families need support to raise their children, do we withhold recognition of the validity of their family unit? Can you imagine raising *your* teenager in a church that questions your parental authority? I can just hear the echoes of surly teens: "You can't tell me what to do! My youth leader said you shouldn't even be a parent!"

Complementarity. Many traditional thinkers say it is the "complementarity" and the "differentiation" between males and females that is crucial in marriage. I appreciate what Neta brings to our marriage as a woman, and I know she appreciates what I bring to it. But many of our gifts are not gender-based and the skills that are have mostly been culturally learned. Furthermore, most gay couples we know end up practicing a functional complementarity in terms of their domestic life, based on their individual gifts and strengths. However, John Piper and Wayne Grudem, among others, believe those roles in marriage must be gender-based with a strict complementarity and differentiation, which requires a man and a woman. But they also carry their theories into how the church should function claiming certain roles of leadership, pastoring, and teaching are only open to men and not to women (perspectives many churches no longer espouse). Some complementarians even extend this subservience of women into the secular realm, suggesting women should not be in executive positions over men.

Along a slightly different vein, Robert Gagnon theorizes about the implications of God's creation of two sexes in the first place and why he thinks marriage between a man and a woman is the only meaningful resolution. He writes:

In Gen. 2:18-24, a binary or sexually undifferentiated human (the *adam*) is split into two sexually differentiated beings. Marriage is treated by the Yahwist as a reunion of two complementary sexual others, a reconstitution of the sexual unity of the original *adam*.[5]

In simpler terms, he claims that Adam was some kind of androgynous being who was sliced in half to create Eve, leaving each being incomplete. Only when the male and the female come back together do we experience the whole image of God. But as James Brownson points out in his book, *Bible Gender Sexuality*, if the reunion of male and female is required to achieve the fullness or image of God, then Adam "had it all" before Eve was created, nothing lacking. So why would God declare that it was not good for him to be alone and in need of a helper?[6] Brownson also notes:

If both male and female must be present together in order to fully constitute the image of God, then those who are single do not fully reflect the image of God. . . . But even more importantly, the New Testament clearly proclaims that Jesus is, par excellence, the image of God. . . . Unless we are to postulate an androgynous savior, something the New Testament never even contemplates, we cannot say that the image of God requires the presence of both male and female.[7]

One further thought on complementarity. Unless we want to return to the stereotypes that put glass ceilings over women and encouraged insensitivity in men, exalting the importance

---

5. Dan O. Via and Robert A. J. Gagon, *Homosexuality and the Bible: Two Views* (Minneapolis, MN: Fortress Press, 2009), 61.

6. James V. Brownson, *Bible Gender Sexuality* (Grand Rapids, MI: Wm. B. Eerdmans Publishing Company, 2013), 28.

7. Ibid., 32.

of gender complementarity could end up focusing on our most obvious differences, which are physical. Admittedly, as a straight guy, the first thing I noticed about my wife over fifty years ago was how she looked, and I still think she looks good. But even then, I knew I needed to look deeper to see the *person* she was. And I was not disappointed. Thankfully, I'd been taught that looks are only skin deep. And I still try to quickly move beyond those first physical impressions in relating to anyone because the deeper, more important character qualities and gifts are not necessarily gender specific. So what exactly are we talking about when we say gender complementarity and differentiation is foundational for marriage? And what are we encouraging people to focus on when we do—prominent breasts and ripped abs? I hope not.

Also, it's not the gender complementarity I model that my grandson needs to see. In fact, contrary to popular culture, he needs to see how, *as a man,* I am not simply defined by stereotypic or transient distinctives. Sure, I learned a lot of mechanical skills from my dad as well as the joy of hunting and fishing, and I hope to pass some of that on to Jacob and my other grandsons. But his birth mom is far more athletic than I am, so, go figure. What I mostly hope my grandson can see in me is that he too—as a boy growing into a young man—can look to Jesus for the character qualities that really matter. Those traits are honorably masculine but not gender exclusive—that is, both men and women can equally express and model such qualities as "love, joy, peace, forbearance, kindness, goodness, faithfulness, gentleness, and self-control" (Galatians 5:22-23).

Common portrayal. There is no question that whenever marriage *as an institution* is actually discussed in the Bible, it is portrayed as between a man and a woman. From the very beginning, we read, "For this reason a man will leave his father and mother and be united to his wife, and they will become one flesh" (Genesis 2:24). In spite of his expansive harem, Solomon's description of married love in the Song of Solomon is between himself and one woman. In arguing for the permanence of marriage, Jesus quotes the Genesis description (Matthew 19:5 and Mark 10:7). In discussing how men should love their wives, Paul also quotes the Genesis passage

(Ephesians 5:31). And when advising on how to deal with sexual temptation, he says, "each man should have his own wife, and each woman her own husband" (1 Corinthians 7:2).

While we've already shown that one man and one woman isn't the only model God has recognized and blessed, these references clearly establish that it is God's most common, basic design to be celebrated and cherished by the majority who are heterosexual. But that doesn't address the dilemma of those with same-sex attraction.

Prophetic symbolism. In his presentation to the 2014 Humanum Conference,[8] theologian N.T. Wright shared his understanding of the fulfillment of God's good purposes for all of creation by bringing together all things in heaven and earth in Christ. He sees this unity of heaven and earth as bookends for creation—how things were in the beginning and how God will restore them in the end. Wright says marriage is the prophetic symbol for this highly longed-for unity. "We know," as Paul says, "that all creation has been groaning as in the pains of childbirth up to the present time. Not only so, but we ourselves, who have the firstfruits of the Spirit, groan inwardly as we wait eagerly for our adoption as sons, the redemption of our bodies" (Romans 8:23). The fulfillment of this longing is described at the end of the Book of Revelation as "the marriage of the Lamb."

Throughout Scripture, God often portrays his relationship with his people—whether the Children of Israel or the Church—as that of a loving husband toward his bride, and this, Wright says, is a signpost for that final fulfillment when all of creation will be brought together in complete unity. So far, so good. But what's not so conclusive is his insistence that the prophetic symbolism of marriage requires opposite genders in order to have eschatological meaning. He begins by pointing to various contrasts in creation: "the sea and the dry land, plants and animals . . . . Within the

---

8. November 17-19, 2014, the Vatican hosted an international colloquium dedicated to "the complementarity of man and woman" and the importance of marriage. N.T. Wright, along with several other non-Catholics, was invited to submit a presentation. https://www.youtube.com/watch?v=AsB-JDsOTwE.

animal kingdom," he says, "we have, of course, male and female. The story reaches its climax in the creating of human beings in the image of God, male and female together." But I think Wright pushes his imagery too far. While it's true that all these entities are juxtaposed, it isn't their differentiation that makes marriage a powerful symbol. It's the love of God for Israel, indeed for the whole world, and Christ's love for the church that's so compelling and foretells the ultimate coming together of all things in Christ. Besides, marriage isn't the only image of God's love for us. Father is the most common, but there's also mother, shepherd, king. Jesus even said, "I have longed to gather your children together, as a hen gathers her chicks under her wings" (Matthew 23:37).

Even the roles of husband and wife aren't gender-dependent in this prophetic vision of marriage either. The union is not characterized by procreation, which is the only aspect of marriage that demands opposite-gender partners. In fact, there really aren't any sexual elements obvious in the biblical symbolism. God and Israel, Christ and the church aren't sexualized as occurs with the deities of some pagan religions. All the emphasis is on commitment, covenant, fidelity, sacrifice, forgiveness, redemption, and relationship—qualities same-sex couples can and do enjoy just like opposite-sex couples.

But doesn't Jesus define marriage as "one man and one woman"?

There are those who believe Jesus' statement in Matthew 19:4-6 (see also Mark 10:2-12), proves he condemned same-sex marriage.

"Haven't you read . . . that at the beginning the Creator 'made them male and female,' and said, 'For this reason a man will leave his father and mother and be united to his wife, and the two will become one flesh'? So they are no longer two, but one flesh. Therefore what God has joined together, let no one separate" (Matthew 19:4-6).

Michael Brown, author of *Can You Be Gay and Christian?* says, "In light of this, it is unconscionable to imagine that Jesus would sanction male-male or female-female unions, since, among other things, they violate God's design and intent 'in the beginning.'"[9]

Indeed, Jesus' answer does affirm God's basic design, but we've already seen that in some circumstances, God didn't limit his blessing only to "*one* man and *one* woman" unions. But Jesus was not commenting on whether or not God allows variations from his basic design. He was answering a specific question posed to him by the Pharisees: "Is it lawful for a man to divorce his wife for any and every reason?" (Matthew 19:3). After reviewing the origin and basic design for marriage, Jesus answered their question: "Therefore what God has joined together, let no one separate" (v. 6).

It's only in our politically correct media culture that we tend to make something out of what Jesus *didn't* say, that he didn't add a footnote to describe or denounce variations on God's basic design for marriage. That's not what he was talking about. He was speaking about divorce and making the point that God's intention for marriage included permanence: "What God has joined together, let no one separate." Claiming Jesus' answer condemns same-sex marriage is at best an argument from silence.

However, apparently the disciples were overwhelmed by how strongly Jesus supported permanence in marriage. Later, when they got him alone (according to Mark 10:10), they said, "If this is the situation between a husband and wife, it is better not to marry."

Jesus replied, "Not everyone can accept this word, but only those to whom it has been given. For there are eunuchs who were born that way, and there are eunuchs who have been made eunuchs by others—and there are those who choose to live like eunuchs for the sake of the kingdom of heaven. The one who can accept this should accept it" (Matthew 19:10-12).

To what was Jesus referring when he mentioned "eunuchs who were born that way"? In ancient times, eunuchs were universally

---

9. Michael L. Brown, *Can You Be Gay and Christian?* (Lake Mary, FL: Frontline, a Division of Charisma House, 2014), 133.

despised and ridiculed, especially in Judaism, because they could not fulfill God's commandment in Genesis 1:28 to "Be fruitful and increase in number." Approximately 1 percent of all males are born with undescended testicles that do not descend spontaneously within a few months, usually rendering them infertile. Today, rather than wait to see if the testes migrate down naturally, the malady is corrected with a simple surgical procedure shortly after birth. But in ancient times, that remedy was unavailable, and those who proved to be completely infertile from this or some other cause would have been designated eunuchs.

The disciples had probably heard of someone with such a birth defect, but the only kind of eunuchs mentioned in the Old Testament (*saris* in Hebrew) were those "who have been made eunuchs by others," Jesus' second category. So when Jesus mentioned "eunuchs who were born that way," the disciples may well have thought of the confirmed bachelors they knew who were inexplicably not interested in "normal" heterosexual marriage, even though procreation was a high expectation in their culture. After all, those who were not interested in heterosexual marriage would have outnumbered those with physical defects by three or four times. So, could Jesus have intentionally included gay people as natural "eunuchs"?

If he did, that virtually ends the debate concerning whether God created gay people, because it was Jesus himself who told us they were "born that way."

A couple of years ago, my good friend, Tim Nafziger, preached a Palm Sunday message in which he pointed out that when Jesus drove the money-changers out of the temple, declaring, "'My house will be called a house of prayer,' but you are making it 'a den of robbers'" (Matthew 21:13), he was quoting from Isaiah 56, which also includes a promise for eunuchs. Eunuchs had previously been excluded from the assembly of God's people (Deuteronomy 23:1),[10] but with the coming Messiah, their faithfulness to God's covenant would be honored. "To them I will give within

---

10. Specifically, this prohibition was for eunuchs who had "been emasculated by crushing or cutting" (i.e., castrated), and no mention is made in Deuteronomy of "eunuchs who were born that way."

my temple and its walls a memorial and a name better than sons and daughters; I will give them an everlasting name that will endure forever" (Isaiah 56:5). If that promise includes "eunuchs who were born that way," have we given them places of honor in our churches?

Furthermore, by including all three categories of eunuchs, Jesus identified himself with the challenge and humiliation heaped upon all eunuchs. Jesus chose not to marry even though by his early thirties he would have been expected to take a wife and have children. In not doing so, he aligned himself with "those who choose to live like eunuchs for the sake of the kingdom of heaven."

Back to Jesus' follow-up on divorce. All three categories of eunuchs he mentions in Matthew 19:11-12 are held up as examples because they *do not* marry. So, even if Jesus is acknowledging naturally gay people, this passage is not in itself an affirmation of gay marriage. However, Jesus is not issuing a new law, not even concerning divorce. He didn't say, if you can't remain married for life, then you *must* remain single. Not at all. He began his little discourse by assuring his listeners, "Not everyone can accept this word," and he concluded it similarly: "The one who can accept this should accept it." He evokes no condemnation for those who can't accept this challenging alternative.

For a matter so close to Jesus' heart as the permanence of marriage, I find it powerfully informative of Jesus' character that he *did not* take this occasion to lay down a universal law. Doesn't this say something powerful about the wideness in God's mercy toward gay people too? Might his word to them be, "The one who can freely accept celibacy—but not out of fear or shame—should do so. But if you can't, I do not condemn you"? Based on this example about divorce, had the disciples explicitly asked him whether *all* gay people had to remain celibate, I doubt he would have issued such a law.

A more effective DOMA (Defense Of Marriage Act)

Obviously, I did not write this chapter (or this book) to advocate gay marriage *over* straight marriage. I unequivocally believe God's basic design for marriage is a life-long, monogamous relationship of equality and love between a man and a woman, which applies to over 95 percent of the population. Our physiology, the joy of procreation with a male and female parent for every child, complementarity (as long as it's not used to subjugate women or deny that single people are fully in God's image), the common portrayal of marriage in the Bible, and as one of the prophetic symbols for God's love for us—all these motifs support marriage between one man and one woman. And I embrace them. I only challenge the *degree* to which they are now being used to claim God has not and could not condone any variations from that basic design.

Straight marriage is not threatened because a small minority of gay people who cannot (and in most cases should not) attempt a straight marriage but already have legally married or wish to marry one another. All the incentives for marriage, all the benefits from marriage remain unthreatened by marriage equality. Genuinely straight people are not going to run out and start marrying people of the same gender just because it's allowed.

What really threatens marriages, *even within the church,* is our failure to place our emphasis on the kinds of things Jesus considers the "more important matters . . . justice, mercy, and faithfulness" (Matthew 23:23) so as to create homes of love and peace and encouragement that everyone wants to be a part of and learn how to make thrive. But people who have grown up in domestic battlefields of abuse and domination or who have attempted marriages only to have them blow up—leaving them with PTSD (post traumatic stress disorder)—are not likely to risk marriage. And so they wait, not sure they ever want to get married and just play around—"friends with benefits." Some shack up to see if they can make it work before committing. Others get married before dealing with their histories and reproduce the same traumas for another generation.

If we really want to defend marriage, we'll put far more of our effort into teaching abstinence before marriage (whether straight or gay), preparing people for marriage, and strengthening our existing marriages and families so we can offer people real hope that a marriage with all the qualities and privileges and rights we espouse are actually achievable, and that the responsibilities and hurdles and challenges are manageable and worthy of persistent pursuit. That would be a truly effective DOMA. And the gay Christians Neta and I know want that too.

Collateral Damage

One of the first things Dawn said as she and Carrie sat down to Sunday dinner at our table was, "Thank you for inviting us. I don't think anyone has ever cared enough to ask us about our story." The story we'd invited them to tell was how they each had realized they were lesbians, how they met, and how they were being received in their church now that they were married.

Neta served everyone steaming helpings of her famous chicken and rice as we exchanged small talk. But once we'd passed around the broccoli and made sure everyone had lemon for their ice water, Dawn began in a soft, melodic voice.

"My grandmother and grandfather always took us kids to church, every Sunday morning and night, Tuesday, and Wednesday. When I was in kindergarten, another girl came on to me, and I kind of liked it. But I'd been taught sex-play was wrong, so I felt guilty and blamed myself. I was eight years old when Grandma died of cancer, and I couldn't understand why God would take her from me. In reaction, I chose to live outside his covering, so to speak.

"When I reached adolescence, I tried to notice boys while secretly beginning to realize I was more attracted to girls. Nevertheless, I kept on trying to fit in until I was about seventeen when the day came that I knew I couldn't continue living a lie. I knew what the social repercussions of coming out might be, but what was far more devastating to me was the thought that God must not love me if he made me this way.

"When my father found out, he disowned me, told me I was no longer his daughter. Thankfully, my mother was more gracious. She said, 'I don't understand it, but I love you. God gave you to me, and I'm going to love you the way he wants me to love you. This is who you are. That's just it.' But when I began bringing my girlfriends around, that was too much for her." Dawn choked up and turned her attention to eating.

Carrie wiped her mouth. "Well, I also grew up in the church and in a very close-knit family." Carrie is a little older and owns a successful beauty salon, the tips of her short Afro dusted as if by a red frost. "I was just a normal kid, but I always knew there was something different about me. And when I moved into my adolescence, I realized I wasn't into the boys. That was no problem in junior high, but by high school, it became more obvious. In church, homosexuality was never talked about until I started asking my pastor's daughter why God made me this way. She said I was wrong, so I decided to keep it a secret and not say anything to anybody else. Finally, however, my mom figured it out, and she blamed herself, wondering what she'd done wrong. 'Well, this is not you,' she said. 'It's me. I should have been around more. I should've paid more attention to you. It's my fault.'

"Maybe because of how it devastated my mom, I determined to become *normal* and started dating boys. In fact, I even allowed one guy sexual privileges to prove I was okay and became pregnant for it right after high school. I love my son to death, but it happened because I just wanted to be accepted by everyone and wanted to be normal and not considered a freak."

Carrie stopped and toyed with her chicken and rice. "But that didn't work out so well, so I decided I wasn't going to be with anyone. All I cared about was becoming successful and raising my son. I avoided relationships for the next ten years. I didn't want to settle down and be with anyone. I just wanted to live Carrie's life. Love Carrie, and that's it. Just love Carrie. But trying to be a heterosexual, even though I wasn't dating, was hiding who I really was. I was living a lie.

"At some point, you look in the mirror and say, 'Who am I, and who am I trying to please?'"

107

By this time Dawn had composed herself enough to continue her story. "Actually, this isn't my first marriage. I was in a civil union when I lived back east. It lasted about five years until I found out that my partner was cheating on me. But before I married her, I knew I wasn't supposed to—not to her and not at that time in my life. So throughout the breakup, I was part of this online sharing group, and that's where I met Carrie. We were just friends, but she was very supportive of me."

"When we would talk," Carrie added, "we'd end up talking for hours even though it was really about nothing. We just clicked, that's all. But one day Dawn said, 'I think I've done something bad.' I told her it couldn't have been *that* bad. But she said, 'No, I really think I've done something terrible.' And without knowing her history or having ever met her face-to-face, I said, 'Did you cut yourself?'"

"I couldn't believe she asked that," Dawn said, almost indignantly, "because I hadn't told anyone I'd been cutting myself on a daily basis."

"I think God gave me the insight to ask that question." Carrie smiled knowingly at her. "That was her secret, but admitting it was the first part of her healing."

"And that was the truth. I'd become seriously suicidal, trying various ways to off myself. One day I mixed charcoal lighter fluid into a pitcher of Kool-Aid and began drinking it, but it just made me sick. Another time I took a whole bottle of pills. But for the first time, someone really understood me and helped me out of my depression. And for that, I'll tell anyone that God used Carrie to save my life."

"But it wasn't only for her," inserted Carrie. "I think God put us together to save me too. I wasn't in a destructive relationship. I just didn't think of love in that way. Online, we developed into close friends, but over time, it developed into love."

"And a lot of our conversations were about God," Dawn added.

"That's right, because my relationship with God is very important. We finally planned a visit, but it was going to be a group visit. I brought one of my friends, and someone Dawn knew was going to join us while we toured her city."

Dawn laughed. "Yeah, but every time we were gonna do something, these other friends reneged, so that left just the two of us. And that's when our relationship really jelled. That was almost four years ago."

It wasn't long after that when Dawn moved to Carrie's city and their relationship deepened. The main focus of their social life was Carrie's church, but that's been hard, because the pastor often preaches against homosexuality. "He harps on this subject all the time," Carrie explained, "and in the most disrespectful fashion. He says he's even received hate letters—not from us, of course. But I can understand why. Right from the pulpit he's said things like, 'I don't care if anyone thinks this is hate speech—this is my opinion. You aren't going to inherit anything in the kingdom, and your children won't amount to anything either.'"

"We knew neither of us would ever be able to have a relationship with a man," she continued, "but we didn't want to 'live in sin,' so the biblical thing seemed obvious—get married." She smiled broadly and gave Dawn a look. "I remember the day I asked her. 'What do you think about being a minister's wife?' That was because I was already involved in ministry—the choir, children's ministry, praise and worship, vacation Bible school, and anything else I was asked to do—that being formally recognized as a 'minister' in our black church—which was where I thought God was leading me."

Dawn said she was cool with the idea. In fact, she'd already finished the New Directions class at the church and had volunteered to join the hospitality ministry.

The problem was, as the weeks went by, no one got back to her, even though she inquired more than once. People were catching on about their relationship. "Though we don't kiss in public or even hold hands," Dawn insisted. "We don't flaunt our relationship. We're not so concerned about what other people may think, but we try to be mindful of how they may *feel*. So we just curb our PDA—our public displays of affection."

The conversation paused as seconds were offered, and we all replenished our plates. Then Carrie continued.

"Sometimes the Lord speaks to me very clearly. And one Sunday when I was going up into the choir loft, I heard God call my name. I didn't know what he wanted, but I was ready to do anything, so I asked him what he wanted. He didn't answer me right then, but a couple weeks later, as VBS was coming to a close, several of us had gathered for an evaluation meeting, and right in the middle of it, God told me, 'This is going to be your last assignment for a while.' At the time, I had no idea why because I'd been so involved. When I told the Sunday school coordinator I was stepping back, he wouldn't accept it and said we needed to have a meeting about it.

"I did have a meeting, but it was to tell the pastor that I was stepping back. He straight out asked me if I was a lesbian, and I told him yes and that I'd been that way all my life. He said, 'You know the Bible says it's wrong. Why don't you quit?' But that'd be like saying the sky is red when I know it's blue. He said, 'You know you can choose to change. It's a choice you made just like I chose to be straight.' I just looked at him, wondering if he ever did make such a conscious choice, and also because I think his own son is gay. At that point, I decided not to divulge any more information to the pastor. It's like all he cared about was keeping it in the closet."

Not long after that, Dawn and Carrie did get married. It was not in the church, and they didn't announce it because almost all their friends were from the church, and they were pretty sure none would come. But it wasn't long before people noticed their rings, and the word got around.

Carrie spent her time "off ministry" studying the Word, and when she felt released from the Lord, she offered to help in the youth ministry. "I wanted to help with the teenagers," she explained. "And so for a couple of weeks, I volunteered on an informal basis to see how it would go, but when the director of the youth ministry spoke to the pastor to formalize my assignment, he said I wasn't eligible to be in any kind of a leadership position. He didn't tell *me*. He just told the director. She was really upset when she talked to me because her own son is gay. She was crying more than I was. Her son had already left the church, saying, 'I came to church, and they rejected me. So now they have to come get me. I'm not going back on my own.'"

"And there *are* other people in our church who are gay too," said Dawn. "I know some of the men are gay. They can serve, sing in the choir, teach, be an armor bearer for the pastor—anything, but they gotta keep their orientation in the closet. Two of them are engaged to women, but they're living on the down-low. Our pastor accepts that. What he won't tolerate is for someone to be really out, which is what our marriage did."

Carrie sighed. "We'd like to leave, but God hasn't released us yet. So for the time being, we continue to attend. We just eat the meat and leave the bones."

Contemplating all they'd said, I looked down at my dinner plate and then at the others. A grin spread across my face. Each plate was clean except for a couple well-picked chicken bones. Suddenly, the somber tension broke as we all burst out laughing.

Chapter 9
God's Justice and His "Wonderful Plan for Your Life"

The Lord has promised good to me.
His word my hope secures.
He will my shield and portion be,
As long as life endures.

"Amazing Grace"
John Newton, 1779, verse 4

THIS SONG NEVER FAILS TO MOVE ME. In spite of his life as a shameless slave trader, John Newton repented and believed God promised him good, secured by God's holy Word, based on some of the same verses that have encouraged most of us when life seems hard.

- "His love endures forever" (1 Chronicles 16:34).
- "Delight . . . in the Lord and he will give you the desires of your heart" (Psalm 37:4).
- "He . . . increases the power of the weak" (Isaiah 40:29).
- "I know the plans I have for you . . . plans for good and not for disaster" (Jeremiah 29:11, NLT).
- "Come to me . . . and I will give you rest" (Matthew 11:28).
- "I have come that they may have life, and have it to the full" (John 10:10).
- "Do not let your hearts be troubled and do not be afraid" (John 14:27).
- "In all these things we are more than conquerors" (Romans 8:37).

- "He who began a good work in you will carry it on to completion" (Philippians 1:6).
- "I can do everything through him who gives me strength" (Philippians 4:13).
- "And my God will meet all your needs" (Philippians 4:19).
- "Cast all your anxiety on him because he cares for you" (1 Peter 5:7).

The list could go on. Of course, some people have selfishly distorted God's promises into health-and-wealth prosperity scams, often designed to fleece followers of their money. Nevertheless, God's promises embody the *good* he intends for us, good most of us can attest to in spite of trials and troubles, heartaches, and failures we regularly face. I know I've found that to be true. God is good, all the time. And all the time, God is good!

Most believers are in such agreement with this fact that we have distilled the Bible's promises of hope into a simple principle, a statement often quoted when presenting the Gospel: "God loves you and offers a wonderful plan for your life."[1]

We're so convinced God really does have a wonderful plan for everyone's life that we're bold enough to offer it to anyone who will listen, whether they are a quadriplegic, suffering from cancer, or have just lost a child. No matter how profound the person's suffering, we believe God offers a way to make it more bearable. And we don't only mean "in the sky by and by." We actually mean this life *with God* can be wonderful in comparison to this life *without God*. We even offer God's "wonderful plan" to people in countries where their conversion to Christianity will almost certainly enroll them in increased hardship, suffering, persecution, and possibly even death.

But do we offer gay people a different plan?

God's wonderful plan for straight people includes the *potential* for one of the most amazing human relationships imaginable—marriage. It is the corrective to the only aspect of God's creation that

---

1. This is the first of the "Four Spiritual Laws," authored by Bill Bright in 1952. It has been distributed 100 million times around the world in numerous languages by Campus Crusade for Christ, now known as CRU.

he declared "not good," the prospect of going through life alone without a suitable partner (Genesis 2:18). Of course, not everyone finds a spouse, and even those who do sometimes lose their spouse prematurely, and not every marriage is as fulfilling as one would hope. But each of those disappointments, which often constitute profound and protracted grief, are the result of *random suffering*, not something that applies to a whole category of straight people.

However, when we take a category of people—in this case, gay people—and say, "God has a wonderful plan for your life . . . but because you are gay and attracted only to someone of the same gender, the possibility of marriage has been canceled in your plan," we have just invoked a *category injustice*.

No individual is promised a good and lasting marriage. But God created the *potential* of marriage as a blessing for all people and a reality for most. We're dismayed when we hear of gay people who promiscuously sleep around. But straight people do the same thing, and they do it with nearly the same frequency.[2] Instead, the Bible offers God's solution: "It is better to marry than to burn with passion" (1 Corinthians 7:9). In fact, married people are told they should "not deprive each other [of marital intimacy] except by mutual consent and for a time, so that you may devote yourselves to prayer. Then come together again *so that Satan will not tempt you because of your lack of self-control*" (1 Corinthians 7:5, emphasis added). It makes me wonder . . . why would God deny all gay people, most of whom are convinced they were created that way, the possibility of a lifetime companion and thereby subject them to what the Bible recognizes is undue frustration and increased temptation?

We all endure *random suffering*

God's plan doesn't promise anyone a "bed of roses," as the saying goes. John Newton knew this over two and a quarter centuries ago when he wrote, "Through many dangers, toils and snares, I have already come . . ." and "When this flesh and heart shall fail,

---

2. Laumann, Edward O., John H. Gagnon, Robert Michael, and Stuart Michaels, *The Social Organization of Sexuality: Sexual Practices in the United States.* (Chicago, University of Chicago Press, 1994), 314, 316.

and mortal life shall cease." He even anticipated cosmic disaster: "The earth shall soon dissolve like snow, the sun forbear to shine." But John Newton's relationship with God made it all worthwhile. "But God, who called me here below, will be forever mine."

These kinds of trials and troubles (unless brought on by our own foolish behavior) occur randomly to all people, at all times, all over the world. Jesus noted in Matthew 5:45 that such troubles (as well as many blessings) fall on the just and the unjust alike. It's how God created the universe to function. The rain that falls indiscriminately on all humanity can, unfortunately, cause floods in some places while producing abundant crops elsewhere. The same virus that kills some people triggers immunity in those who survive their first exposure to it.[3] That doesn't make such events any less painful. And God is fully mindful of and compassionate toward us as we go through them. Psalm 56:8 tells us he records our laments and collects our tears in a bottle. Anticipating the coming Messiah, Isaiah wrote, "Surely he took up our infirmities and carried our sorrows" (Isaiah 53:4).

Sometimes God intervenes in our lives through the still small voice of the Holy Spirit guiding us to something better. Occasionally he miraculously relieves our suffering. But usually we just come to terms with it and carry on, calling it "our lot in life" or calling natural disasters "acts of God." We resort to these figures of speech, inaccurate as they may be, as a way of coping with things we find hard to understand.

Suffering from our sinful choices

There are also times when God does use tragedies as a wake-up call for us to change. The destitute condition of the Prodigal Son

---

3. Karl W. Giberson & Francis S. Collins, *The Language of Faith and Science* (Downers Grove, IL, IVP Books, 2011), 104, provide helpful insights into understanding pain and suffering in the world by pointing out that "the same forces that produce a life-sustaining planet, including the laws of physics, chemistry, weather and tectonics, can also produce natural disasters. As with the free will of humans, God cannot constantly intervene in these areas without disrupting the inherent freedom of the creation and disrupting his consistent sustaining of all the matter and energy in the universe. Without this consistency, science would be impossible, moral choices would be subverted and the world would not be as rich with meaning and opportunity."

brought him to his knees where he repented and returned to his father to confess, "I have sinned against heaven and against you" (Luke 15:18). However, in Luke 13:1-5, Jesus warned us not to interpret random tragedies we observe *in someone else's life* as a measure of their sinfulness, because we're all on level ground when it comes to sin (see Romans 3:23).

In the Old Testament, we also read of rare occasions when the sin of a whole people was so grievous God decided the entire culture had to be eliminated—for example, the generation of Noah, the residents of Sodom and Gomorrah, and the Amalekites. Those judgments were not random. They were God's just verdicts concerning an unredeemable situation. But *we* are never authorized to declare someone unredeemable. To do so is to play God.

God opposes *category injustice*

Human suffering that results from injustice, particularly injustice that targets whole categories of people—foreigners, different language groups, different religions, people with a different skin color or ethnicity, the poor, or in this case, gay people is category injustice. But it happens. It's never random, and the victims always know they are being targeted because they are black or brown or poor or a minority—or in some places in the world, because they are Christians.

Whenever a category of people is discriminated against, our sense of injustice rightly ignites and we insist on redress. Why? Where did we get such an ethic? It comes from God! He never approves of us treating people differently than we want to be treated ourselves. In fact, our very ability to recognize when an injustice has occurred coincides with Jesus words: "In everything, do to others what you would have them do to you, for this sums up the Law and the Prophets" (Matthew 7:12). We trust God to treat every group fairly and to judge everyone fairly. It is God who "so loved the [whole] world . . ." (John 3:16). And it is God who is "not willing that any should perish but that all should come to repentance" (2 Peter 3:9 NKJV).

Even what at first appeared like favoritism when God selected the Jews, was so "through [their] offspring *all nations* on earth will be blessed" (Genesis 22:18, emphasis added). When they thought their status as his special people exempted them from God's universal standard for justice, he reminded them in Amos 9:7 how he had delivered neighboring pagan nations because of his passion for justice for all people. Jesus said, "Will not God bring about justice for his chosen ones, who cry out to him day and night? Will he keep putting them off? I tell you, he will see that they get justice, and quickly" (Luke 18:7-8).

For this reason, God becomes particularly displeased when his people perpetrate category injustice. To the powerful religious people of Israel who had been oppressing the poor and helpless, he said, "I despise your religious feasts; I cannot stand your assemblies. Even though you bring me burnt offerings and grain offerings, I will not accept them. Though you bring choice fellowship offerings, I will have no regard for them. Away with the noise of your songs! I will not listen to the music of your harps. But let justice roll on like a river, righteousness like a never-failing stream!" (Amos 5:21-24).

When we amend God's "wonderful plan" for people's lives by saying he doesn't want a certain group of people to have what he has clearly said was beneficial for everyone else, we have attributed to him a position that is distinctly atypical of his character as revealed in the sweep of Scripture and in the life of Jesus. For those of us who believe "All Scripture is given by inspiration of God" (2 Timothy 3:16, NKJV), we have to look beyond isolated verses that can be misinterpreted as proof texts for our own opinions to see how God is characterized in the whole Bible.

Why do we keep returning to marriage equality?

We return to the issue of marriage equality because marriage is the most profound and valuable of human relationships . . . but a gift many Christians deny gay people.

My devotions this morning brought me to 1 Timothy 4, where I read the following:

> The Spirit clearly says that in later times some will abandon the faith and follow deceiving spirits and things

taught by demons. Such teachings come through hypocritical liars, whose consciences have been seared as with a hot iron. They forbid people to marry and order them to abstain from certain foods, which God created to be received with thanksgiving by those who believe and who know the truth. For everything God created is good, and nothing is to be rejected if it is received with thanksgiving, because it is consecrated by the word of God and prayer.... Have nothing to do with godless myths and old wives' tales; rather, train yourself to be godly (vv. 1-5, 7).

I confess that after the first sentence, my breath caught because I know that many traditionalists and neo-traditionalists believe any support for marriage equality—and in some cases, even warm acceptance of gay people—comes from the devil. So, have I been following deceiving spirits, things taught by demons?

I reread the passage and was reassured that though I have questioned some old *traditions*, I have certainly not abandoned my faith in Jesus Christ as my Lord and Savior. Furthermore, Paul's first example of these deceivers involved teachers who forbade people to marry. I'd come across that heresy before. When I was growing up, segregationists resisted the civil rights movement with all kind of tactics, one of which was claiming that if we allowed the races to mix, the "horrors of miscegenation" would become rampant.[4] I recall wondering what my parents would say if I married a black girl. They pointed out that interracial marriages often face serious social pressure from both sides of the family as well as the rest of society. But they also admitted that God supported Moses' black wife to the point that he punished his sister, Miriam, with leprosy for her racist remarks when she resisted Moses (Numbers 12:1-15).

Segregationists, however, offered isolated verses claiming that the dividing of the "races" at the Tower of Babel and verses like Deuteronomy 7:3 ("Do not intermarry with them") and 2 Corinthians 6:14 ("Do not be unequally yoked . . . [For] what

---

4. For instance, fundamentalist Bob Jones University adopted a ban on interracial dating in the 1950s and did not rescind it until 2000. See http://www.christianitytoday.com/ct/2000/marchweb-only/53.0.html.

communion has light with darkness?" NKJV), among other passages "proved" interracial marriage was sinful. It was an ugly time . . . which hasn't entirely passed.

And now we are dealing with another instance when some church leaders are telling gay people *they* cannot marry. Could opposition to marriage equality be another fulfillment of Paul's warning for these "later times"? In looking more deeply at the passage, Paul called these deceivers "hypocrites." What constitutes hypocrisy for someone who forbids people to marry? By definition, Paul almost certainly was speaking of leaders who themselves were married while finding an excuse to prohibit others from doing so, which is what many heterosexual leaders (usually married) are telling gay people. And the consciences of these end-times leaders have been "seared as with a hot iron" to the point that *they simply don't care* how much misery their teachings load on people.

But we can also learn something from Paul's other example—the deceivers who prohibited certain foods. Paul refutes this falsehood by showing us something about "the wideness in God's mercy," as the old hymn describes it. God is primarily concerned about where our heart is. So Paul said, "nothing is to be rejected if it is received with thanksgiving [an attitude of the heart], because it is consecrated by the word of God and prayer." And finally, one way we constrict God's grace is by heeding "godless myths and old wives' tales," which are by definition falsehoods people have believed for a long time, perhaps including some age-old traditions of the church regarding gay people that deserve a review.

It is within the church that we have declared gay marriage the Rubicon, the line that must never be crossed. And so, at this point in history, almost all discussions concerning how we should relate to gay people come down to that one question: Can they marry? Or when you want to know where someone else stands, where some church stands, where some denomination or college or ministry stands, *that* is the defining question.

Of course, not all gays want to marry. Some are convinced they should remain celibate, some will attempt a cross-orientation marriage, some will not find a suitable partner, and sadly, some will continue to reject the importance of permanent marriage in the first place—*just as many straight people do.* Nevertheless, all gay people were profoundly emancipated when gay marriage became legal in this country, whether they take advantage of it or not. But for most gay Christians, marriage equality is not primarily about having sex. If that were their goal, they'd just do it in the same way so many unmarried straight people do it whether or not Christians approve. No. What they seek is *family,* the kind of partnership God envisioned when he said it was not good for humans to be alone. And we all know this kind of partnership—a true marriage, a true family—requires support from relatives, friends, the community, and especially the church. When that kind of support is withheld, the potential for survival of the relationship declines. This is why many gay Christians seek the blessing of their family, friends, and church.

Where that is given, those who practice faithful, committed marriage earn a respectable place in the church without suspicion of practicing an "immoral lifestyle." Those with children should be given the same protections and respect for their families as you and I have. And for those of us who are straight, once we recognize the normal aspirations of gay families, we begin seeing them more and more as *people like ourselves,* with hopes and dreams, fears and failures, who love and struggle and sacrifice for their children and need our support and friendship just as we need theirs.

So whose "wonderful plan for life" are we offering gay people? Are we sure it's God's plan, or might it be a plan we have amended with a footnote (often as large as a billboard) that conforms to our natural inclinations and the biblical interpretations we grew up with, without ever seriously evaluating it in light of Jesus' life and ministry.

Psalm 33:5 says, "The Lord promotes equity and justice; the Lord's faithfulness extends throughout the earth" (NET). Shouldn't we also promote the Lord's equity and justice, admitting that what's generally good for us is good for others as well? For our gay friends and family, this is what "marriage equality" is all about—nothing more, nothing less.

Collateral Damage

Susan and Robert Cottrell host private online support groups for moms and dads of gay kids. You can apply to participate through www.freedhearts.com. Neta met Gail through the private moms group, and Gail agreed to let me share her story here.

* * * *

Gail's eighteen-year-old son, Scott, came out as gay almost two years ago at age sixteen. She and her husband had always suspected he might be gay from the time he was only four years old, mostly based on his likes and dislikes and various things he would say. Overwhelmed at the prospect, they started counseling with Dr. Joseph Nicolosi, founder of the National Association for Research and Therapy of Homosexuality (NARTH), who practices reparative therapy and authored the book, *A Parent's Guide to Preventing Homosexuality.*

They prayed daily for Scott not to be gay because they believed that together, they and God could prevent it. But thinking back now, Gail says, "I can't believe we put our son through all that 'crap,' and it was nothing more than that—utter absurdity!"

What made things worse was the environment of the evangelical church they were deeply involved in and the private Christian school to which they sent all their kids. "All together," she says, "Scott ended up feeling unloved and unaccepted by us, by others who were our close friends, and by God. I can't believe we didn't see what was happening to him."

The result is that now, at age eighteen, Scott is so angry—mostly with his father for trying to change him—that, according to Gail, he's become an atheist with the Bible being the main focus of all his hatred.

Gail admits their whole family has stopped going to church primarily because of the hurtful incidents and the spoken and unspoken judgments people keep doing and saying. "I think half of our church knows about our son coming out. But even though the others don't, I truly don't care anymore who knows at this point. There's no going back for me. I'm proud of our son and who he is.

"We're now trying to repair the damage we caused by whatever means possible. I'm not even sure how to do that other than both of us apologizing to our son, loving him, and accepting him unconditionally." But this whole thing has opened floodgates of questions about Christianity for Gail, about her beliefs, and the beliefs of others, and she doesn't like what she sees.

Beyond that, Gail says her biggest challenge is to continue to love those "Christian" friends who are so anti-gay and who "randomly mouth off about it," as she puts it. "This is a huge struggle for me. I'm obviously staying away from them for the time being, but I know I have resentment in my heart for them and most evangelical churches."

PART II

THE "PROHIBITIVE" TEXTS

Chapter 10
Was Sodom Burned for Being Gay?
Genesis 19, Judges 19—20

Down in the human heart, crushed by the tempter,
Feelings lie buried that grace can restore;
Touched by a loving heart, wakened by kindness,
Chords that were broken will vibrate once more.

Rescue the perishing, care for the dying,
Jesus is merciful, Jesus will save.

"Rescue the Perishing"
Fanny J. Crosby, 1869, verse 3, refrain

IN 2012, THERE WAS AN INCIDENT OF HAZING at Main West High School not far from us in Des Plaines, Illinois, in which several soccer players allegedly "initiated" new players by tackling them, giving them wedgies, and sodomizing them with fingers or sticks. There was no testimony at the trial of Coach Michael Divincenzo to suggest the perpetrators or the victims were gay, even though such violent acts had a sexual component and were perpetrated on same-sex victims.[1]

The fact is, throughout history sexual assault has been used by straight people to subdue, demean, and emasculate those they

---

1. A similar event was reported on October 1, 2014 involving the Sayre-ville War Memorial High School football team in Sayreville, New Jersey. According to the national study *Hazing in View: Students at Risk* conducted by Elizabeth Allan, Ph.D. and Mary Madden, Ph.D. from the University of Maine, 1.5 million high school students are hazed each year, and sexual acts are common forms of hazing.

wished to dominate—whether in battle, prison, the workplace, or sports. It is also true that the presence of a stranger in ancient cities and towns after dark was considered a threat. Vestiges of this suspicion can still be found in some cities where hotel registration requires information (home address, car license, and other information) that has nothing to do with paying the bill.

God's destruction of the cities of Sodom and Gomorrah is often offered as an example of how much God hates homosexuality, but . . . was homosexuality the focus of God's wrath? Many Bible scholars agree the sin of Sodom involved the people's inhospitality, an offense that may seem insignificant today, even though God certainly considers hospitality a prime obligation.[2] When Jesus instructed the disciples before sending them out on mission, he said, "If anyone will not welcome you or listen to your words, leave that home or town and shake the dust off your feet. Truly I tell you, it will be more bearable for Sodom and Gomorrah on the day of judgment than for that town" (Matthew 10:14-15). Here he clearly associated a lack of hospitality with Sodom's sin. And later, when a Samaritan village denied Jesus and the disciples hospitality as they passed through, James and John said, "Lord, do you want us to call fire down from heaven to destroy them?" (Luke 9:54).[3] Jesus rebuked them and led the disciples on to another village, but the incident gives us modern readers an insight into the serious nature of inhospitality. It was far more than rudeness. Motels and restaurants weren't at every highway off-ramp like they are today. Without shelter and food, travelers could be subject to the elements, thirst, and become prey to bandits.

However, God's verdict against Sodom had been levied *before* the angelic messengers were even sent. (See Genesis 18.) Therefore, the city's behavior must have been habitually against vulnerable people—the poor and needy and particularly strangers and sojourners—who would have had no defense or anyone to protect them. The incident with the messengers simply revealed what had been happening all along.

---

2. See Exodus 22:21, 23:9; Leviticus 19:33,34; Job 31:32; Matthew 25:40; Hebrews 13:2, and many others.
3. Some manuscripts include, "even as Elijah did."

But what had been happening?

Genesis 19:4 says, "All the men from every part of the city of Sodom—both young and old—surrounded [Lot's] house." It's not surprising that everyone took part if this was a mob action because that's the way mobs behave. And we already know from chapter 18 that God could not find even ten righteous men in the whole city who would do the right thing. But was that because "all the men"—every single one of them—were homosexual? Not likely. That would be a most unusual population, and according to the Scripture, the mob included "young" assailants, so the inhabitants had been procreating. Furthermore, the only two natives of Sodom the Bible specifically mentions—the "sons-in-law" of Lot—were sufficiently *opposite-sex attracted* to be pledged to marry Lot's daughters. That is, they may have been rapists, but they weren't gay. Add to this the fact that if all the men were homosexual, Lot would have known his desperate and despicable offer of his daughters to the mob was utterly futile (v. 8). Therefore, it's unlikely the crime that involved "all the men from every part of the city" was homosexuality per se even though their crime had a sexual component and targeted victims of the same sex.

The Scriptures say the city dwellers demanded the guests be brought out to "*yada*" them. Some form of the Hebrew term *yada* appears 944 times in the OT, usually meaning to know, perceive, understand, etc. For instance, God knows (*yada*) us (Psalm 139), but occasionally the term includes a sexual connotation as in Adam knew (*yada*) Eve (Genesis 4:1). Certainly, in the Sodom context, there's no denying the sexual element. However, we can understand it in various ways. If it's translated as "to have sex with them," as the NIV does, it conjures the image of a sex orgy. We then think, "Ah, men having sex with men. It must be describing homosexuality." But the narrative demonstrates a far more evil intent. Actually, the mob's call to "*yada*" the visitors, mocks the biblical sense of the term, which is never malicious. Think of a white mob calling for the release of a black prisoner. "Come on, Sheriff. Bring him on out. We just want to have a little sport with him. Ya know, get to *know* him. Teach him a lesson," when their true intent is to lynch the man. The mob in Sodom had nothing benign in mind when it yelled, "*yada.*" They intended to gang rape the visitors, demean, subjugate, dominate them, do them fatal bodily harm—the same thing victorious warriors might do to a spy or a prisoner to terrify and warn off others. It's the same tactic used by ISIS in public beheadings, crucifixions, immolations, and rape to gain power by instilling absolute terror.

A very similar incident is recorded in Judges 19—20. However, this time it didn't involve a pagan city but the Israelite city of Gibeah, which was not otherwise known for sexual deviance. The traveling strangers weren't angels but a Levite, his concubine, and a servant. The mob demanded the householder surrender his guest "so we can have sex with him." Again, the term is *yada*, but later (Judges 20:5) their intent is clarified and we find that *from the outset*, they were "intending to kill him." In fact, when he sent his concubine out, that's exactly what they did. They gang raped her to death!

The point is, these violent mobs don't represent our gay friends and family desiring a life-long monogamous marriage any more than serial rapists represent those of us who are heterosexual. And yet, our gay loved ones are still stigmatized by the label, "sodomites."[4] More importantly, homosexuality is not the primary characteristic the Bible uses in recalling the gross sins of Sodom. After its destruction, the Bible refers to the city and its evil nearly thirty times, but only in 2 Peter 2:7 and Jude 7 is there any mention of sexual perversion. Certainly rape for the purpose of emasculating and even killing someone is perverse. Gay Christians don't deny that what happened in Sodom and Gomorrah was "sexually perverse." They simply plead that what happened in Sodom shouldn't characterize them any more than the rest of us.

Several biblical passages that mention Sodom say God's chosen people were *worse* than the people of Sodom. Worse, but

---

4. Though some older translations of the Bible use the term "sodomite" to describe sexual immorality, that definition is not derived from the original Hebrew or Greek. It was simply a term of convenience, which better translations no longer employ. In fact, "sodomite" was not used to describe sexual sin until about 394 A.D. in letters between Saint Jerome and a priest, Amandus, but even then, the nature of the sin is not described as a same-sex act. http://www.newadvent.org/fathers/3001055.htm.

how? There's no evidence they were largely homosexual, if that would make them worse, but they *did* indulge in child sacrifice and idolatrous shrine prostitution, which we'll discuss in Chapter 11. As for Sodom, Ezekiel 16:49, 50 explicitly describes *in detail* the nature of Sodom's sin: "Now this was the sin of your sister Sodom: She and her daughters were arrogant, overfed and unconcerned; they did not help the poor and needy. They were haughty and did detestable things before me." *Arrogant, unconcerned, haughty, detestable, refusing to help the outsider*—for sure, similar to bullies everywhere who are abusers, predators, and manipulators who cheat, beat, rob, emasculate, seduce, and even rape to maintain and advance their power.

It's not the biblical writers who were homophobic, putting all the emphasis on the homosexual aspects of what happened in Genesis 19. It's our *interpretations* that went astray when we chose to ignore the specific description in Ezekiel and add our own interpretation. Therefore, we who take the Bible seriously must be honest enough to admit there's no evidence homosexuality of the faithful, life-long, monogamous variety is how the Bible describes the sin of Sodom.

But if the traditional interpretation of the passage is wrong, why was such an erroneous view adopted in the first place? Perhaps it's because over 95 percent of us are straight. The story of Sodom is shocking. God's anger is scary. We wouldn't want any of it to be focused on us. One way to avoid that is to redirect it toward someone else. Subconsciously, we needed a scapegoat. "Why not blame God's wrath on the homosexuals, whose proclivities are so incomprehensible, and so unnatural (to us)? *Voila!* We can sigh in relief. God's warnings don't threaten us so long as we "flee Sodom" and everyone and everything associated with it—meaning, from our prejudiced point of view, gay people and any accommodation to them.

But the price of such a parry (as in fencing when you deflect the sword just enough to miss you) has been very high.

This story is one of the strongest condemnations in the Bible of predatory and abusive power and how much God hates it. But when was the last time you heard a sermon on the subject of predatory power? When has a Sunday school lesson told children what God thinks of bullies based on the story of Sodom? When that city is mentioned, do we examine our lives for arrogant, haughty, predatory business practices? Do we rise up against *all* forms of sexual abuse? For too long arrogant, haughty abusers have been tolerated and sometimes, even lauded in sports, the military, business, the workplace, on campuses and school grounds, and even in families and churches. They're the tough guys, the winners (by any means)!

But now the bill comes due! Half of our children experience physical assault by bullies before the age of twelve.[5] *These* mostly straight "sodomites" sexually abuse one in four girls and one in six boys before their eighteenth birthday.[6] They seduce, commit date rape, manage the sex traffic, and profit from pornography. They are the supervisors, priests, counselors, professors, pastors, military officers, coaches, husbands, and wives who use the power of their position to demean, humiliate, or entrap those under them, not necessarily out of base sexual lust, but because of their appetite for power and control. They simply manifest the same predatory power exercised by those soccer players at Main West High School in Des Plaines, Illinois, on their incoming teammates. After all, it was "just an initiation." And next year, the recipients will get their chance to do the same thing to someone else.

When I was six years old, my parents were home missionaries who were not stationed overseas but in small rural towns in the northwest. Small towns don't easily receive newcomers, especially not a preacher's kid. When the teacher of the one-room school asked why I was always late, my parents turned the question to me because they usually sent me out the door in plenty of time. But by hiding off the school grounds until after the bell rang, I'd been avoiding getting "beaten up" by the school bully.

---

5. Finkelhor, D., Ormrod, R.K., Turner, H.A., & Hamby, S.L. (2005). "The victimization of children and youth: A comprehensive, national survey. Child Maltreatment," 10(1), 5-25. http://www.unh.edu/ccrc/statistics/index.html.

6. "National Statistics about Sexual Assault," Cleveland Rape Crisis Center. http://www.clevelandrapecrisis.org/resources/statistics/national-statistics-about-sexual-assault.

My father took me aside and taught me how to slug his open hand as hard as I could. Then he said, "Aim only at the nose. But don't let me ever, *ever* hear of you hitting anyone younger or smaller!" The next morning I went to school on time and was assaulted as usual, but this time I did exactly what Dad said and landed a solid punch that bloodied the bully's nose. He fell down crying, got up and kicked me in the shins (which hurt more than any of his previous attacks), but I bore it bravely and was never attacked again.

Far more memorable to me than Dad's lesson on self-defense, however, was his warning to never ever bully other people. It stuck!

If we read the story of Sodom rightly, might it be like my dad's warning to me? Might we see the story as a lesson for *us* rather than a justification to fear, hate, and exclude gay people?

This is not to say that Genesis 19 affirms homosexuality. It neither affirms nor condemns it because it's not about gay people. The Bible's focus in reporting this incident does not condemn either same-sex attraction or gay people who desire or are involved in a life-long monogamous marriage. So let's be more—not less— biblical when we speak of Sodom, and for certain, let's stop calling gay people sodomites.

Collateral Damage

Six weeks after the President of Uganda signed into law the Anti-Homosexual Act of 2014,[7] we were visited by a couple from Uganda who had been guests in our home on two previous occasions. We love them and support their remarkable work with over six-hundred orphans by arranging occasions for them to present their ministry to people in churches near us who might contribute. Over

---

7. http://en.wikipedia.org/wiki/Uganda_Anti-Homosexuality_Act,_2014.

dinner on the fourth day with us, they shared a quarterly magazine they produce representing their fellowship of churches. I knew the man was a pastor in addition to their orphanage work. But they are such unassuming, humble people, I had no idea he was also the bishop over more than three hundred churches.

However, we were shocked to see that the magazine's feature article praised their country's president for signing the Anti-Homosexual bill into law. The headline said, "Bravo Mr. Y. K. Museveni!" Subheads continued: "Our Heroes: Members of the Ugandan Parliament. Congratulations fellow Ugandans upon graduating from the Anti-Homosexuality bill to Anti-Homosexuality law." Then the article began, "As [a] fellowship, on behalf of Uganda, we would like to thank our President for taking such a bold stand . . ."

This law, as the article pointed out, provided for life imprisonment for gay sex and gay marriage and between five and seven years in jail for "the promotion of homosexuality." (The original version of the law called for the death penalty for anyone convicted of being a homosexual.) The article also quoted "our Brother, David Bahati," the sponsor of the bill, who "insisted homosexuality was a behavior that can be learned and can be unlearned. . . . Bye-bye to Sodomists, bye-bye to Gomorrists," he said.

We were so shocked we could hardly respond, though I did say that one of the most serious problems in the States has been the degree of hate fomenting among some Christians toward gay people. But after tossing and turning much of the night, by breakfast the next morning I needed to respond more frankly. "You have had a chance to meet our son and his family when they came over to visit," I began. "But now I want you to meet our daughter's family." I got up and took their picture off the wall and returned to the table, pointing out, "This is our daughter and this is our *daughter-in-law*." I paused and watched his blank eyes. "And this is our granddaughter and our grandson."

Consternation wrinkled our guest's brow. "What do you mean?"

"I mean, our daughter and daughter-in-law are married. They are a gay couple."

His eyebrows arched as shock ignited his features before I proceeded.

"You have been encouraging us to come and visit you in Uganda, and we would love to do that, but if we did—if we brought our family—you would put our daughter and our daughter-in-law in prison. In trying to help and defend them, we might also be jailed, since who knows how your country's law against anyone who 'in any way abets homosexuality' might be interpreted. And then our grandchildren would be orphans."

Even though I'd hinted at my concern the evening before, the drama of my words probably blindsided him. But I hoped the personal and practical nature of my response would bear more fruit than a theoretical challenge to his position. As if to distance himself from the issue, he quickly said he'd never met a gay person.

I said, "And you're not likely to, either. After announcing your support for this cruel law, they might run from you out of fear you will turn them in."

Much of his position, which he kept saying wasn't as harsh as the law, was based on his conviction that people weren't born gay but that it was a learned behavior that could be unlearned. Neta and I disagreed with him, based on the best studies and the fact that actual change in orientation seems very rare. However, we kept pursuing the contention that whatever was true about the origins of homosexuality, these laws didn't express the way Jesus related to society's outcasts.

The bishop claimed his rule of thumb was, "Hate the sin, but love the sinner."

"But that's not working, is it?" I asked. "You already admitted that you've never even met a gay person. So, how could they feel loved? How could they be drawn to Jesus?"

We talked for two and a half hours, and I think our guests took what we were saying seriously. I concluded by challenging them to make an effort to get to know real gay people. They have hearts of compassion for orphans, and I want to believe God can give them hearts of compassion for gay people too.

One insight for me came out of this conversation. Polygamy is legal in Uganda, and the bishop thinks its incidents may be as high as 60 percent. (As of 2007, the Uganda Bureau of Statistics said 28 percent of women were in a polygamous union.[8]) Whatever the number, it's high enough that the bishop's churches have encountered several polygamous families. While the bishop calls polygamy a form of adultery, his churches welcome these families without asking the men to put away their extra wives. Nevertheless, when faced with *this* situation that doesn't conform to their understanding of God's basic design, they found a response far more gracious than life imprisonment.

We are rightly appalled by the detestable behavior of the mob in Sodom, but it's possible to incite *Christians* to do detestable things too. The film, "God Loves Uganda,"[9] documents how anti-gay Christians from the States played a major role in spreading attitudes that made possible the anti-gay legislation. Beyond the legislation, these attitudes have given rise to vigilante gangs that have killed several gay people and caused over four hundred to flee the country for their lives.[10]

Scott Lively, an American author who wrote several books opposing homosexuality, and Don Schmierer, a former board member of Exodus International, crusaded hardest, but other American evangelicals as well as many Ugandan clergy joined the effort. UK-based evangelical preacher, Paul Shinners, commended the bill by saying, "There is no other nation the world over that has such a plan and through this, Uganda is going to be blessed."[11]

Once the law was passed, some American evangelicals backpedaled, saying they never condoned the death penalty or

---

8. Uganda Bureau of Statistics, "Uganda, 2006 Demographic and Heath Survey—Key Findings," page 5. http://www.ubos.org/onlinefiles/uploads/ubos/pdf%20documents/Uganda%20DHS%202006%20Key%20Findings.pdf.

9. *God Loves Uganda*. Directed and produced by Roger Ross Williams. Brooklyn, NY: Full Credit Productions, 2013.

10. "Six LGBT Murders by Stoning Reported in Rural Uganda," Friends New Underground Railroad, August 18, 2014, http://friendsnewunder-groundrailroad.org/six-lgbt-murders-by-stoning-reported-in-rural-ugan-da-others-flee-vigilante-backlash-to-repeal-of-antigay-law/.

11. "Calls to pass the anti-gays Bill dominate New Year messages," *Saturday Monitor*, September 20, 2014. http://www.monitor.co.ug/News/National/Calls-to-pass-the-anti-gays-Bill-dominate-New-Year-messages--/688334/1655670/-/11vv8ob/-/index.html.

imprisonment. Perhaps they didn't, but they should have foreseen that their rigorous preaching concerning the evil and dangers of homosexuality would stir up fear and hatred, ultimately inciting a kind of legislative mob violence.

A year later, our pastor friend returned to stay with us once again. Presuming he'd have stories to eagerly tell if he'd taken my suggestion to meet gay people, I chose to leave the initiative to him. But when he hadn't said anything by the time I was ready to take him to the airport, I asked whether he'd met any. "No," he said, "I think if there are any gay people, they're kind of underground."

Hmm. I'm sure.

The Ugandan Supreme Court has since declared the Anti-Homosexuality law unconstitutional, but its advocates are retrenching to reintroduce it with bullet-proof wording.

Chapter 11
What Don't We Understand about "Do Not"? Leviticus 18 & 20

> *Not the labor of my hands*
> *Can fulfill Thy law's demands;*
> *Could my zeal no respite know,*
> *Could my tears forever flow,*
> *All for sin could not atone;*
> *Thou must save, and Thou alone.*

> *"Rock of Ages, Cleft for Me"*
> *Augustus M. Toplady, 1776, verse 2*

STACEY CHOMIAK, WHO GREW UP IN A CHRISTIAN HOME and gave her heart to Jesus at a young age, was totally immersed in church life including summer camps, Friday night youth groups, and conventions. Her church was her home . . . until as an older teen she admitted she was gay. She spent years doing her best to "pray the gay away" without success. As her orientation became known, she later wrote, "I endured extreme hurt, neglect, shame, loneliness, and guilt from my church family. . . . What had been my refuge since birth became a dark place that made me question everything and hate myself and my futile prayers. [My church] made me believe I had to choose—embrace God, or be damned and embrace this capital sin."

She couldn't make that choice. "I spent an intense week crying out to God at the end of my rope. I told him I loved him so much and was going to walk toward him . . . with my girlfriend of seven years, Tammy (Tams), by my side. Hours later, I felt a peace that can only come from him."

The journey was long, but they finally found a small Christian and Missionary Alliance church in British Columbia where the pastor and the congregation, with the full knowledge of their married state, welcomed them with open arms and without restrictions to serve among them in ministry. However, within six months, the denomination discovered they had joined the church. But this church was different. Even though the denomination closed the doors of the building and relieved the pastor of his position, the pastor and members stood with Stacey and Tams rather than kick them out.[1]

What causes denominations, churches, or even parents to take such harsh measures? Undoubtedly Leviticus 18:22—"Do not lie with a man as one lies with a woman"—plays a part, especially with its companion verse in 20:13 that designates death as the penalty for its violation. Perhaps a sense of urgent obligation arises to do *something*—if not the death penalty, then at least something drastic enough to match the unequivocal tone of the law.

In the past, liberal gay apologists simply threw the verse out, claiming it was so incompatible with a loving God that he couldn't have issued it. But I take Scripture more seriously, so I felt compelled to study the passage carefully to see if we were justified in thinking it applied to all gay people, because I knew there are many Old Testament laws that we dismiss rather freely—not because we doubt they were God's word for that time, but because they do not apply today. Consider the satirical treatment in this partial list.

- How can a guy know if a woman is having her menstrual period to be sure not to touch her as the Bible instructs in Leviticus 15:19-24? If he asks, she'd have reason to slap him.
- Would it solve the immigration problem if we simply bought slaves from other nations like Leviticus 25:44 recommends?

---

1. Stacey Chomiak, "The Church that Loved," Rachel Held Evans blog, February 4, 2014, http://rachelheldevans.com/blog/church-loved.

- Whenever Red Lobster has one of those "all the shrimp you can eat" specials, who can resist like Leviticus 11:10-12 requires? Shrimp doesn't seem so "detestable" (and neither does catfish). So what's a person to do?
- We're supposed to keep the Sabbath holy by not working on it. But many pastors use Saturday to put the final touches on their sermons, even if they take a break on Monday. Are they in danger of the death penalty as Exodus 35:2 says?
- Suppose a veteran just back from Iraq wants to become a minister even though he's lost a limb or an eye. Leviticus 21:16-23 says such a person is disqualified for the priesthood. Does that include this veteran?
- So you got a tattoo, a beautiful peacock on your shoulder before you read Leviticus 19:28. Should you have it removed?
- A family with a cash flow problem noticed that Exodus 21:7-8 would allow them to sell their daughter into slavery . . . of course not to a foreigner. But if they offer her on Craig's list, how will they know who answers the ad?
- Leviticus 11:7-8 forbids touching a hog, but footballs are called "pigskin." Is it okay to play football if you only use footballs made of cowhide or rubber?

Ridiculous, right? And the list could go on. But Christians have more thoughtful reasons for dismissing many Old Testament rules, usually reflecting some form of dividing the Law into various man-made categories such as moral law, ceremonial law, and civil law. (We will discuss these in Chapter 17 and show Jesus' better way of discerning how and when to apply various laws.)

How can gay Christians affirm Leviticus 18:22 while asking for marriage equality?

Initially it surprised me to learn that many gay Christians *don't* dismiss Leviticus 18:22 and don't feel they have to because they see it as applying to historically specific practices that don't represent their desire for a faithful, monogamous relationship of equality.

Matthew Vines says in *God and the Gay Christian*[2] that the evil prohibited in verse 22 stemmed from the cultural glorification of male domination. Putting another male in the submissive, receptive role was degrading and therefore wrong. To "lie with a man as one lies with a woman" is to reduce a male to the status of female, which in that culture was an enormous humiliation. Vines offers considerable historical support for his observations, and I'm personally convinced of its significance even though the penalty for violating the law—"They are to be put to death" (Leviticus 20:13)—makes no moral distinction between the guilt of the dominate perpetrator and the passive partner, which in many cases was a genuine victim—a slave, a vanquished enemy, or a mere boy.

But not everyone agrees with Vines' analysis. For instance, Owen Strachan, an assistant professor of Christian theology and the executive director of the Council on Biblical Manhood and Womanhood challenges Vines by citing other historical authorities he claims contradict Vines' thesis.[3] What lay readers are left with—if they are diligent enough to read competing views—is a "he said, she said" dilemma. Without the scholarly means to evaluate who is most accurate, they are likely to go with the view that coincides with their preconceived ideas.

Considering the biblical context

But without trying to evaluate which extra-biblical historical documents are most accurate, whether all sources have been considered, or the technical nuances of translation, there is much to be found in the biblical narrative itself.

There are two ways to read, "Do not lie with a man as one lies with a woman." One way is to see it as a stand-alone command, included among other commands but without any setting or back-

---

2. Matthew Vines, *God and the Gay Christian: The Biblical Case in Support of Same-Sex Relationships*, (New York: The Doubleday Religious Publishing Group, Kindle Edition, 2014), Chapter 2.

3. Owen Strachan, "Have Christians Been Wrong All Along? What Has the Church Believed and Taught?" *God and the Gay Christian?: A Response to Matthew Vine*, edited by R. Albert Mohler Jr., (Louisville, KY: SBTS Press, 2014), 67-69.

ground. If you look at it that way, you have nothing other than the words by which to understand its intended application. It stands stark and without context. It applies to everyone who might be encompassed by the specific words whether the author intended it that way or not.

During the latter part of the last century when controversy raged over the role of women in the church, many people treated Paul's instructions in 1 Corinthians 14:34-35 in much the same way. "Women should remain silent in the churches. They are not allowed to speak. . . . It is disgraceful for a woman to speak in the church." Period! What could be clearer? Paul included no exemptions within the rule itself, and this command cannot be dismissed as part of the Old Covenant since it was written under the New Covenant. Therefore, if you don't consider context, it's just out there, to be obeyed by *all* women under *all* circumstances or blatantly violated in outright rebellion against God's Word.

Some people still see it that way. (Though few of them apply it literally to mean women can't say *anything*. They just prohibit women from preaching or teaching.) But to invoke it universally disregards two important rules of hermeneutics—to whom was this spoken and why? Fortunately for most churches, wiser theologians prevailed by pointing out that even Paul didn't apply it universally and was addressing it to a specific situation for a specific reason. Hence modern women willing to abide by the basic decorum we expect from everyone are exempt.

Unless you insist on reading the verses of Leviticus 18 as disconnected from one another, you have to explain why most Christians easily dismiss verse 19—"Do not approach a woman to have sexual relations during the uncleanness of her monthly period."— while insisting verse 22, just three verses later, must be obeyed by all gay people.

Pagan idol worship

The other way to read Leviticus 18:22 is to consider the context, which includes a preamble at the beginning of the chapter where God identifies to whom he's speaking and why.

The Lord said to Moses, "Speak to the Israelites and say to them: 'I am the Lord your God. You must not do as they do in Egypt, where you used to live, and you must not do as they do in the land of Canaan, where I am bringing you. Do not follow their practices'" (Leviticus 18:2-3).

So the context is clear and the danger is great. The Israelites faced the very real risk of continuing the pagan practices of the Egyptians from which they came and/or adopting the pagan practices of the Canaanites among whom they would settle. What follows is a catalog of incestuous and adulterous practices they must not emulate. Verse 19 remains something of an enigma, but it is nevertheless related to the cleanliness code.[4]

One might think the last three prohibitions in the chapter (verses 21, 22, and 23) merely continue the list of sinful cultural habits the Israelites were in danger of emulating. But actually, *as a group*, they address the specific category of pagan idol worship.[5]

1. "Do not give any of your children to be sacrificed to Molech, for you must not profane the name of your God. I am the Lord" (v. 21).
2. "Do not lie with a man as one lies with a woman" (v. 22).
3. "Do not have sexual relations with an animal and defile yourself with it. A woman must not present herself to an animal to have sexual relations with it; that is a perversion" (v. 23).

We might overlook the connection and the significance of these last three prohibitions if we know nothing about the depraved religious practices of the region, but the following information is in itself not disputed so you aren't forced to choose between which scholars are more accurate.

Molech was the god of fire, to whom the Canaanites sacrificed their firstborn infant in order to bring good fortune. It was a huge idol portrayed as a man with the head of a bull standing upright

---

4. See Leviticus 15:19-24; 20:18, Ezekiel 18:6; 22:10.
5. James V. Brownson, *Bible Gender Sexuality* (Grand Rapids, MI: Eerdmans, 2013) 269-70.

with its arms outstretched. Inside its stomach was a furnace, within which—when heated red-hot—children would be placed and sacrificially consumed.

Baal and *Asherah* (Baal's female counterpart) were the primary fertility gods, said to be the powers behind the rain and dew, the abundance of crops and fertility among the livestock and humans. To appease these gods, supplicants would visit their shrines and temples and pay to use the services of male and female cult prostitutes in an attempt to ensure fertility and prosperity in all areas of life.

Baal was also said to practice (and thereby encourage) bestiality. Poetry from the Ugaritic tablets reads, "Mightiest Baal hears / He makes love with a heifer in the outback / A cow in the field of Death's Realm. / He lies with her seventy times seven, / Mounts eighty times eight; / [She conceiv]es and bears a boy."[6] Again, a practice said to ensure fertility.

For any agrarian people in a semi-arid land, prosperity and even survival depends on the weather. One region can be lush and rich while the adjoining one suffers famine. One season can bring abundant crops while the next ushers in a dustbowl. At the time of God's warnings in chapter 18, the Israelites were no longer experienced herders and farmers as they had been when they first migrated to Egypt four hundred years earlier. In the interim, they'd become construction slaves and escaped only to become wanderers in the desert for forty years. They knew next to nothing about farming. Therefore, it was hard for them—as interlopers—to ignore the local "wisdom" of the experienced Canaanites when the local people claimed to know the secrets of survival and prosperity.

This was the context in which God said, do not sacrifice your children to Molech, do not engage temple prostitutes, and do not practice bestiality! Though verse 22 only addresses men, the command, "Do not lie with a man as one lies with a woman" coincides perfectly with Deuteronomy 23:17—"No Israelite man or woman is to become a shrine prostitute."

---

6. Marcus S. Smith, trans., in *Ugaritic Narrative Poetry*, ed. Simon B. Parker, (Atlanta, GA: Society of Biblical Literature, 1997), 148.

And yet, again and again, Israel violated these commands. It was a repeated offense that angered God because of the idolatry involved. Shrine prostitution, often connected with the Asherah poles (a phallic symbol), is mentioned nearly forty times in the Old Testament. 1 Kings 14:22-24 says,

Judah did evil in the eyes of the Lord. By the sins they committed they stirred up his jealous anger more than their fathers had done. They also set up for themselves high places, sacred stones and Asherah poles on every high hill and under every spreading tree. There were even male shrine prostitutes in the land; the people engaged in all the detestable practices of the nations the Lord had driven out before the Israelites.

In 2 Kings 23:7 King Josiah was affirmed because Hilkiah, the high priest, "tore down the quarters of the male shrine prostitutes, which were in the temple of the Lord and where women did weaving for Asherah."

Most Bible scholars of the last century recognized that Leviticus 18:22 was about shrine prostitution, and it's only been in more recent times, as gay people sought approval to marry one another, that scholars expanded the verse's meaning to prohibit that. Even Robert Gagnon, one of the most outspoken anti-gay scholars of our time admits: "I do not doubt that the circles out of which Lev. 18:22 was produced had in view homosexual cult prostitution, at least partly. Homosexual cult prostitution appears to have been the primary form in which homosexual intercourse was practiced in Israel."[7]

But I still struggled with the question: Is idolatry the only valid application?

Case law helps define any statute

The need to periodically purge the fertility cult of prostitution from Judah and Israel as well as the prophets' frequent appeal for

---

7. Robert A. J. Gagnon, *The Bible and Homosexual Practice: Texts and Hermeneutics*, (Nashville, TN: Abingdon Press, 2002), 130.

the people to repent of prostituting themselves with the Canaanite deities is well-documented in Scripture, confirming how necessary Leviticus 18:22 was to curtailing these sins. If the law were also meant to prohibit life-long same-sex relationships, we would expect to see similar prosecutions, purges, or denouncements by the prophets or in narratives. But within Scripture we don't find this concern mentioned even once. In fact, though Leviticus 20:13 establishes the death penalty, there is no account of capital punishment *ever* occurring for any private same-sex behavior in all of Jewish history.[8] On the other hand, temple prostitution was a huge part of the idolatry that led to Israel's punishment in the Babylonian exile.[9]

While that contrast doesn't *prove* God never intended this law to prohibit same-sex marriage, the absence of any recorded incidents is, admittedly, an argument from silence. However, we're all familiar with the role "case law" plays in defining the scope and application of a statute. In many instances, even well-worded laws can have some ambiguity in terms of how broadly they apply. But these ambiguities are cleared up through case law—the record of when and how the law is invoked.

One of the things attesting to the Bible's inspiration and authenticity is its boldness, even its raw reporting of the sins of individuals, both small and great. There's no question that Leviticus 18:22 applied to temple prostitution because God's prophets and priests addressed those violations as part of the "case law." If it were also meant to condemn permanent, monogamous gay relationships, we would expect to see some record of response in that regard, especially since, percentage-wise, several people in every significant gathering were probably same-sex attracted. Inevitably, liaisons would have formed, some would have been exposed if they were so scandalous as to fall under the Leviticus 18:22 prohibition, and the Bible, which does not censor for the sake of appearances, would have reported it, and that too, would have become part of the "case law." But there's no such record.

---

8. "Homosexuality and Judaism," http://en.wikipedia.org/wiki/Homosexuality_and_Judaism.
9. See Lamentations 1:5; Ezekiel 39:21-24, Nehemiah 9:29-31.

This is not to say that in post-biblical eras the rabbis didn't addressed this question. The Babylonian Talmud obliquely addresses same-sex marriage.

Non-Jews accepted upon themselves thirty mitzvot [divinely ordered laws] but they only abide by three of them: the first one is that they do not write marriage documents for male couples, the second one is that they don't sell dead [human] meat by the pound in stores, and the third one is that they respect the Torah.[10]

But that was some time after the third century A.D., considerably removed in time from the inspired biblical record. Today, Jewish scholars are nearly as divided on the subject as Christians. However, Orthodox Rabbi Chaim Rapoport, Chief Medical Advisor in the Cabinet of the Chief Rabbi of Great Britain and the Commonwealth (a rather authoritative position), writes,

The Bible does not condemn homosexuality in general, but it does condemn three things: homosexual rape, the ritual prostitution that was part of the Canaanite fertility cult that was apparently, at one time, in Jewish practice as well, and homosexual lust and behavior on the part of heterosexuals.[11]

In the Genesis 19 narrative of the destruction of Sodom, it was clear that God condemned attempted rape, sexual violence, intimidation, and domination—all of which took place in the context of the sins of Sodom described in Ezekiel 16:49. But there was nothing in the Genesis narrative or Ezekiel's indictment that condemned committed same-sex relationships. Here in Leviticus 18, there's no question God condemned temple prostitution and anything associated with idolatry, but again, without any direct denouncement of gay marriage. Scholars with equally impressive credentials debate the history, the archeology, the technical language of the text without

---

10. Chullin, 92ab.
11. Rabbi Chaim Rapoport, *Judaism and Homosexuality: An Authentic Or-thodox View*, (London: Vallentine Mitchel, 2004).

a convincing conclusion, while the more fundamental biblical narrative of Leviticus may hold the key to its intended application: *three verses condemning three idolatrous practices.*

There is, of course, the option of ignoring the questions and insisting gay Christians are prohibited from marrying one another because "God said it. I believe it. That settles it!" But to be consistent, anyone taking that approach would need to do the same with Jesus' command, "If your eye causes you to sin, pluck it out" (Mark 9:47), and I haven't noticed very many blind pastors, even though half of them admit to viewing pornography.[12]

These passages are challenging, and because of the simplicity of its wording, this command in Leviticus is particularly hard if you ignore the context. There are other explanations for how to interpret it—the idea that the verse prohibits only domineering, degrading sex or that this verse is just part of the obsolete purity code. But I am far more moved by the cultic, temple prostitution explanation because it's so intrinsic to the context of the verse. I think it is worth considering. And it is with this explanation that some gay Christians say, "Yes, Leviticus 18:22 *is* an important command. We *do* understand what 'Do not' means. We are totally opposed to any activity that smacks of idolatry and temple prostitution, but don't expand the verse's application to those of us who eschew those activities as much as you do."

Collateral Damage

While working on this book, I signed up for a Google Alert for any articles having to do with "gay Christian." I don't recommend it.

---

12. "In March of 2002 Rick Warren's (author of the *Purpose Driven Life*) www.pastors.com website conducted a survey on porn use by 1351 pastors: 54 percent of the pastors had viewed Internet pornography within the last year, and 30 percent of them had visited sites within the last 30 days." http://talkingthewalk-cal.blogspot.com/2010/02/pastors-and-porn.html.

You'll be inundated by a plethora of stuff written on the subject every day. Some are inspiring personal stories of courage and love, some are thoughtful reflections from various points of view, but far too many are vitriolic diatribes, usually by people claiming to be Christians, I'm embarrassed to admit.

But hoping for some thoughtful input one day, I clicked on the title: "Stop Comparing Your Lust to My Sexual Orientation," and was taken to a blog by Matthias Roberts that did not disappoint. I reached out to him and arranged for an interview to put his ideas into the larger context of his personal story.

Matthias's parents were working in a Christian camp in Wisconsin when he was born, but when he was ten years old, they moved to Iowa and continued in another ministry. He was homeschooled and deeply involved in the life of the church from an early age. Matthias loves the Lord, and once he was old enough, he returned every summer to attend the same Christian camp in Wisconsin where his parents had once worked.

Thinking back on his childhood, he says he was about eleven when he realized he was attracted to other guys in a way that was more than just being buddies. "And it terrified me. I'm not sure anyone ever said it explicitly, maybe it was just cruel comments by other kids, but I definitely got the message that my interests were unacceptable."

Religious instruction regarding sexuality took place in various settings—youth group, Sunday school, and camp—beginning at about junior high age. For instance, one night each week at camp the leaders scheduled a sleep-out for the men and boys in the woods while the girls and women stayed back. Everyone soon learned these separate sessions were for "the talk." Sitting around the campfire, the leaders would discuss resisting lust and maintaining sexual purity and relating to girls. What they had to say was solely based on the presumption that everyone there was straight.

"I don't blame them for that," Matthias says, "but for a young gay kid, that was scary, especially when we broke into small groups for more intimate conversations where we were expected to talk about our personal experiences and our questions about sexuality. I knew if I didn't participate, people might begin to wonder why. So I had to make translations from my experiences into vague comments that would fit in without revealing that I actually wasn't attracted to females. There was a lot of shame within me doing that and a lot of fear that someone might figure out how I was different."

As Matthias reflects on those times, he realizes that out of all the ways suggested to guard against lust, no one ever said, "Hey, I know the solution. What if we just stopped liking girls?" No, their strategies never proposed eliminating one's *attraction* for women. For the straight guys, such a solution was preposterous—neither possible nor desirable.

And yet when he got older and began to admit he was attracted to men, that was the primary prescription many Christians offered: Just stop being attracted to them! From age eleven to eighteen, Matthias tried to find a way to do that, believing he could somehow change his orientation. Maybe it was just a phase. Maybe he could pray hard enough and God would do a miracle to take it away. He just wanted to grow up, get married, and have kids like everyone else.

When he was about fifteen, his parents discovered his orientation. They were shocked and not very happy, but they didn't break off their relationship with him. In fact, Matthias says, they have done their best to love him. When at eighteen he went off to John Brown University, a small Christian school in Arkansas, his parents urged him to see a therapist. Maybe, Matthias hoped, that would help.

But the therapist gently guided him into realizing the truth that his *orientation* wasn't likely to change. It was something he was going to have to accept. So the question evolved from how to change himself, to how to live faithfully for Christ within this new understanding. "At that point I thought it would be celibacy," he says. "But before I made such a dramatic lifelong commitment, I needed to learn why some gay Christians thought they could marry with God's blessing."

While he was looking into various interpretations of Scripture, he also recognized a very subtle condition many Christians attach to their "welcome" of celibate gay people. They may say "experiencing same-sex attraction isn't a sin," but they

147

simultaneously tell LGBT people they must be constantly "fighting it," "battling it," or "taking up their crosses." In that sense, they don't really believe the desire is not in itself sinful.

As Matthias pointed out in the example of the "sex talks" around the campfire, heterosexuals are only expected to avoid *lust*, not eliminate their fundamental desire. But when it comes to being gay, he says there is a lot of pressure in many churches for LGBT people to not accept their fundamental sexual orientation. "If you say you are 'same-sex attracted' or are 'struggling with homosexuality,' that's acceptable because it essentially agrees with their unspoken belief that your orientation is fundamentally wrong and sinful. But if you outright own your orientation and call yourself gay [whether or not you've ever had any actual sexual experience], you've stopped short of condemning your orientation. And most don't consider that acceptable, even though they would never expect straight people to renounce or condemn their orientation."

He points out that while homosexual people *can* experience lust, that's not characteristic of being gay any more than the lust heterosexual people experience is the inevitable result of being straight. "For a lot of Christians, when they hear you say you're gay, they assume a stereotypical 'gay lifestyle,' which doesn't represent my morals and standards at all. Lust may have been what those campfire talks were all about, but it's not necessarily what bisexual, lesbian, and gay people are 'embracing' when they come to terms with their sexuality."

To help clarify this, Matthias wrote that blog titled, "Stop Comparing Your Lust to My Sexual Orientation" in which he pointed out, "By accepting our sexualities, we are naming something that is true about our experience. But admitting my sexual orientation—to myself and others—is not the same as acting upon it. It is possible to be certain of one's sexual orientation without engaging in sexual activity. Case in point, I've never even held hands with someone in a romantic way, and yet I am *certain* that I am gay. It's just a matter of honesty. For me, to say that I am gay is to say that I am sexually attracted to men. Anything else would be a lie."

If sexual orientation is misunderstood as being sinful, or is compared to something that is sinful, an environment is created where it is not safe for LGBT people to be honest. "We cannot turn off our sexual orientations with a switch, we cannot simply confess them and stop experiencing them, but they *are* something that we can hide from others." Unfortunately, one of the places where hiding is often required is in the church.

To combat this, Matthias believes it is important for faith communities to foster understanding around what sexual orientation is (attraction towards certain genders and gender expressions) and what it is not (lust, sin). This understanding builds the ground work for open conversations around sexuality, morality, and theology. And he is working toward that end while pursuing two master's degrees—one in Theology and Culture and the other in Counseling Psychology—at The Seattle School of Theology and Psychology. You can read his blog at www.matthiasroberts.com.

Personally, his extended study of the Scriptures led Matthias to conclude that God can indeed bless same-sex marriages for those whom he has created that way, and therefore God does not require permanent celibacy of all LGBT people. If God leads Matthias to the right person—someone to whom he is naturally attracted—he intends to make it a relationship based on Christ, not on lust.

Chapter 12
Does Romans 1 Describe Your Gay Loved Ones?

Marvelous, infinite, matchless grace,
Freely bestowed on all who believe!
You that are longing to see His face,
Will you this moment His grace receive?

"Grace Greater Than Our Sin"
Julia H. Johnston, 1911, verse 4

CHRISTOPHER YUAN, AUTHOR AND ADJUNCT INSTRUCTOR at Moody Bible Institute, is a gay man whose history corresponds at several points to the progression into debauchery described in Romans 1:18-32. His story[1] also parallels some old stereotypes concerning homosexual males—a cool and distant father, a smothering and manipulative mother, persistent rebellion and rejection of God, a lonely and socially awkward childhood (until he came out), involvement in gay clubs, the gay party circuit, gay orgies, short-term hookups, and finally, the drug scene . . . until he was infected with HIV and finally arrested for major drug trafficking. Praise God for rescuing Christopher! And there's no denying there are many people—both gay and straight—who live similarly destructive and sinful lives.

For years the media gave all their attention about gay people to flamboyant, in-your-face, thong-wearing exhibitionists who may have begun their life of debauchery by rejecting God, a stereotype

---

1. Christopher Yuan & Angela Yuan, *Out of a Far Country*, (Colorado Springs: WaterBrook Press, 2011).

150

that reinforced all our presumptions. But as marriage equality was legalized in state after state—and now for the whole country—we have seen a steady stream of more staid, mature couples, many of whom have been together ten, twenty, thirty years, or like Patrick Bova and James Darby, committed for 52 years, their marriage vows legalized as soon as Illinois recognized them in November of 2013.

I don't know Patrick and James, but back when I helped Ed Hurst write his book, *Overcoming Homosexuality*, Romans 1:18-32 was touted—as many do today—to be the preeminent New Testament condemnation of homosexuality, resulting from a denial of God. Ed himself had found an excuse to "walk away from the Lord," telling God, "You are a crutch; I don't want a crutch; I don't need a crutch"[2] until he took a pretty deep dive into homosexual debauchery and drug use. At the time, his pattern seemed to fit the Romans description.

But since then, I've realized it doesn't fit all or even most gay people, certainly not our family—Leah and Jane—or the married women across the street, or the guys around the corner with the twelve-year-old adopted son. And in recent years, we have come to know other gay couples and many gay singles who don't fit this description. Some are believers who have never denied the existence of God, which Romans 1:18-20 pegs as the beginning step. And none of these gay family and friends could be described as "filled with every kind of wickedness, evil, greed and depravity . . . full of envy, murder, strife, deceit and malice . . . gossips, slanderers, God-haters, insolent, arrogant and boastful [who] invent ways of doing evil . . . disobey their parents . . . are senseless, faithless, heartless, ruthless," which verses 29-31 claims are characteristic of the kind of people Paul was describing.

So perhaps the theme of these verses is not a cause-and-effect description of naturally gay people—how they began and how they end up. Maybe it's more about confirmed idolatry, which can lead to a specific kind of same-sex indulgence as well as many other grave evils.

---

2. Ed Hurst with Dave and Neta Jackson, *Overcoming Homosexuality*, (Elgin, IL: David C. Cook Publishing Co., 1987), 8.

Putting it in context

To better understand Paul's message, it's important to place this passage in context. At the beginning of this epistle, Paul identifies his audience in verse 7: "To all in Rome who are loved by God and called to be saints." They include both Jews and "people from all the Gentiles" (v. 5) whom he desires to encourage in the faith and provide a sweeping overview of God's redemption, which we can receive only by grace through faith in the atoning sacrifice of Jesus Christ. Then Paul proceeds with the other themes he addresses in Romans.

Paul wrote to a mixed congregation that undoubtedly struggled to understand how the Gospel applied, given their differing backgrounds. Some members had come out of a debauched life of the worst kind, while other Gentiles may have lived as "good" people though without much knowledge of Christ, and some were Jews who had done their best to obey God's Law all their lives. So Paul had to begin by building a sweeping case that "Jews and Gentiles alike are all under sin. As it is written: 'There is no one righteous, not even one'" (Romans 3:9-10). This all led to the one solution: God's grace!

> But now a righteousness from God, apart from law, has been made known, to which the Law and the Prophets testify. This righteousness from God comes through faith in Jesus Christ to all who believe. There is no difference, for all have sinned and fall short of the glory of God, and are justified freely by his grace through the redemption that came by Christ Jesus (Romans 3:21-24).

It's in this broader context that we can begin to understand verses 18-32 of chapter 1, a passage many take out of context in their attempt to indict all gay people.

The "wicked," the "good," and the "chosen"

In building his case that "all have sinned and fall short of the glory of God" (Romans 3:23), Paul describes three groups of people, beginning with the most wicked people and how they got that way by suppressing the truth about God.

> Since what may be known about God is plain to them, because God has made it plain to them. For since the creation of the world God's invisible qualities—his eternal power and divine nature—have been clearly seen, being understood from what has been made, so that men are without excuse. For although they knew God, they neither glorified him as God nor gave thanks to him, but their thinking became futile and their foolish hearts were darkened. Although they claimed to be wise, they became fools and exchanged the glory of the immortal God for images made to look like mortal man and birds and animals and reptiles (Romans 1:19-23).

Notice that this descent into idolatry was not inevitable: "what may be known about God is plain" to everyone. They could have acknowledged God's "eternal power and divine nature" and lived as members of the second group, which we might call the "good" people. Good people may not have had God's written Law like the third group, the "chosen" Jews, but according to Romans 2:14-15, God does write his basic requirements on everyone's heart. And "if those who are not circumcised keep the law's requirements, will they not be regarded as though they were circumcised?" (v. 26).

Perhaps Cornelius, a centurion in what was known as the Italian Regiment, was part of this second group, one of the good people. Acts 10:2 says, "He and all his family were devout and God-fearing; he gave generously to those in need and prayed to God regularly." He was not a Jewish proselyte or Peter would not have needed divine permission to enter his house. And he was not yet a believer or Peter would not have needed to tell him the Good News of Jesus Christ and baptize him. So, he was simply a good man, representative of the second group, but someone who needed the Gospel of Christ, nonetheless.

Pioneer missionaries sometimes reported encountering remote people groups that worshiped the Creator God, maintained an orderly, peaceful, and fair life, and quickly welcomed the Gospel. For instance, two hundred years before any contact with white men, shamans in the Nez Perce, Spokane, Flathead, and Coeur d'Alene tribes foretold the coming of "fair-skinned men wearing long black robes with crossed-sticks under their belts" who would teach them a "new way to the heaven trail."[3] The Nez Perce worshiped *Hanyawat*, the Great Spirit and maker of all things. Contact with Lewis and Clark revived the old prophecy, followed by its more literal fulfillment by traveling Jesuit priests. Beginning in 1831, the Flathead and Nez Perce sent three successive delegations (one of which was attacked and wiped out by Sioux warriors) twelve hundred miles down to St. Louis to request someone to come and teach them about this "new way to the heaven trail."

So there are examples of good people, clearly distinguishable from utterly wicked groups.

Nevertheless, many traditionalists and neo-traditionalists claim the idolatry described in Romans 1:18-23 is not about the path of a specifically wicked group of people, but they say it's a metaphor for the general sinfulness of all humanity. Such a generalization, however, undermines the argument Paul was building over all three chapters, which was—no matter what one's category— wicked, good, or chosen—"all have sinned and fall short of the glory of God" (Romans 3:23). It weakens his argument to ignore these obvious differences because there *are* people who don't fit the description of Romans 1:18-23 for a variety of reasons, not just regarding homosexuality. And the Bible never claims there is no difference between grossly wicked people like Hitler and relatively good people like Gandhi. But Paul describes the wicked path of this particular group because they were well-known to the Roman believers.

Describing their descent into wickedness doesn't excuse the good people or the chosen people as being without sin. Paul

---

3. Rodney Frey and Ernie Stensgar, *Landscape Traveled by Coyote and Crane*, (Seattle, WA: University of Washington Press, 2001), 62.

maintains "there is no one righteous, not even one" (Romans 3:10), and the only antidote for sin is the "righteousness from God [that] comes through faith in Jesus Christ" (Romans 3:22).

What can we learn?

Homosexual activity unquestionably features prominently in the descent into wickedness described in these verses in the first chapter, so what can we learn from them?

1. *Their depravity resulted directly from denying God*, his existence, and the fact that he created the world, is all-powerful, and is eternal. Their denial of what was obvious led to their first "exchange." They "exchanged the glory of the immortal God for images made to look like mortal man and birds and animals and reptiles" (v. 23). Modern people seldom worship idols of wood and stone, but once a person jettisons a belief in God, it is not uncommon for them to replace God with some other compelling, organizing focus. I'm intrigued by stories of people who sacrifice absolutely everything—family, relationships, health, and sometimes their very integrity—to achieve the "impossible." They are usually very sad stories even though the world lauds and envies them as the greatest, the richest, the fastest, the first, or the only. We, too, make idols that "look like mortal man."

2. *Initially, they were heterosexuals.* Verses 26 and 27 say, "Even their women *exchanged* natural relations for unnatural ones. In the same way, the men also *abandoned* natural relations with women and were inflamed with lust for one another" (emphasis added). When someone first pointed out to me that the words "exchanged" and "abandoned" must mean that these people were originally straight, I didn't see the significance because back then because I assumed everyone involved in homosexuality began as straight and made a *choice* to become gay. I even thought that was what Leah had done, even though I could only speculate on her reasons. But as I faced her testimony, and that of the multitude of other gay Christians who maintain they never made such a choice (and there are thousands), I had to reexamine the implications of Paul's word choices here. Traditionalists might dismiss all gay people as either lying or self-deluded, but as the evidence mounted, I could not

155

presume I knew more about so many people than they knew about themselves.

So what was Paul saying? If he was just being descriptive as to how these people were, he might have said something like, "rather than natural relationships, they practice unnatural ones." That could describe all sexually active gay people—what they do is considered uncommon, atypical, not according to the "basic design." Instead, Paul used very active verbs, implying that they deliberately *exchanged* and *abandoned* who they naturally were for something unnatural to them.

Even more significant, Paul created a literary parallelism that emphasizes the deliberate nature of the choices these people made.

- They "suppress[ed] the truth" (v. 18).
- They "exchanged the glory of the immortal God for images" (v. 23).
- "They exchanged the truth of God for a lie" (v. 25).
- "Their women exchanged natural relations for unnatural ones" (v. 26).
- "The men also abandoned natural relations with women" (v. 27).

It becomes a drumbeat of a deliberate choice to move from one state to another. So it's not unreasonable to conclude that the people Paul was describing were originally heterosexuals who chose to abandon what was natural to them.

Paul's readers would have had no problem following this line of thinking. They lived in Rome replete with two prominent examples of heterosexuals *departing* from their normal sexuality to "degrade their bodies with one another." There were the Greco-Roman fertility cults in which men and women engaged in sexual orgies that included both heterosexual and homosexual rites, much as was condemned in Leviticus 18:22. And there was the practice of dominant men—conquerors, masters, the rich—subjugating the vanquished, the slave, or younger boys as a matter of sport and to demonstrate their prowess.

The significance of this understanding is that "naturally gay people" make no such choice. They never were heterosexual; they abandoned nothing. As Matthew Vines says, "Same-sex attraction is completely natural to me. It's not something I chose or something I can change."[4] Therefore, we cannot assume they are included in Paul's scathing condemnation.

3. *These people were "inflamed with lust."* Both gay and straight people can be inflamed with lust. But not everyone is. The stereotypic reading of this passage presumes that attraction is the same as lust, which it is not. Most of us who are straight realize that we are broadly attracted to people of the opposite sex, but that does not mean we continually imagine committing adultery with every good-looking person we see, and if we do, we need to deal with that directly without attempting to eliminate all attraction to the opposite sex. Likewise, we should acknowledge that just because gay people are attracted to others of the same sex does not necessarily mean they are inflamed with lust. In fact, most gay people manage their attraction just like you and I do . . . or should.

This distinction should help us realize that your gay family or friends may not be among the wicked people Paul was describing in this passage.

4. *They became filled with every kind of wickedness.* As we saw earlier, Paul's objective in the first three chapters of Romans is to demonstrate that "all have sinned." But this first group of people has devolved to the lowest of the low. "They have become filled with every kind of wickedness, evil, greed and depravity. They are full of envy, murder, strife, deceit and malice. They are gossips, slanderers, God-haters, insolent, arrogant and boastful; they invent ways of doing evil; they disobey their parents; they are senseless, faithless, heartless, ruthless" (Romans 1:29-31). And they actively encourage other people to do the same.

Tragically, there are people today who qualify as members of this group just as there were in Paul's day. It's an apt description of wickedness and depravity. And as Paul began this section,

---

4. Vines, Matthew. *God and the Gay Christian: The Biblical Case in Support of Same-Sex Relationships,* (New York: The Doubleday Religious Publishing Group, 2014, Kindle Edition), 29.

"The wrath of God is being revealed from heaven against all the godlessness and wickedness of men who suppress the truth by their wickedness" (Romans 1:18). But this isn't the only category. There are the "wicked," the "good," the "chosen," . . . and there are also the "saved by grace." Many of our gay family and friends do not fit the wicked profile of Romans 1 in any of the four points that Paul so graphically described.

Therefore, if they don't fit, don't put them there. Don't even put them there simply because they need the "righteousness from God [that] comes through faith in Jesus Christ to all who believe." Because we all need that.

Seamless Scripture

Finally, this passage is very informative in the larger sweep of Scripture. As you will recall, Leviticus 18 addressed the Israelites as they were preparing to reclaim the Promised Land, warning them not to emulate the idolatrous practices of the Canaanites they were invading or repeat the practices of the Egyptians they'd left. However, they did not obey. Idolatry, including temple prostitution, reared its ugly head repeatedly for hundreds of years until the Israelites were carried off to Babylon in punishment. But apparently they learned their lesson during their exile because, after their return, we no longer read of the Jewish people broadly practicing idolatry.

However, as the Gospel of Jesus spread through the Gentile world, the danger of idolatrous pollution again arose, including temple prostitution as well as the sexual subjugation of weaker boys, slaves, and vanquished foes by dominant men.

To any who doubt the inspiration of the Scriptures, the cohesion between Leviticus 18, where God told his people not to follow the idolatrous practices of the Canaanites (v. 3), and here in Romans where he warns of the same danger from Greek and Roman culture, demonstrates that "prophecy never had its origin in the will of man, but men spoke from God as they were carried along by the Holy Spirit" (2 Peter 1:21). In fact, the same Holy Spirit who inspired the Leviticus laws, here in Romans 1:18-32 provides—through Paul— an explanation of *how* people fell so low as to burn their infant

children in the furnace of an idol, participate in temple prostitution, and practice the bestiality decried in Leviticus 18:21-23.
It all fits together.

Collateral Damage

By David Khalaf[5]

© 2016, David Khalaf. Used by permission.

Someone finally pointed the finger of sin at me.

It came from a casual friend from my old church, who had recently caught wind of Constantino's and my engagement. He emailed his grave disapproval for our choice to marry and offered an earnest appeal for me to come to my senses. In a subsequent exchange, he accused me of "sin creep" (my term, not his) by likening my faith to a frog in a pot of heating water. I have been changing my theology by degree, he asserted, so gradually that I can't see how I am warping my faith to serve my own desires and not God's. *Whew.*

This isn't a post about how I responded or all of my sassy retorts (there were many; none were sent). It isn't even about trying to change someone's mind. Rather, it got me thinking about how I can remain a Christian who is open to God's correction while still standing confident in the beliefs I've developed about God and the nature of his love.

I'm someone who wants to be endlessly correctable by God. It's how we change. It's how we grow. Thomas Merton, a Trappist monk and social activist, once wrote, "If the you of five years ago doesn't consider the you of today a heretic, you are not growing spiritually." I see truth in that claim. If our fists grasp too tightly to

---

5. This story first appeared as a post on the Modern Kinship blog at www.daveandtino.com. http://daveandtino.com/blog/2016/2/3/a-friend-called-my-engagement-profane.

what we think we know about the Bible and the nature of God, our hands will be too full to hold any revelations God may have for us.

For me, God speaks revelatory truth most often through other people. Consequently, I've tried to cultivate an ear that is open to receiving the words others have for me, even when my natural response is to disregard them. I don't believe everything someone offers me, but I try to make space in my heart to listen to people without dismissing them.

So what do I do when a friend calls me a sinner? Do I have a responsibility to listen? Could it be God speaking truth to me through someone else? How do I navigate these questions now, rather than after I'm married, when the stakes are so much higher? The answer, I think, lies in discerning both the message and the messenger.

The problem with my casual friend as messenger is that we don't have any real relationship. He admitted as much. He's a sweet guy and a true lover of Jesus, but we were never close enough to speak meaningfully into each other's lives. He hasn't gotten to know Constantino, and has never spent time with us to see the fruit borne of our relationship. So, when he wrote me with his scripture-spattered disapproval, my heart had little generosity to listen. I didn't trust what he had to say, and I was suspicious that his motives were less out of genuine love for me, and more out of a sense of duty to convey truth as he understands it. In short, the messenger was wrong.

I've heard similar reservations about my relationship with Constantino from much closer friends, and my heart has been far more attuned to their concerns. The difference is that I trusted their words as being spoken with love and a desire to understand, and not with the hubris of righteousness. These friends loved me first, and only then offered their concerns. The lesson for all of us is this: Your authority to speak into someone's life is directly proportional to your investment in the relationship.

What about the message itself? The thing is, I've wrestled with the issue of homosexuality for 20 years now—through agonizing therapy, amazing books, thoughtful discussion, Bible study and prayer. I doubt the friend who wrote me has been so diligent about this issue. So when he asserted my wrongness with so much confidence, it felt to me like an insolent kindergartener criticizing a Ph.D.'s solution to a calculus problem. The message he was delivering to me is one I'm all too well acquainted with. I've been ruminating on this problem for years, whereas he just opened up to the answers in a book and pointed to them. But the Bible isn't an answer key.

Remaining open to God's correction does not mean revisiting a difficult decision every time someone raises questions about it. I've worked through this long and complex problem many times now, and I'm satisfied with the answer I've come up with. Trying to solve it over and over again is not only futile but destructive. As my wedding approaches, I'm beginning to understand how crucial it is for me to solidify my opinions on the nature of homosexuality once and for all. It won't serve our marriage if, year after year, I continue to question its spiritual validity.

I liken the issue to a rope bridge crossing a chasm. I can argue for days with someone about whether it is structurally sound, but at some point I have to choose whether or not I'm going to cross it. And if I do, once I'm on that bridge, it doesn't serve me to turn around to the person standing on solid ground and argue whether the bridge will hold. I've made my choice. I'm on that journey. And my focus should not be on whether the bridge will hold, but on my faith in God to see me safely across.

[Because this was a blog, followed by several encouraging responses, there was one celibate gay reader who raised the question—very respectfully, by the way—of whether by entering a marriage covenant, David and Constantino were in fact locking themselves into a commitment that would make it harder to hear God if in the future he were to try and convict them that gay marriage was wrong. What follows is David's response.]

Thanks so much for your thoughtful comments. I can relate to so much of it. For many years, I lived as a celibate gay Christian, not because I felt that was my calling (as many do) but because I understood that to be my only option. I lived in a state of "fear paralysis"—although I could theorize about God blessing same-sex unions, I wouldn't actually take a step toward it for fear of entering into sin.

This may sound radical: I've come to believe that inaction based on fear is more sinful than stepping into a questionable situation with a genuine intention to follow God. If I refuse to make decisions for fear of sinning, I have as much usefulness to God as a clod of dirt. And if I only make "reversible" decisions that can be undone, how can I ever truly commit to anyone or anything in life? I firmly believe we need to jump into life with a God-focused heart and trust that he will correct our missteps so long as we listen to him.

Keep in mind that I'm not jumping straight from singleness to marriage with nothing in between. I've dated Constantino for over a year, and in the first seven or eight months I prayed *every day* that God would convict me if I was doing something out of line with his intentions for me. That was the "reversible" opportunity, the months waiting for God to gently push me back on track if I was off. He never did. How much longer must I keep praying for God to convict me? How much prayer is enough before I take action? Or should I never move at all? I think we reach a point of insanity if we are receiving an answer from God but keep praying the same question *just in case* he wants to change his mind.

I don't see God as fickle. If I genuinely believe that he is blessing our union now, I have to trust that this promise is good for the rest of our lives. And while I must remain open to hearing what he has to say to me in the future, I don't have the responsibility to revisit the issue every time someone else disagrees. Thanks again for your thoughts.

Chapter 13
Are 1 Corinthians 6:9-10 &
1 Timothy 1:9-11
about Sexual Abuse?

O perfect redemption, the purchase of blood,
To every believer the promise of God;
The vilest offender who truly believes,
That moment from Jesus a pardon receives.

"To God Be the Glory"
Fanny J. Crosby, 1875, verse 2

ONE OF THE GREATEST FEARS AMONG STRAIGHT PEOPLE is that some teacher, some priest, some Scout leader will sexually molest their boys. It's a valid concern because it happens, and every precaution should be taken to prevent it. Unfortunately, the concern is often too narrow. It has scapegoated homosexual men when *everyone* working with children should be thoroughly screened, supervised, and kept accountable—gay, straight, male, and female.

The National Center for Missing and Exploited Children estimates there are at least 100,000 American children trafficked for sex each year.[1] And it's not boys who are at greatest risk, but girls from predatory *heterosexuals*. A shocking four times as many girls are sexually abused as boys.[2] According to Professor Gregory Mof

---

1. Malika Sasda Saar, "The myth of child prostitution," CNN, July 29, 2015, http://www.cnn.com/2015/07/29/opinions/saar-child-trafficking-united-states/index.html.
2. "Child Sexual Abuse Statistics," The National Center for Victims of Crime, 2012, http://www.victimsofcrime.org/media/reporting-on-child-

at the University of California, we are foolish to confine our concern to the stereotypic gay teacher, priest, or Scout leader. The conclusion "among researchers and professionals who work in the area of child sexual abuse is that homosexual and bisexual men do not pose any special threat to children."[3]

Nevertheless, anytime someone in power—straight or gay—takes sexual advantage of anyone who is weaker, more vulnerable, or in any way dependent on them, it is a crime! And because this was happening in an organized and socially acceptable way in the Roman world during New Testament times, it should not surprise us that Scripture addressed it. And that is how some theologians understand what Paul was talking about in the following two passages, particularly in regard to a couple of Greek words he uses.

Do not be deceived: Neither the sexually immoral nor idolaters nor adulterers nor male prostitutes [*malakoi*] nor homosexual offenders [*arsenokoitai*] nor thieves nor the greedy nor drunkards nor slanderers nor swindlers will inherit the kingdom of God (1 Corinthians 6:9-10).

We also know that the law is made not for the righteous but for lawbreakers and rebels, the ungodly and sinful, the unholy and irreligious, for those who kill their fathers or mothers, for murderers, for adulterers and perverts [*arsenokoitai*], for slave traders and liars and perjurers—and for whatever else is contrary to the sound doctrine that conforms to the gospel concerning the glory of the blessed God, which he entrusted to me. (1 Timothy 1:9-11).

That is how the New International Version of the Bible read prior to the revisions for the 2011 edition. In the older version, the team of translators rendered the Greek words *malakoi* and *arsenokoitai* as "male prostitutes" and "homosexual offenders"

sexual-abuse/child-sexual-abuse-statistics.

3. Gregory M. Herek, "Facts About Homosexuality and Child Molestation," 1997-2013. http://psychology.ucdavis.edu/faculty_sites/rainbow/html/facts_molestation.html.

in 1 Corinthians 1:9 and *arsenokoitai* as "perverts" in 1 Timothy 1:9. However, influential advocates of the traditional view of homosexuality objected and lobbied for change, claiming that the earlier translation allowed "a loophole for mutual consenting homosexual sex," as Rev. Canon Phil Ashey put it. He and others like him wanted a phrase that would "apply to every conceivable type of same-sex intercourse."[4]

Not much of a loophole, you may think. To what were they objecting? Well, they realized that with the original translation, gay-friendly readers might agree that *prostitution* is wrong (whether in or out of a pagan temple) and that those who practiced pederasty or other forms of homosexual domination—as had become popular in the Greco-Roman world—were certainly gross moral offenders. But those two categories didn't describe mutually consenting adults in life-long, committed relationships. Similarly, the reference to "perverts" in 1 Timothy could be dismissed as not applying to gay Christians wanting to marry if their conduct was governed by the same standards of faithfulness, love, and mutual sacrifice to which heterosexual marriages aspire. And therefore, as Ashey said, the traditionalists wanted language that would "apply to every conceivable type of same-sex intercourse."

Perhaps Paul did intend to say it that way. Perhaps everyone involved in any type of a same-sex relationship, even if they've placed their faith in Jesus, will not "inherit the kingdom of God." But I find it troubling that people with a particular point of view could lobby to change a leading translation of the Bible so it agrees with their perspective as though the NIV was their personal paraphrase. But that is what they succeeded in doing. Beginning with the 2011 edition of the NIV, *malakoi* and *arsenokoitai*—the two separate and specific Greek words Paul used in 1 Corinthians 6:9— were summarized in the much broader catch-all phrase, "men who have sex with men." And where *arsenokoitai* had been translated in

---

4. Michael Gryboski, "Theologians OK with Latest NIV Bible's Handling of Homosexual Sins," CP Church & Ministry, January 5, 2012, http://www.christianpost.com/news/theologians-ok-with-latest-niv-bibles-handling-of-homosexual-sins-66500/.

1 Timothy 1:9 as "perverts," it was broadened to include all "those practicing homosexuality," whether they were perverts or not.

I understand that translators have to strike a balance between a more literal translation that might be very cumbersome to read and a more readable version that still aspires to accuracy. But if any adjustment were merited, it should have been toward a more accurate rendering of the specific words in a way that allowed readers to prayerfully recognize and apply their implications.

However, before we complain too much about the NIV, it might be helpful to consider how some other translations handled these two words.

	malakoi 1 Cor. 6:9	*arsenokoitai* 1 Cor. 6:9	*arsenokoitai* 1 Tim. 1:10
KJV	effeminate	abusers of themselves with mankind	defile themselves with mankind
NKJV	homosexuals	sodomites	sodomites
NASB	effeminate	homosexuals	homosexuals
NLT	male prostitutes	who practice homosexuality	who practice homosexuality
NRSV	male prostitutes	sodomites	sodomites
NIV pre-2011	male prostitutes	homosexual offenders	perverts
NIV post-2011	men who have sex with men		those practicing homosexuality
ESV	men who practice homosexuality		men who practice homosexuality
HCSB	anyone practicing homosexuality		homosexuals

As you may recall from what I said in Chapter 10 about Sodom, the practice of calling gay people sodomites is utterly unjustified and highly offensive. However, in the context of these verses, if the translators intended to refer *only* to rapists and murderers, then the term might actually be "gay-friendly" because it would clearly not be talking about most gay people . . . creating an explicit "loop-hole," as the traditionalists would call it. But I'm quite certain that was not the intention of the publishers of these translations.

Use of the word "homosexuals" (NKJV, NASB) by itself or speaking generally of those "who practice homosexuality" (NLT,

NIV post-2011), or "anyone practicing homosexuality" (HCSB) editorializes in a way that includes women when the Greek words in no way allude to women. Again, traditionalists would probably prefer the broader concept so it would include lesbians as well as gay men.

You don't need to be a Greek scholar to find the following about the use of these words.

Malakoi

According to *Strong's Concordance*, *malakoi* means soft (as in fine clothing) or effeminate. When questioned about John the Baptist, Jesus asked, "What did you go out to see? A man dressed in fine [*malakoi*] clothes?" (Matthew 11:8 [twice] and Luke 7:25). The only other scriptural occurrence of this word is the one we've been looking at in 1 Corinthians 6:9. *Thayer's Greek Lexicon* also mentions that in Greek, the word can refer to catamites (as the *Jerusalem Bible* translates it), meaning boys kept for homosexual practices. This may be how the original NIV and the NRSV came up with "male prostitute," though prostitution implies receiving payment and a catamite could easily have been a slave. According to K. Renato Lings, "Renderings based on classical Greek literary usage include, 'mild,' ' tender,' 'delicate,' and 'gentle.' Occasionally the term acquires derogatory nuances such as 'feeble,' 'morally weak,' and 'cowardly.'"[5]

Other translations—King James Version, New American Standard Bible, J.B. Phillips New Testament, Young's Literal Translation—render the word as "effeminate." Perhaps the NIV translators and those of other versions wisely thought using "effeminate" unnecessarily called into question men who might *appear* effeminate completely apart from their sexual orientation or activity.

Arsenokoitai

An accurate translation for the Greek word, *arsenokoitai*, is particularly challenging. As David Gushee, one of America's leading evangelical ethics scholars points out:

5. K. Renato Lings, *Love Lost in Translation: Homosexuality and the Bible*, (Bloomington, IN: Tafford Publishing, 2013), 501.

The only two times the word appears in the New Testament are found in 1 Corinthians 6:9 and 1 Timothy 1:10, and most scholars believe Paul coined the phrase. It appears only very rarely in ancient Greek writings after Paul, mostly also in vice lists. . . . *arsenokoitai* (plural for *arsenokoites*) is a composite word, made up from two previously existing words that do not seem to have been put together before in Greek literature.[6]

Gushee and several other scholars have speculated that Paul made up the word by combining two words, *arsenos* (man) and *koiten* (bedder), from the Septuagint (Greek) translation of the Hebrew Bible's Leviticus 18:22: "Do not lie with a man as one lies with a woman." And perhaps that was Paul's intention. But Gushee agrees with Dale Martin that "of the few uses of the term *arsenokoites* in Greek literature outside of the New Testament [i.e., after Paul], in four instances it concerned economic exploitation and abuses of power, not same-sex behavior; or more precisely, perhaps, economic exploitation and violence in the sex business, as in pimping and forced prostitution."[7]

But if Paul's intention in coining or using the word, *arsenokoitai*, was to literally identify "man-bedders," Matthew Vines, author of *God and the Gay Christian*, explains it this way:

The most common forms of same-sex behavior in the ancient world were pederasty, prostitution, and sex between masters and slaves. Pederasty, in fact, was so common that Philo described it simply as the union of "males with males." He rightly expected his readers to grasp his specific reference despite the generic nature of his word choice. Given the prominence of pederasty in the ancient world,

---

6. David P. Gushee, *Changing Our Mind: A call from America's leading evangelical ethics scholar for full acceptance of LGBT Christians in the Church*, (Canton, MI: David Crumm Media, 2014), Kindle Locations 1164-1167.

7. Ibid., Kindle Locations 1197-1199.

Paul may have been taking a similar approach through his use of the word *arsenokoitai*.[8]

Vines also points out that "Most of the other vices listed in 1 Corinthians 6 . . . can be understood as sins of excess or exploitation: general sexual immorality, adultery, thievery, greed, drunkenness, slander, and swindling."[9] That is to say, committed relationships between gay people are no more driven by excess and exploitation than between married straight people, which would tend to imply that they were not envisioned in Paul's condemnation.

Again context, particularly as Paul uses the term in 1 Timothy 1:9, may provide a fuller understanding. In sequence, Paul names those who are "sexually immoral" (or prostitutes), "practice homosexuality," and "slave traders" (or kidnappers). James Brownson, professor of New Testament at Western Theological Seminary and author of *Bible, Gender, Sexuality*, says, "Many scholars believe that the three terms belong together in this list: that is, we see kidnappers or slave dealers (*andropodistai*) acting as 'pimps' for their captured and castrated boys (the *pornoi*, or male prostitutes), servicing the *arsenokoitai*, the men who make use of these boy prostitutes. Scholars have noted that the Roman Empire tried on several occasions to pass laws banning this practice—but with minimal success."[10]

Robin Scroggs, Professor of Biblical Theology at Union Theological Seminary in New York, agrees that in 1 Corinthians 6:9-10 "A very specific dimension of pederasty is being denounced with these two terms [*malakoi* and *arsenokoitai*]." In fact, he goes so far as to conclude: "What the New Testament was against was the image of homosexuality as pederasty and primarily here its more sordid and dehumanizing dimensions."[11]

---

8. Matthew Vines, *God and the Gay Christian: The Biblical Case in Support of Same-Sex Relationships*, (New York: The Doubleday Religious Publishing Group, Kindle Edition, 2014), 124.

9. Ibid., 128.

10. James Brownson, *Bible Gender, Sexuality*, (Grand Rapids, MI: Wm. B. Eerdmans Publishing Co., 2013), 274.

11. Robin Scroggs, *The New Testament and Homosexuality*, (Minneapolis, MN: Augsburg Fortress, 1984), 108, 126.

Back to the future

One thing that lends weight to the idea that both the Corinthian and Timothy passages address temple prostitution or pederasty rather than committed and faithful same-sex relationships between peers is that women aren't mentioned. Certainly there were gay women at that time (though largely closeted), but they probably would not have been involved in this sadistic sex trade.

If Brownson and others are correct that these three terms are interrelated, then it brings us back to our very contemporary crisis of sex trafficking. The crisis in Paul's day may have focused on the abuse implicit in the power differential between older men and young, sometimes castrated boys, but today, the crisis we face is as evil and tragic as was the problem in Rome even though it most commonly involves young girls.

We can take heart in Paul's promise that no one practicing such destructive, hurtful behaviors mentioned in 1 Corinthians 6:9-10 "will inherit the kingdom of God," since that would ruin heaven. And of course, the list is much broader than the sexually immoral. As previously noted, it includes thieves, the greedy, drunkards, slanderers, and swindlers.[12] But there is even better news in the next verse: "That is what some of you were. But you were washed, you were sanctified, you were justified in the name of the Lord Jesus Christ and by the Spirit of our God."

While most scholars agree that in these two passages, Paul condemns same-sex sins involving idolatry, prostitution, exploitation, and pederasty, they divide on whether Paul was ignoring (and thereby giving a pass to) committed relationships between gay people. Wesley Hill, a gay Christian, doesn't think so. He believes the terms *malakoi* and *arsenokoitai* rule out any possibility of same-sex marriage. Therefore, he is committed to celibacy, even though the washing, sanctifying, and justifying described in 1 Corinthians 6:11 has not changed his orientation. As he wrote to a friend, "I . . . cannot imagine what 'healing' from my orientation would

---

12. It follows that the behaviors found in other vice lists such as Romans 1:29-31, 2 Corinthians 12:20-21, Galatians 5:19-24, Ephesians 4:31; 5:3-8, and Colossians 3:5-9, among others, would not be welcome in the kingdom, either.

look like, given that it seems to manifest itself not only in physical attraction to male bodies but also in preference for male company, with all that it entails, such as conversation and emotional intimacy and quality time spent together."[13]

Washed and waiting

But Paul declared, "You were washed, you were sanctified, you were justified," as though all three were a done deal. Still, as the title of Wesley's book, *Washed and Waiting*, declares, he is still *waiting* for God's sanctification (being made holy) and finds his hope in Romans 8:23-25:

We ourselves, who have the firstfruits of the Spirit, groan inwardly as we wait eagerly for our adoption as sons, the redemption of our bodies. For in this hope we were saved. But hope that is seen is no hope at all. Who hopes for what he already has? But if we hope for what we do not yet have, we wait for it patiently.

Because those verses are preceded by, "We know that the whole creation has been groaning . . ." (v. 22), the phrase, "the redemption of our bodies" has a distinctly physical connotation. We all face the deterioration of our bodies and empathize with those with physical handicaps. But Wes, whom I've met and deeply respect, waits for "the redemption of [his] body" in terms of release from his homosexuality. He writes, "When God acts climatically to reclaim the world and raise our dead bodies from the grave, there will be no more homosexuality."[14] (And no more heterosexuality? one might ask.) But there's something of a paradox in this perspective. The more his homosexuality is seen as a physical condition, the more it is the way God made him. The more it is a spiritual thing (a product, aspect, or source of sin), the more victory and freedom should be possible. "If the Son sets you free, you will be free indeed" (John 8:36). Though in this life, our sanctification process remains unfin-

---

13. Wesley Hill, *Washed and Waiting: Reflections on Christian Faithfulness and Homosexuality*, (Grand Rapids, MI: Zondervan, 2010), 42.
14. Ibid., 50.

ished—at least for me—genuine ongoing progress should be the normal Christian experience. And yet thousands of gay Christians report that while they may be able to control their behavior, they remain gay with little or no change no matter how earnest their prayers or how rigorous their spiritual disciplines.

There is another conundrum with paraphrasing the Greek words in these passages to include "every conceivable type of same-sex intercourse." Each of the vices in the list involves a sinful *activity*. When sinners repent, they are "washed" and "justified." But they are also "sanctified" or changed and set apart for God's purposes. When the adulterer quits committing adultery, he is sanctified in the sense that he is no longer an adulterer. When the thief stops stealing, he is changed and no longer a thief. When the swindler quits cheating people, he is no longer a swindler, etc. Likewise, when the idolaters, slave dealers, pimps, and pederasts repented and ceased their behavior, they were no longer what they had been. That's the marvelous grace of being washed, sanctified and justified "in the name of the Lord Jesus Christ and by the Spirit of our God." But while Wes lives as a celibate and doesn't even believe he should marry a person whom he might desire, he remains . . . gay. He is still a homosexual.

So from what were the Corinthian believers "sanctified" as Paul declared them to be? Certainly all forms of same-sex idolatry, prostitution, exploitation, and pederasty, as well as heterosexual sins—fornication, prostitution, pedophilia, adultery. But if Paul intended to include people with same-sex attraction, how were they changed? And if they did not experience any more orientation change than do modern gay Christians, in what kind of freedom did they live out their lives?

Taking these possibilities into account, there seems to be valid reasons for considering the alternative interpretation that these passages explicitly condemn abusive same-sex behaviors so common in that day but not necessarily the traditional assumption that all gay people are included.

Collateral Damage

Crystal Hodges is now a communications professor at a college in Chicago, but she grew up in a large extended family on Chicago's south side where her parents, brothers and sisters, grandma, aunts and uncles, and cousins all lived in the same neighborhood. That gave her a lot of security, but it also meant there were always eyes on her, and word soon got back to Mom if Chrystal wasn't doing what she was supposed to be doing.

Nobody else noticed, however, the day some neighborhood boys walked by her house where she and three other girls were sitting on the steps. "Lesbians," they sneered. She had no idea what that meant, but later she figured out that it might have been because she was a tomboy, always dressed in T-shirts and jeans. And it might have been because the youngest girl in their little clique often rested her head on Crystal's shoulder while they sat on the stoop talking.

Even before this, Crystal realized the shape of the female body intrigued her, particularly that of her sixth grade math teacher, Miss Parker. One day when the whole class was supposed to be doing their math homework, Crystal sat studying her favorite teacher's tightly corseted torso. Almost without realizing it, she began drawing it on a fresh sheet of paper, studying each line intently to get the three-dimensional perspective of her full breasts just right. Suddenly, she felt a hand slip over her shoulder and pick up the paper.

Crystal froze, not only because she hadn't been doing her math but because of what she had been drawing. Without saying a word, Miss Parker carried the paper to her desk, looked at it a moment, and slipped it into a drawer as Crystal scrambled to catch up with her math problems.

But apparently her teacher wasn't angry, because she submitted the picture to the Art Institute of Chicago, which resulted in a scholarship for Crystal in a special course for promising young artists.

More and more the girls Crystal hung out with spent their time talking about boys. But she was not interested in boys, unless it was to beat them on the basketball court. And nothing made her happier than the day a crew of older guys invited her to play full-court with them. But Crystal drifted away from those girls and took up with a couple of younger girls who weren't always talking about boys. Her mom noticed and said, "Find somebody your own age to play with."

She did find some older girls to hang with, girls from church "But they soon learned that if they wanted to relate to boys, they needed to do it away from me, because I wasn't participating in that."

Church was an all-day-Sunday and several nights-a-week marathon, and some meetings were held in their house with all the relatives and some neighbors in attendance. When they weren't conducting church or eating dinner, the men and women often separated—the men and boys in the living room while the women and the girls worked in the kitchen cooking or cleaning up. The kitchen was the elder women's classroom often conducted in veiled gossip about the sins of other people. Sometimes they tried to talk over the younger girls' heads, but Crystal soon got the message that the worst of all sins was homosexuality.

Later, in a conversation with one of her uncles, she also learned that there were several lesbians in their extended family, going back four generations. It put the fear of God into Crystal.

That fear haunted her when the horseplay among some of the girls that included grabbing at each others' breasts turned serious one night when she slept over at a friend's house. They were sharing the same bed when the touching was no longer horseplay. Crystal stopped her friend. "Dee, sometimes I'm afraid of myself."

"Whadda you mean?"

"I don't think we outta be doin' that anymore. Ya know?"

"Yeah. Me neither."

It rocked Crystal that someone else had the same feelings she had. They talked some more without really understanding what they were talking about. But in the end, they agreed not to play like that again.

In high school, Crystal sensed that it was important to fulfill her family's expectations. But it wasn't enough to excel in music and art. They were hoping she would be the first one from their family to go to college. There was also the push toward boys, perhaps because of her tomboy style. So she started dating . . . sorta. And she took note that her mother let her go down to the privacy of their basement with any boyfriend when she would never allow her brothers and sisters to do that. "What's with that?" Crystal thought. "Is she trying to stir up my interest?"

She tried and did develop a deep friendship with one guy. In fact, she thought she was in love with him . . . in love with his soul, that is, not his gender.

After high school Crystal received a full scholarship to the University of Arkansas. Off to college she went that fall, but she got so homesick, she gave up and came home after the first semester. She transferred to the Chicago Conservatory of Music, and to make things look even more normal to her family, she married that high school boyfriend who had been pestering her to get married. He seemed a nice enough guy, and it was a way to get out of the family home environment.

A month or two after they were married, she saw her mom downtown. "So how's married life?"

"I hate the nights."

"Oh, you'll get used to it."

It made Crystal angry. She had no *desire* to "get used to it." At most it was something she had to tolerate to fulfill her family's expectations. She learned how to check out during sex—put her mind in a completely different zone—and just let him have his way with her.

But when her new husband began to get physically abusive, there was no more tolerating it, and she cut him off cold. It wasn't long before he divorced her because she wouldn't have sex with him. As far as she was concerned, the only good thing to come out of that marriage was her beautiful baby daughter.

It wasn't long after her divorce that something strange began to happen. She began to have daydreams about being with a beautiful faceless woman, just hugging and kissing. And it was so overwhelming. It almost became something that tormented her. Though she'd never enjoyed sex with her husband, she began to realize that there was

175

another part of her that she couldn't deny. "That attraction terrified me," she says, "because I didn't want to go to hell."

Her solution was to get married again . . . not right away, of course, but by the time she was twenty-five. In between she'd dated a very boring guy because he was safe and made a good cover to her family. When he got serious, however, she dumped him. But there was always that daydream in the back of her mind. "I was terrified that it might become a reality," she recalls, "and I would disappoint my mom. My grandmother would kill me. My aunts would be ashamed of me. This is why I kept fighting." Maybe all she needed was the "right guy." And she finally thought she found him at a dance club. He was attractive, seemed to be nice, loved her daughter, *and* she was three years older and wiser than he. She could handle that. In fact, her friends teased her that they knew she'd be wearing the pants in their family.

About a month into their marriage, however, he lost his job. And just like some people are mean drunks, he became a mean out-of-work guy. "He picked the wrong person to hit," she says. "And that ended that!" It wasn't long until she put him out, but by then she was pregnant with her second child, a wonderful boy.

Perhaps it was on the rebound, but when her childhood friend showed up to console her, they talked, and Crystal told her about her daydreams, and one thing led to another until they ended up in bed together. "It was like I was born," she says. "I was suddenly in love with life. It created a desire in me to know more, because I didn't know anything about anything."

The same dance club where she'd met her second husband had a lesbian night, and Crystal decided to give it a try. She loved to dance, but she'd often ended up the one holding the other girls' purses. But not at this club, on Wednesday nights. There, the other women looked at her amorously. She relaxed and received the approval she'd never known.

As much as admitting she was a lesbian terrified her, she knew it expressed the authentic self that had always been trying to get out in spite of her family's constraints.

She met Martha, and they moved in together. It was before marriage equality in Illinois, but they were committed to each other, in the good times and the bad. And they made a life, a good life (that ultimately lasted twelve years) if it weren't for the continuing hammering from her family.

By this time, her mother and most of the family had moved to Michigan, but she continued on the warpath, coming back to Chicago to try again to change Crystal. It was an ugly row, but in it Crystal confirmed something she'd suspected for a long time when her mother said, "Well, I had those thoughts too. But I fought, I fought, and you can too!"

"Mom, you're making my life a living hell, but this came through your genetics,[15] your side of the family. And you want to make me feel bad, but I'm a product of you, and you just admitted that. I didn't choose this."

She loved God, and she didn't want to make God angry as her family told her she was doing. She also didn't want her mom, her aunts, or other family members angry or embarrassed by her. She was afraid of them. She stayed away from her family a whole year, feeling like her mother wanted to kill her. Her mother called her at her job and sent her propaganda about how she was going to get HIV and die. She even tried to scare Crystal with, "You know, when one of the parents are gay, the kids are likely to be gay too."

Crystal played along with her theory. "So who was it with me, you or dad?"

Her mom hung up.

The confrontations took their toll.

She and Martha found a church that seemed to accept them, though they took care not to flaunt that they were a couple. In that church Crystal met a Biblical scholar who was well trained in Hebrew and Greek and she met with him for some extended conversations about whether or not all those verses her mother kept quoting to her were really what the Bible said. He explained that some verses simply didn't mean what traditionalists assumed they meant, but there were others where the interpretations were gray, hard to speak in absolutes one way or the other. That was

---

15. No single source has been identified for sexual orientation, but various studies suggest a combination of genetic, in utero, hormonal, and social factors may play a part.

both comforting and troubling to Crystal. She didn't want to do anything against God's will, so she threw herself into praying that if this wasn't his will, he would change her.

But when the question came up of whether she could actually serve in the church, one of the pastors told her that wouldn't be possible. More devastation.

She prayed so hard that God would make her straight that she ended up having an emotional breakdown, crying uncontrollably all day. Ultimately her relationship with Martha dissolved, but that did not change who she was inside. No matter how hard or long she prayed, there was no change. "I'd tried being with a man—twice—and I can't. I simply can't. And I had no desire to try again." She felt so discouraged that one day she walked out on the overpass over a busy highway and stood there contemplating whether to jump into the traffic below.

God's grace brought her back, and that summer, she read the whole Bible like a history book because she was tired of other people telling her what it said. "So many new realities opened up to me. I think some of the prohibitions in the Bible are about the idolatry that took place at those fertility altars. But mostly I'm 95 percent sure God made me just the way I am, like it says in Psalm 139, 'I am fearfully and wonderfully made: marvelous are thy works.' But I have to admit that sometimes little doubts creep in. Whether they are from God or just the echoes of what my family keeps saying to me, I don't know."

Crystal's single now. "I have a totally different relationship with God now that I understand my faith is not about my mom or my family. It's about him—God and me. And it's not about a spouse. It's about him and me. God is bigger than anything we can understand, and we're not expected to understand everything about him. We're just supposed to follow Jesus.

"But I'm still never happy when I'm at my mother's house. I'm still 'guilted.' I go and I sit and I observe and I listen and I die until I cann't take it anymore. And then I leave. It's not that the family says anything overt anymore. It's just the system, set up over time, that's never been dismantled."

Chapter 14
"Did God Really Say . . . ?"

Just as I am, without one plea,
But that Thy blood was shed for me,
And that Thou bidst me come to Thee,
O Lamb of God, I come, I come.

Just as I am, Thou wilt receive,
Wilt welcome, pardon, cleanse, relieve;
Because Thy promise I believe,
O Lamb of God, I come, I come.

"Just As I Am"
Charlotte Elliot, 1835, verses 1, 5

TODAY I WAS READING A BLOG BY A PASTOR who was reviewing the same six passages we have looked at in Part II of this book, and his study caused him to conclude that gay marriage was compatible with the *whole* witness of Scripture, even though many have interpreted these passages through culturally "straight" lenses in the past. Reader comments ranged from thankful appreciation to vitriolic condemnation. But one reader brought me up short when he accused the pastor of "preaching the same message as the serpent in the garden:

Why would God make a tree with such attractive fruit yet command you not to eat it (lest you die)? Why would God create in man such a strong desire to eat the fruit from the tree if it weren't ok to do so? That's not fair. Listen to your own body, your own desires and your own reasoning. God has lied to you. Surely, if you disobey God, you will not die.[1]

He was, of course, fictionalizing the incident in the Garden of Eden where the serpent began by challenging Eve with, "Did God really say . . . ?" (Genesis 3:1) in his attempt to entice Adam and Eve to disobey God's direct command. But to put things in perspective, there was never any question about what God had said. Adam and Eve *knew* the answer, and Eve replied without hesitation, "God did say, 'You must not eat fruit from the tree that is in the middle of the garden'" (Genesis 3:3). That should have settled it. There were no Scriptures to search, no long-held interpretations that might have been rooted in cultural bias, and no alternative applications that better fit the character of Jesus as the Bible reveals him.

And the attraction of the fruit—it appeared "good for food and pleasing to the eye" (v. 6)—is a trite parallel to the deeply embedded nature of one's sexual orientation. Many of us resist the foods we shouldn't eat with relative ease compared to the struggles of thousands of gay Christians who attempted reparative therapy for years without appreciable change. On that level, the reader's critique introduced an uninformed and unfair comparison.

In fact, it wasn't some overpowering "desire to eat the fruit from the tree" that the serpent played upon when tempting Adam and Eve. It was the promise that they would "be like God" (v. 5), the same jealous ambition many scholars believe motivated Satan to challenge God's authority as described in Ezekiel 28 and Isaiah 14.

Nevertheless, I still took the main thrust of the reader's challenge seriously. Was this pastor's blog—or am I—tempting people to sin by questioning whether our traditional interpretations about homosexuality are right? In other words, is it wrong to ask the question, "Did God really say . . . ?" regarding any issue and especially same-sex marriage?

---

1. Rev. Jared C. Cramer, "Christian marriage 'only man and woman'?" (*Grand Haven Tribune*, August 2, 2015), http://www.grandhaventribune.com/opinion/opinion/2219021.

Arriving at our moral convictions

As evangelical Christians, we are committed to basing our moral convictions on what the Bible reveals about God's position on ethical issues. And there are typically two general ways we arrive at what we think is "God's position" on any specific subject.

1. *According to the topic.* The first is to scour the Bible for every passage that touches on the issue. What appears to be right or wrong according to those passages becomes the basis for our moral convictions on the subject. Is the passage a "law" of God? Does it apply for all time and all circumstances? Is it some other statement attributed to God? Is it a narrative that seems to reveal God's favor or displeasure? and so forth. Scholarly opinions concerning translation, cultural setting, and other interpretative elements can play a major role in deciphering the implications of these passages. But those opinions are sometimes in dispute, and the average Christian is ill-equipped to evaluate which scholar is right. Furthermore, this approach doesn't necessarily consider whether the conclusions coincide with broader revelations of God's character and sentiments that might indirectly apply to the subject.

2. *According to the character of Jesus.* The second approach is to begin with broader, though sometimes more amorphous, biblical revelations about the nature and character of God and his purpose and relationship with humans. Jesus, "the image of the invisible God" (Colossians 1:15), "the exact representation of his being" (Hebrews 1:3), takes center stage, so much so that all our ideas about God must be interpreted through the lens of what the Bible tells us about Jesus. If other passages—even if they directly mention the subject in question—*appear* to conflict with what we know about Jesus, then we look for plausible alternative interpretations for those direct passages or hold them in tension while we allow our morals to be governed by the character of Jesus. One advantage of this approach is that it is more accessible to the common believer. One does not need to be a Hebrew and Greek scholar or have a Ph.D. in ancient Middle Eastern cultures to get to know the person of Jesus Christ quite well from the Bible.

Jesus actually demonstrates his preeminence over other biblical precepts in his Sermon on the Mount where he repeatedly said, "You have heard that it was said . . .. But I tell you . . .." For instance, "You have heard that it was said, 'Eye for eye, and tooth for tooth.' But I tell you, do not resist an evil person. If anyone slaps you on the right cheek, turn to them the other cheek also" (Matthew 5:38-39). The Old Testament appears to establish the "eye for an eye" ethic as totally prescriptive—how we are required to behave[2]—and therefore representative of God's heart. But then along came Jesus with a corrective: No! "If anyone slaps you on the right cheek, turn to them the other cheek also," which he backed up with his life and especially his conduct at his trial. In so doing, Jesus unequivocally revealed God's heart, which we must not nullify or even qualify by any other statement, no matter how clear it may seem. This does not diminish our conviction that "All Scripture is given by inspiration of God" (2 Timothy 3:16). But it creates a proper priority for application. *After* we are clear about Jesus' character from what he said and did, then we are free to try and figure out why seemingly contrary statements appear elsewhere in the Bible, mysteries we may never completely solve. But we do not allow them to redefine Jesus.

Another example can be seen in the history of Christians' moral convictions regarding slavery. There are numerous biblical passages that presume the institution of slavery, laws on how to treat slaves, and even Paul sending the slave, Onesimus, back to Philemon.[3] For hundreds of years, slave traders and slave owners and their supporters—claiming to be Christians—used these passages to justify the institution of slavery, often with the support of highly placed and well trained religious leaders. It was only by setting aside those topical references and concentrating on how God values all human beings, "from every tribe and nation," especially as demonstrated by Jesus, that the old convictions were overturned.

As C. S. Lewis said in a letter to Mrs. Johnson:

---

2. See Exodus 21:23-25, Leviticus 24:17-20, Deuteronomy 19:21.
3. Paul encouraged Philemon to receive him "no longer as a slave, but better than a slave" (v. 16), but still he honored the institution of slavery rather than acted as an abolitionist.

It is Christ Himself, not the Bible, who is the true Word of God. . . . We must not use the Bible (our ancestors too often did) as a sort of Encyclopedia out of which texts (isolated from their context and read without attention to the whole nature and purport of the books in which they occur) can be taken for use as weapons.[4]

Determining what "did God really say" about gay people requires more than looking at the "prohibitive texts." We must base our moral convictions on the whole witness of Scripture for which Jesus is the "chief cornerstone" (Matthew 21:42, NKJV), and that is why I'm desirous of "loving our gay family and friends *like Jesus.*"

Sincerity and Humility

I certainly do not want anyone to disobey God. And even though God's grace is not dependent on being on the "right side" of the gay marriage question, we're not playing games here. It's always a grave thing to misrepresent God's wishes regarding right living; therefore, our inquiry must proceed with sober sincerity and profound humility.

But God never seems upset by genuine questions. Job, Abraham, Moses, Joshua, Elijah, Elisha, David, Isaiah, and many others all questioned God. Even Jesus said, "My God, my God, why have you forsaken me?" (Matthew 27:46). After hearing Paul preach the Gospel, the Bereans were commended for taking the time to examine the Scriptures and to ask that daunting question, "Did God really say . . . ?" and thereby determine whether Paul's message was true. So it's okay to question long-held interpretations in light of new information. How else would faithful people have given up the belief that the earth was the center of the universe? Or that God condones slavery? Or that women must be silent?

Genuine questions aren't a problem when we are open to receiving and acting on *God's* answers. I have been impressed by gay people like Justin Lee, who entered the process of searching

---

4. C.S. Lewis to Mrs. Johnson, November 8, 1952, *The Collected Letters of C.S. Lewis*, Vol. III, 1st edition, (New York: HarperOne, 2007), 245-48.

the Scriptures about same-sex committed relationships with the declared willingness to remain celibate should it be biblically clear that gay marriage is against God's will. That's the kind of obedience to which we all should aspire . . . and it works the other way too. We should be just as open to changing our minds if we discover the objections to marriage equality are more a human command than God's command.

So, when it comes to the traditional *interpretations* of the "prohibitive texts," it's legitimate to ask, "Did God really say that?"

Points of agreement

There is nearly unanimous agreement among theologians—whether they are traditional, neo-traditional, or inclusive—that the six prohibitive texts we reviewed in the previous four chapters express God's wrath against all behaviors involving . . .

Rape	Temple idolatry
Coercion	Domination
Sexual violence	Prostitution
Pederasty	Lust
Trafficking	Adultery

Every one of the six prohibitive passages addresses one or more of these commonly known destructive and idolatrous behaviors. No matter what their bias, nearly all the scholars agree these behaviors constitute *porneia*, the Greek word usually translated "sexual immorality."

The primary point of contention

Where the scholars differ is whether the prohibitive passages *also* condemn committed same-sex marriage.[5]

New Testament scholar N.T. Wright thinks they do because the Greeks and Romans "knew a great deal about what people today would regard as longer-term, reasonably stable relations between

---

5. Of course, because traditionalists believe that in one way or another same-sex attraction is a choice, they would say merely *being* gay is also a sin that must be resisted.

two people of the same gender. This is not a modern invention, it's already there in Plato."[6]

Other neo-traditionalists think the prohibitive passages apply, but for the exact *opposite* reason. They *don't* think ancient people were familiar at all with the concept of some people being "gay" and, therefore, desiring a permanent same-sex relationship. Richard B. Hays, a professor of New Testament at Duke University Divinity School says, "The idea that some individuals have an inherent disposition towards same-sex erotic attraction and are therefore constitutionally 'gay' is a modern idea of which there is no trace either in the [New Testament] or in any other Jewish or Christian writings in the ancient world."[7]

Glenn Stanton supports this point in his book, *Loving My (LGBT) Neighbor*, when he says, "What we're experiencing in our generation is historically unprecedented:

> It was not until the 1960s and 1970s, starting in the United States, and then spreading to England and Western Europe, that anyone had either identified or proclaimed himself as 'gay.' And this was not just because the word itself had never been used, but because it was developed to describe something altogether new in history.[8]

Actually, N.T. Wright is correct in that ancient literature and other historical records did occasionally mention committed same-sex relationships, but Ken Wilson points out that Plato's description of the relationship between Nero and Sporus was nothing like the monogamous gay unions between equals the church is being asked to bless.

---

6. John L Allen, Jr., "Interview with Anglican Bishop N.T. Wright of Durham, England," *National Catholic Reporter*, May 21, 2004. http://www.nationalcatholicreporter.org/word/wright.htm.

7. Richard B. Hays, "Relations Natural and Unnatural: A response to John Boswell's Exegesis of Romans 1," in the *Journal of Religious Ethics*, Vol. 14 (1986), 199-201.

8. Glenn Stanton, *Loving My (LGBT) Neighbor: Being Friends in Grace and Truth*, (Chicago: Moody Publishers, 2014), 28, referencing David F. Greenberg, *The Construction of Homosexuality* (Chicago: University of Chicago Press, 1988), 458–81.

Nero eyed Sporus, then a male child by today's standards, had him castrated, dressed him as a woman and referred to him as his "wife." . . . Given the prevalence of pederasty [in the Greek culture] it is possible, likely even, that at least some continued their sexual relationship well into the adulthood of the minor party. But this can hardly be regarded as anything but exploitative.[9]

But would the common people in New Testament times have been familiar with Plato's writing? They may have gossiped about the nice old maids who shared a room in the city wall or the bachelors who lived in the winery at the edge of town, but more because of the cultural stigma attached to being childless than that they might have been "couples."

However, by insisting that committed same-sex relationships were completely unheard of, Hays and Stanton introduce a point that seriously undermines—perhaps even contradicts—their perspective. In claiming that we are experiencing "something altogether new in history," they are inadvertently acknowledging that biblical authors and readers would have had no cause to be thinking of *that kind* of "gay" when writing or reading the prohibitive texts condemning "sexual immorality." This is essentially what inclusive or affirming scholars have been saying all along: The Bible essentially doesn't address gay marriage; therefore in condemning it, we're adding a modern bias to God's command.

Toxic consequences

Adding a human command to God's command always gets us in trouble. It's part of what happened in the Garden of Eden. Eve compounded the serpent's deception by *adding* something to what God had said. God only told Adam and Eve they could not *eat* of the fruit of that particular tree, but Eve added, "and you must not touch it," which God had not said.

---

9. Ken Wilson, *A Letter to My Congregation: An evangelical pastor's path to embracing people who are gay, lesbian and transgender in the company of Jesus*, (Canton, MI: David Crumm Media, LLC, 2014), 66, 67.

Many of us who believe in the inspiration of the Scriptures are rightly concerned when people dismiss verses they don't like. We remind them of Deuteronomy 4:2, "do not subtract from [God's law]" and Revelation 22:19, "if anyone takes words away from this scroll of prophecy, God will take away from that person any share in the tree of life and in the Holy City." But God's warnings cut both ways. Like Eve, we have often added to God's commands, ignoring the accompanying warnings in the above texts: "Do not *add* to what I command you" and "if anyone *adds* to them, God will add to him the plagues which are written in this book" (emphasis added). Think of how easily throughout church history we have done just that with extra-biblical rules concerning how to dress, how to talk, what to eat, what music is appropriate, who you may marry (including race and class and now gender restrictions). At one time or another, the list has touched almost every area of life.

So it seems legitimate to ask whether or not God *meant* to include committed same-sex relationships along with the other condemnations even though he didn't inspire the biblical writers to explicitly mention them, *not even once*. And one would have expected any good author (especially one inspired by the Holy Spirit) to have done so since their readers wouldn't have otherwise even thought of the closeted gay people in their midst.

Therefore, to ask the question, "Did God really say gay marriage is wrong?" requires looking at alternative interpretations of passages that have long been read through the traditional lens. Admittedly, some of these alternatives are more compelling than others, but I cannot dismiss them beyond a reasonable doubt. It was Jesus who told us how to discern true from false prophets: "By their fruit you will recognize them" (Matthew 7:15-23). And in Acts 15, that is exactly how the apostles and elders in Jerusalem were convinced of the authenticity of the Gentile converts. It was undeniable that they had been given God's Holy Spirit. And therefore, even if you do not fully agree with our Christian gay brothers and sisters, we owe it to them to respect their integrity when the fruit evident in the lives of many demonstrates the "love, joy, peace, patience, kindness, goodness, faithfulness, gentleness, self-control" which are the fruit of the Holy Spirit (Galatians 5:22-23).

187

Collateral Damage

My parents served with Village Missions, planting churches in small logging and ranching towns in the northwest. To raise financial support, they often went on "deputation trips," speaking in mission-minded churches in larger towns and cities.

I sometimes felt their tension of not knowing how they would be received among total strangers. But it was usually followed by joyful relief that the Body of Christ always welcomed its own. Neta and I have also traveled all over this country (as well as in China) leading writing seminars for kids or speaking on subjects related to our adult Christian novels and other books. Our experience was similar as we were welcomed, often into people's homes by brothers and sisters we hadn't previously known.

That's why I felt alone while I drove a moving truck down the highway this last Sunday as I passed church after church with their parking lots full of the cars of loyal attendees. Neta and I were helping Leah and her family move across the country to a new city and new jobs for both her and Jane. But rather than feel confident that those churches held brothers and sisters who would welcome me if I had time to stop and join them or if—God forbid—I had trouble with the truck and needed help, I felt apprehensive.

If I came knocking, would I find good Samaritans or aloof Pharisees ready to cast stones as soon as they discovered my heart toward gay people. Too much has happened over the last few months that has shaken my confidence in Christian institutions.

It began with events at World Vision, the Christian humanitarian organization dedicated to working with children, families, and their communities. As a boy, my family sponsored an orphan through them, and I have respected World Vision ever since. But on March 14, 2014, World Vision announced a policy change to allow married gay Christians to serve on its U. S. staff of over 1,100 employees. It was a momentous decision that encouraged gay Christians everywhere who longed to serve Jesus in this way. Maybe evangelical ministries were about to let them serve even if they were married or contemplating marriage to someone of the same sex.

However, within forty-eight hours, a crew of conservative evangelical leaders—Al Mohler, president of the Southern Baptist Theological Seminary; Russell Moore, president of the Ethics and Religious Liberty Commission of the Southern Baptist Convention; the Evangelical Council for Financial Accountability; the National Religious Broadcasters Association; theologian John Piper; evangelist Franklin Graham; George Wood, general superintendent of the Assemblies of God—all denounced (in some cases publicly) World Vision's new policy. In fact, according to *Christianity Today*, the Assemblies of God denomination actually urged its members to withdraw their support. The initial uproar from all these leaders incited over 2,000 child sponsors to drop their support with greater opposition threatened. Though 2,000 is a small percentage of the total number of children World Vision helps, the ministry reversed its policy rather than abandon those children, and sent a letter of apology for their "mistake" out to all their sponsors and friends. However, before all the blood-letting ended, World Vision had "lost about 10,000 of its child sponsors" according to *The Washington Post*.

When I heard about this debacle, I *presumed* World Vision's board initially had been responding to an appeal by some existing or potential staff members who were already in a gay marriage or desired to be, and I wanted to hear their story of how such a one-step-forward-and-two-steps-back impacted them.

In trying to track them down, I had a phone interview with Richard E. Stearns, president of World Vision. He assured me the policy change was not made to accommodate any specific individuals within or without the organization. Furthermore, the board had not been responding to pressure. No lawsuit was threatening. No group was lobbying them. "We were just facing the hypothetical: What do we do about someone who applies for

189

a job at World Vision who is in a legal same-sex marriage that may have been sanctioned and performed by their church? Do we deny them employment or not?" World Vision's staff comes from over fifty denominations, some of which accept same-sex marriage, and the board felt that different convictions about this, and other challenging issues, were better handled by the churches themselves while World Vision focused on serving the needy.

In the letter of apology to their supporters, the board "strongly affirm[ed] that all people, regardless of their sexual orientation, are created by God and are to be loved and treated with dignity and respect."[10] But that was too little, too late. The pressure tactics from other evangelical leaders and organizations willing to sacrifice 10,000 orphans as pawns forced World Vision back into line.

This was not the first or only time evangelical institutions were disciplined for stepping out of line. That same year, when Convergent Press released Matthew Vines' book, *God and the Gay Christian* (in which he supports marriage equality), the National Religious Broadcasters threatened WaterBrook Multnomah Publishers with expulsion. Both Convergent (catering to a more progressive Christian audience) and WaterBrook Multnomah (tailored to more conservative Christians) are imprints of the Crown Publishing Group, a subsidiary of Random House, the secular giant based in New York. Furthermore, they shared the same Colorado Springs offices, some staff, and were overseen by Steve Cobb, the chief publishing executive.

Soon, other evangelical heavyweights jumped in to pressure WaterBrook Multnomah. Albert Mohler, president of Southern

---

10. Information for this account came from my personal phone interview with Richard E. Stearns on May 11, 2015, as well as from articles by Celeste Gracey and Jeremy Weber, "World Vision: Why We're Hiring Gay Christians in Same-Sex Marriages," *Christianity Today*, March 26, 2014; Celeste Gracey and Jeremy Weber, "World Vision Reverses Decision to Hire Christians in Same-Sex Marriages," *Christianity Today*, March 28, 2014; Morgan Lee, "World Vision Board Member Resigns Following Charity's Reversal on Same-Sex Marriage for US Employees," *Christian Post Reporter*, April 4, 2014; Sarah Pulliam Bailey, "World Vision, recovering from gay policy shift, tries to shore up its evangelical base," *The Washington Post*, June 26, 2014.

Baptist Theological Seminary, warned, "I believe that Multnomah is in serious danger of crashing its brand in terms of evangelical trust."[11]

At first, WaterBrook Multnomah chose to resign from the NRB rather than be bullied by them. However, approximately six months later, Crown announced it was separating WaterBrook Multnomah and Convergent and moving Convergent's offices to New York. Steve Cobb's retirement was also announced for the following March.[12]

Even though senior executives at four major evangelical publishing houses expressed personal openness to *Risking Grace*, they finally determined they couldn't publish it. One mentioned the likelihood that CBA retailers would balk. Another took the time to write me, "Personally, I regret this as I feel what you have written is unique and can contribute constructively to the ongoing dialogue that continues on this subject. And where you have ended up biblically is close to where I am in my own thinking."

Anticipating the release of *Risking Grace*, I contracted with *Christianity Today* magazine for a half-page ad to run in the September 2016 issue. But when the editor-in-chief briefly scanned a review copy of the book and found a perspective with which he disagreed, he canceled the ad, saying, "Why you imagine that we'd advertise your book in CT is surprising, since you know full well we think this both a theological and ethical error of some magnitude."[13] That's his call, yet *Christianity Today* often features articles presenting diverse views on controversial issues, and the ads they sell go even further afield. But apparently on this subject they have concluded the

---

11. Ruth Moon and Ted Olsen, "NRB Forces Out WaterBrook Multnomah Publishers Over Sister Imprint's 'Gay Christian' Book," *Christianity Today*, May 16, 2014.

12. Sarah Eekhoff Zylstra, "Not So Convergent: Leading Publisher Separates How Evangelical and Progressive Books Are Made," *Christianity Today*—"Gleanings," November 4, 2014.

13. According to the time stamps on the emails from when he got the book to when he fired back his decision (a couple of hours), it's unlikely he considered my journey—personal and theological—of how God changed my mind from agreeing with him to a position he wouldn't want others to consider.

conversation is over, even though many evangelical churches still convulse over how to respond to gay people and have no idea what to do with gay married couples who walk through their doors.

Wheaton College is one of my alma maters, and for Neta, our son, our daughter-in-law, my brother-in-law, sister-in-law, my mother- and father-in-law . . . The list goes on. When it became undeniable that most gay people could not become "straight" through prayer, counseling, or the heroic efforts of reparative therapy that had been attempted for decades, the college transitioned to a neo-traditional position and set up "Refuge," an on-campus group for students questioning their gender identity or sexual orientation. As Melanie Humphreys, Dean of Student Care and Services explained, "Research indicates that this is one of the most at-risk student groups on campus. And what I mean by 'at-risk' is at risk for self-harm or suicide. Each of the students I have come to know has experienced significant loneliness and isolation on our campus."[14]

Julie Rogers was subsequently hired under the chaplaincy program as a counselor to work with these students because she was something of an evangelical "poster child" for gay Christians. In Julie's own words, she "wanted to be the good kind of gay," that is, remain celibate. For twelve years before coming to Wheaton, she spoke publicly in support of this position. But something happened to her the more "gaybies" she counseled and cared for on campus, and it drove her deeper into the Scriptures until on her personal blog on July 13, 2015, she wrote:

> Though I've been slow to admit it to myself, I've quietly supported same-sex relationships for a while now. . . . While I struggle to understand how to apply Scripture to the marriage debate today (just like we all struggle to know how to interpret Scripture on countless controversial topics), I've become increasingly troubled by the unintended

---

14. "Refuge Becomes an Official Group for Students Questioning Their Gender Identity or Sexual Orientation," *The Wheaton Record*, February 22, 2013, http://www.wheaton.edu/Students/The-Record/Archives/Spring-2013/February-22-2013/Refuge-becomes-an-official-group-for-students.

consequences of messages that insist all LGBT people commit to lifelong celibacy. No matter how graciously it's framed, that message tends to contribute to feelings of shame and alienation for gay Christians.[15]

Knowing the administration would not tolerate the change in her position, she submitted her resignation. However, in her blog she added, "I feel the need to say that I'm not dating anyone . . . . I'm as single as ever and have remained celibate throughout my twenties."

The institutional stonewall became personal shortly before Leah and Jane moved out of state. In changing jobs, they faced a medical insurance gap, and at first COBRA appeared excessively expensive, so they asked if any of us had better suggestions. I noticed an ad in a Christian magazine for Medi-Share, an alternative to insurance where thousands of Christians share each other's healthcare bills, a "Christian Care Ministry" that purported to be far less expensive than conventional insurance.

So I called Medi-Share and explained that my daughter and her family were moving and were caught between work-related health programs, "So I was wondering if Medi-Share might be a short- or long-term solution for them?"

The agent welcomed me with a warm voice. "I'm sure we would, just so long as they are Christians and non-smokers."

"Great!" But a bell was ringing in my head. Of course, smoking involves direct health liabilities, but the mention of it reminded me of a line in the magazine ad that said something about not having to pay for things you don't believe in. At first I'd thought of abortion, an actual procedure. But the bell was still ringing. "Uh . . . there's one other thing I should mention. My daughter and her spouse are in a gay marriage. They have two children. Would that be a problem?"

"That would be a *big* problem. A deal breaker."

I guess I should have known before I even phoned. But it made me angry. On the one hand, I can understand people not

---

15. Julie Rogers, "An Update on the Gay Debate: evolving ideas, untidy stories, and hopes for the church," July 13, 2015, from her blog at https://julierodgers.wordpress.com.

wanting to pay for medical procedures they don't believe in. But it's unlikely *any* healthcare issue would arise for my daughter's family that would require other members of Medi-Share to pay for anything that might go against their conscience . . . unless they crassly objected to keeping gay people alive and healthy. And Leah and Jane's lifestyle is supremely healthy, probably superior to many Medi-Share members!

It boiled down to these Christians disowning other Christians because they have the "wrong" biblical view. But even if they are opposed to their views, even if they consider gay people their enemies, what happened to Jesus' instructions to "love your enemies" (Matthew 5:44)?

So as I drove the moving truck down the interstate that Sunday morning, caravanning with my wife, daughter, and grandson in another car, I missed the warm sense of security I used to feel as I passed one church after another. Who was inside? And after a life of feeling embraced by other brothers and sisters in Christ, was I now alone?

Then I recalled Elijah hiding in a cave because he thought he was alone and no one else followed God until God enlightened him that there were still seven thousand faithful believers (see 1 Kings19:18). Undoubtedly in every church I passed, there were also faithful believers. They might be temporarily confused by the "commandments of men" (Matthew 15:9, NKJV), but in the end, I believe many are committed to obeying Jesus' supreme command: "Love one another. As I have loved you, so you must love one another" (John 13:34). Christians are more than mere allies in a cause; therefore, as we learn to love like Jesus loves, we will embrace even those with whom we disagree.

But I do grieve for all those gay people who have no confidence that this is so because they have only experienced a stone wall of rejection when it comes to Christian institutions.

PART III

LOVING OUR GAY FAMILY AND FRIENDS

Chapter 15
Can You "Love the Sinner, and Hate the Sin"?

There is a fountain filled with blood
drawn from Emmanuel's veins;
And sinners plunged beneath that flood
lose all their guilty stains.
Lose all their guilty stains,
lose all their guilty stains;
And sinners plunged beneath that flood
lose all their guilty stains.

"There Is a Fountain"
William Cowper, 1772, verse 1

BEGINNING WITH THIS CHAPTER, I want to explore ways to love our gay family and friends *whether or not* we agree with them. There are things we are sometimes tempted to say which we don't intend as hurtful but come across that way to gay people who have heard far worse and don't know where our hearts and boundaries are. "Love the sinner, and hate the sin" is one of those phrases. "God loves you too much to leave you the way you are" is another. And recently, I heard a radio preacher resurrect, "There's tender love and there's tough love, and you've got to know when to use which."

All of these slogans reflect the presumption that we have the responsibility to make someone else our project and fix their life. Few people want that "distinction," especially when becoming your project presumes they aren't acceptable to you the way they are. But let's look more closely at the notion of fixing other people.

According to Scripture, God does hate sin. It damages our relationship with him, hurts other people, and hurts us. Proverbs 6:16-19 provides a short list of the sins God hates.

There are six things the Lord hates, seven that are detestable to him: haughty eyes, a lying tongue, hands that shed innocent blood, a heart that devises wicked schemes, feet that are quick to rush into evil, a false witness who pours out lies and a person who stirs up conflict in the community.

You can add to that divorce (Malachi 2:16), robbery of the poor (Isaiah 61:8), and hypocrisy (Amos 5:21). So, if God hates these sins, shouldn't we hate sin? After all, David as much as boasted that "I hate what faithless people do" (Psalm 101:3). In fact, it's hard to avoid hating heinous crimes like those of ISIS or child molesters. And we may not even pretend to "love" such sinners or notorious criminals like Hitler, Stalin, or Pol Pot. They deserve whatever punishment comes to them in this life or the next. And we would not think it a just universe if they escaped. But the fact that hatred comes easily to us when we see the pain and suffering sin causes doesn't mean it is an attitude we should cultivate.

Apparently, God doesn't throw the term "hate" around loosely. He seems to reserve it for the sins that create the most suffering. And while any sin separates us from God—apart from forgiveness through the blood of Jesus Christ—it's obvious some sins create far more suffering than others. John points out this distinction: "All wicked actions are sin, but not every sin leads to death" (1 John 5:17, NLT).[1] And the same contrast was reflected in the Old Testament where there were proportionally different punishments for breaking different laws: Steal someone's livestock, and you were required to restore it four or five fold (Exodus 22:1). But kidnap a

---

1. Some theologians speculate that the sin that "leads to death" is the rejection of Christ as savior: obvious. Others suggest it refers to blasphemy against the Spirit (Matthew 12:31). But the point I'm making is simply that not all sins are the same.

person, and the penalty was death (Exodus 21:16). Jesus scorched the Pharisees for failing to recognize the relative difference between sins: "You blind guides! You strain out a gnat but swallow a camel" (Matthew 23:24).

But if hatred is not God's primary response to every infraction, perhaps we should hold it in check as well. In fact, Jesus never instructed us to hate anyone or anything. Instead, he repeatedly commanded us to love our neighbor, to love one another as he loves us, and even love our enemies.[2] Furthermore, love is the only response we can be sure won't backfire. Think of all the wars that were supposed to save the world or a country or a people. Some may have stemmed the tide of evil for a time, but the price was always higher than anticipated and too often made things worse. Similarly, introducing hatred into any aspect of a personal relationship is liable to backfire even when we try to tell the person we still love them. Nevertheless, we often justify our hatred because we don't know how to love someone unconditionally.

We don't know how to love unconditionally

After reading this far in *Risking Grace*, hopefully you empathize even more with your gay family and friends, you grieve over how badly they've been treated by many Christians, and even though you may not agree with them if they hold alternative interpretations of the "prohibitive texts," you're not calling for them to be burned at the stake as heretics. But with a heavy heart, you still cannot affirm gay marriage. You think it displeases God, and therefore you feel compelled to let them know.

How do you do that in a godly way?

It has become popular for Christians to appeal to the motto: "Love the sinner, and hate the sin!" in relation to gay people. In fact, even though we all commit many sins, this particular phrase has become primarily reserved for gay people. It's a flag phrase. If

---

2. In his earthly ministry, Jesus only used the word "hate" to label the animosity others expressed *toward* him or his followers or in a rhetorical sense to establish a strong contrast, such as John 12:25, "Anyone who loves their life will lose it, while anyone who hates their life in this world will keep it for eternal life." (Also see Luke 14:26; 16:13.)

you overhear just that phrase these days, the speaker is probably talking about homosexuality. Christians picked it up because it seems to express the only way we know how to live in the tension of loving someone while remaining true to a conviction that the other person is wrong. But does it work, and more importantly, is it biblical?

First of all, that phrase is not found in Scripture, neither is anything like it prescribed by Scripture . . . perhaps because any time hate is introduced into actual human relationships, people get hurt. Even if you could hate only what a person *does* while perfectly loving them as an individual, that's not the way the other person is going to experience it.

The phrase, "Love the sinner, and hate the sin," attempts to communicate love and acceptance of one part of a person while rejecting—in the strongest possible terms—another integral part of that person. Some claim they intend to separate the person from the behavior, but the phrase itself ties them together. The person is a "sinner"—not in the same universal way we all are; otherwise it would be "Love the *saint*, and hate the sin"—but precisely because of their hated sin. Again, that is why this slogan is used almost exclusively in relation to homosexuality.

Many of us can recall a time in our childhood when some bully mocked something about us—our teeth, hair, size, walk, voice, whatever. Were you comforted by, "Oh, don't worry, honey. That's not the real you"? Of course it was the real you! Whether the criticism was valid or not, whatever was being mocked, whatever was hated, was you! We've all known children who were bullied so long and so intensely that they ended up hating themselves and living under a cloud of shame and self-loathing.

Complicating this matter, people who use the phrase seldom clarify what exactly they hate. Is it extramarital gay sex, gay marriage, support for marriage equality, or merely same-sex attraction? Sometimes it's just the way the person looks, walks, or dresses. But often the speaker hasn't even thought through what he or she hates. It's just anything related to homosexuality. A church I'm familiar with is technically neo-traditional, but sometimes the pastor speaks in shorthand. When someone asked him whether

Jesus ever said anything about homosexuality, he admitted that Jesus never used that word (or any equivalent), but he referred to Mark 7:21 where Jesus said, "For it is from within, out of a person's heart, that evil thoughts come—sexual immorality, . . . [along with a list of other sins]." Then he went on to claim that in his opinion "sexual immorality" (translated from the Greek word, *porneia*) included homosexuality.[3] "So," he claimed, "Jesus *did* speak against homosexuality." But at the very least, an answer like that needs more clarification regarding *what kind* of homosexuality. The pastor officially welcomes gay people to his church, expecting them to remain celibate, but simply saying that Jesus spoke against homosexuality can create significant anxiety. For instance, did he mean one's sexual orientation? Were the "evil thoughts" Jesus mentioned the same as same-sex attraction? Some would say not necessarily, but leaving it ambiguous cannot help but foster insecurity and shame among gay people, especially if they cannot alter their orientation.

We need to focus on saying, "I love you," period! No buts, no exceptions, no qualifiers, no conditions. But we fear that love all by itself will cause the other person to assume we agree with everything they do. So we have to add a qualifier, a condition to our love that reminds the person there's something about them we

---

3. The King James Version of the Bible translated *porneia* as "fornication" twenty-six times. However, several theologians claim the term became inclusive for all kinds of sexual sin. If that were true, all idolatrous, abusive, or unfaithful sexual activities—whether straight or gay—would be included. But as Chapter 14 summarized, that does not answer whether faithful, gay marriage was ever envisioned by the biblical writers or their readers since that was not a widely understood concept for centuries to come.

Those who would *now* like to retrofit same-sex marriage into the definition of *porneia*, claim that by the New Testament era it referred to "all the prohibited sexual activity in the Levitical Holiness Code, which included incest (Leviticus 18:6-18), adultery (18:20), homosexuality (18:22), and bestiality (18:23). Therefore whenever Jesus refers to this term, he is prohibiting all of these activities" ("Pastoring LGBT Persons," Stafford, TX: Vineyard USA, 2014, 18). But that doesn't answer the question of whether gay marriage was ever envisioned by the Old Testament writers. Additionally, the logic of this argument breaks down if those who espouse it fail to include *all* the prohibitions, such as the prohibition to having sex during a woman's menstrual period (Leviticus 18:19), separated by only two verses from verse 22 about men not sleeping with men. Perhaps a better definition for *porneia* would simply be, "marital unfaithfulness."

don't love, that we consider borderline and dangerous. Perhaps something we even hate. And the only way for them to escape our hatred with certainty is for them to remove that part of their person. Hence, our love is conditional.

But aren't we helping a person by hating their sin?

In Romans 7:15, Paul lamented how difficult it was to live the righteous life he desired: "I do not understand what I do. For what I want to do I do not do, but what I hate I do." So if a person can hate their own behavior, isn't it legitimate to join in hating what you believe is sin in your family member or friend's life?

Not unless they ask you to! And maybe not even then.

And here's why: Your fervor is likely to be—or become— greater than theirs, and then you are no longer supporting them in their fight but pressuring them to comply with *your* convictions. Furthermore, they may not so much hate who they are or what they do as hate the ostracism it elicits. There have been myriads of gay people who endured depression, self-loathing, and even attempted suicide because they hated *being* gay. If you had approached them at that point—as many well-meaning Christians did—they might have welcomed your alliance in hating their "gayness" because they were ready to do whatever would make them straight. Many attempted grueling reparative therapy, thinking it would overcome and do away with their homosexuality. But part of the problem was many of these gay people were responding to, reacting to, drowning under the rejection and shame their homosexuality engendered in Christians, family members, and other people from whom they longed for acceptance. For many it wasn't the "gayness" per se they hated but the price of being gay that was too heavy to bear.

This is one reason the gay rights movement has gained so much momentum. Gays aren't trying to stamp out straight people or man-woman marriage as some alarmists claim.[4] All they ask

---

4. Theodore Shoebat, a self-proclaimed—though discredited—terrorism expert says, "Do not think for a second that the sodomites would treat us peacefully! Do not think for a second that the sodomites do not want to commit persecution against Christians. I do not hesitate at all to say that the

is that we, the majority, lift the stigma of being gay and let them live as normal, contributing members of society . . . and for gay Christians, as normal, faithful members of the church.

The Holy Spirit's unique role

Confusing acceptance with sanctification is the primary complication that arises whenever we try to do the task God reserved for the Holy Spirit. Jesus said, "When he [the Holy Spirit] comes, he will convict the world of guilt in regard to sin and righteousness and judgment" (John 16:8). He did not recruit us as deputies to police other people's behavior or to fix their sins. Does this mean we have nothing to say about right and wrong living? Not at all. The New Testament is full of counsel regarding godly living. But there is a right and a wrong way to share that counsel. The right way is an appeal to people through the preaching and teaching of the Word that explains, lifts up, inspires, warns, and encourages. The wrong way is to exert pressure to force someone to change through threats, shame, ostracism, or—as so often occurred throughout church history—violence and punishment.

The Inquisition, holy wars, and centuries of persecution *between* Christians (who thought the others were sinning) represent totally unbiblical attempts to force people to change. Emotional, relational, and social pressure that shames people may seem to be an improvement, but the grandiose presumption behind both is the same: that it is our responsibility to *make* people change. That's not our job, and usurping it from the Holy Spirit, even under the cloak of genial and polite language, can destroy people all the same. Telling someone there is something about them you hate, something that is despicable, something they can't seem to change but remains a stigma, disqualifying them from marriage,

---

sodomites—and I say this with confidence—that the sodomites would not hesitate to kill people like me, . . . to kill other Christians, to kill anyone who is opposing their agenda." http://shoebat.com/2015/09/10/homosexual-activists-tell-kim-davis-we-will-kidnap-your-husband-tie-him-up-and-force-him-to-watch-us-raping-you-we-will-burn-you-alive-civil-unrest-is-coming-to-america/. The quote comes from five minutes into his video.

from full acceptance, from serving God in ministry or leader-ship—it's the gamut of shame.

Who is the author of shame?

Revelation 12:10 says, "For the accuser of our brothers and sisters who accuses them before our God day and night, has been hurled down." We can look forward to Satan's defeat, but in the meantime, he wields *shame!* And we can sometimes become his unwitting henchmen. After Alan Chambers, former president for ten years of Exodus International, closed down that umbrella organization over 250 "ex-gay" ministries, he admitted, "I know there are people who have taken their life because they felt so ashamed of who they are, felt like God couldn't love them as they are, and that's something that will haunt me until the day I die."[5]

With marriage equality now legal in this country, more and more churches will find gay couples and gay families coming through their doors seeking a spiritual home. Many neo-traditional churches claim to welcome gay people provided they remain celibate, but most of those churches have not considered how to respond to *already married* gay couples. Should they subtly encourage them to find another church? Convince the couple that their situation is sinful and require them to separate in spite of their children? Or allow them to stay married but prohibit them from full participation in ministry and leadership since that might imply their situation was acceptable?

Try putting yourself in such a couple's shoes. You have a bright six-year-old daughter who is going through a shy stage and needs a secure home to counter some bullying at school. But she's astute and can put two and two together when she hears the pastor and other teachers say same-sex marriage is sinful, so she concludes that God and the church don't approve of her family, the family she desperately needs for security and support. Or you have a fourteen-year-old son who's kicking up his heels and occasionally testing the boundaries. The church is looking for a Sunday school teacher,

---

5. Alan Chambers on "Anderson Cooper 360," CNN, June 11, 2014, 20:00 ET, http://www.cnn.com/TRANSCRIPTS/1406/11/acd.01.html.

but when your name is proposed, your son hears someone object because the Bible attaches moral requirements to church leadership—especially teachers—and you are "living in sin." Is he going to throw that back in your face as a reason not to obey his parents?

Would you stay in that church living under a cloud of shame that undermines your authority as a parent or your best efforts to provide security and safety for your children?

Are we doing Satan's work when we establish policies that enshroud people in shame? In some instances, the policies don't even come in the guise of *fixing* people. People just have to live under them because they can't change their life circumstances, as in the case of a married gay couple raising children.

"Open and welcoming" used to be a term employed only by churches that affirmed gay people, including those in gay marriages. But in recent years, some neo-traditional churches have begun saying they are "welcoming" or even "radically welcoming" (as our church claims). And they do welcome anyone to come, receive, and participate in the life of the church. But that does not mean they are "affirming." In fact, their welcome comes with some hidden caveats. Who the gay person is—their intrinsic sexual orientation—can never be blessed in marriage and is even a liability that can cause shame, fear, and public suspicion. *Shame* because the church teaches that the same longings in their heart for a lifetime companion that are celebrated in a straight person's heart are sinful. *Fear* that they might succumb to those longings and marry (or have an illicit affair since marriage is not an option). And subtle *suspicion* coming from other church members and perhaps the leadership that they aren't completely "safe" to work with children or influence other people. Or, even if they are deemed safe, they still represent a "poor example."

Such an environment constitutes a very tenuous welcome at best.

Does God make allowances for human circumstances?

Jesus said, "From everyone who has been given much, much will be demanded" (Luke 12:48), indicating that God takes into account our circumstances in what he expects of us. This is not about "earning" salvation, which only comes by faith, but it is evidence

204

that the Holy Spirit follows his own timetable and methods and extends great grace in dealing with us.

Let's suppose God *does* object to gay marriage. Is there any evidence that he might extend grace to people who don't conform? Or do we see God as inflexible, a God who gives no mercy to those who cannot or think they cannot meet his expectations? Nehemiah described our God as "a forgiving God, gracious and compassionate, slow to anger and abounding in love" (9:17). And even when things were so bad in Sodom that God planned to destroy it, Abraham appealed to God. Surprisingly, God was willing to spare the city even if there were only 50, 40, 30, 20, or even just 10 righteous people in it. This was not a lesson in negotiating with God, but it does tell us a great deal about God's character. He does not treat us as if he were a computer where even one wrong character in your password prevents the program from opening. No, he looks at our heart and understands our human circumstances and what we've been given to work with . . . or haven't been given. That was the whole point of Jesus coming to live among us: "For we do not have a high priest who is unable to empathize with our weaknesses, but we have one who has been tempted in every way, just as we are— yet he did not sin. Let us then approach God's throne of grace with confidence, so that we may receive mercy and find grace to help us in our time of need" (Hebrews 4:15-16).

God understands when we can't—or think we can't—do what he wants and sometimes makes allowances. In Chapter 7 we looked at the story of Moses' encounter with God in the burning bush. When God commissioned him to confront Pharaoh, Moses offered many objections, finally saying, "O Lord, I have never been eloquent . . . I am slow of speech and tongue" (Exodus 4:10). Surprisingly, God did not dispute this. In fact, he said, "Who gave man his mouth? Who makes him deaf or mute? Who gives him sight or makes him blind? Is it not I, the Lord? Now go; I will help you speak and will teach you what to say." That was still more than Moses thought he could manage, and he begged God to send someone else. Moses' resistance to God's obvious and perfect will was so strong, the Bible says, "The Lord's anger burned against Moses" but only briefly before he agreed to have Moses' brother

Aaron do the speaking (v. 14). In the years that followed, we don't see God holding this "compromise" against Moses or hesitating to bless him on account of this resistance.

Later, in 1 Samuel 8, the Israelites asked Samuel to appoint them a king. The Lord was displeased but assured Samuel, "It is not you they have rejected, but they have rejected me as their king" (v. 7). And then he went on to warn them of all the grief having a human king would bring. Nevertheless, the people rejected God's counsel, and God finally told Samuel to go ahead and give them a king. Samuel anointed Saul and later David. And God blessed every king in Israel's history who honored him, even though that was not God's preferred plan for the nation.

A further example can be seen in God's response to divorce. In Malachi 2:16, God explained, "I hate divorce," and yet in Deuteronomy 24:1, he had approved a procedure to allow it (which Joseph almost took advantage of when he discovered Mary was pregnant). In Matthew 19:8, Jesus said, "Moses permitted you to divorce your wives because your hearts were hard. But it was not this way from the beginning." That is, it was not God's preferred plan, but in his mercy, he allowed it.

Most of our evangelical churches include remarried people. Divorce ended their first marriage for a variety of reasons, some seemingly justified, while others . . . well, let's just say they threw themselves on God's mercy. But can you imagine the damage if we went around saying, "We love remarried people; we just hate their sin"?

Pointing to God's benevolence concerning divorce is not a tit-for-tat argument, like a child wailing, "Well, he got a lollipop, so I should get one too." But it does show the nature of God's heart and how he responds, even to something that grieves him deeply, because he understands our frailty and does not hold it against us. This is not to justify outright rebellion against God. That's a fatal mistake: "For the wages of sin is death, but" the Bible adds, "the gift of God is eternal life in Christ Jesus our Lord" (Romans 6:23).

These examples demonstrate that God takes note of our circumstances, who we are, what experiences brought us to the challenges we now face, and the light and understanding we've been given. He takes all of these things into consideration, and then, in many cases and for his own purposes, he grants remarkable, gracious latitude, and often to our consternation, pardons and even blesses those who turn to him in faith and give him thanks and praise in the middle of their less than perfect life. That is true even when we don't fully comprehend—and therefore have not repented of—specific sins. We just know we need God's salvation, and he gives his grace freely because "love covers over a multitude of sins" (1 Peter 4:8).

Do not judge

This is why we should not attempt to take over the Holy Spirit's job of trying to fix people, certainly not by increasing the pressure through the shame of hating something about them. In so doing, we risk focusing on the wrong spiritual agenda and end up judging. Jesus was pretty unequivocal in saying, "Do not judge" (Matthew 7:1). It is one thing to be confident in our own convictions as they pertain to us, our conduct, and our beliefs. But judging someone else presumes we are absolutely right and have the authority to dispense a consequence. And that's something only God has the authority to do.

When the serpent tempted Eve in the Garden, he claimed, "You will be like God, knowing good and evil" (Genesis 3:5). In his book, *Benefit of the Doubt*, pastor and theologian, Greg Boyd, explains it this way:

> The forbidden tree was meant to serve as a sort of "No Trespassing" sign. It was God's warning, placed in the garden out of love, not to try to take on God's role of defining and judging good and evil. God was essentially saying, "Your job is to love like I love, not judge like only I can judge. And to do the first, you can't do the second." When non-omniscient beings like us start to judge, we stop loving and begin to look more like Pharisees, who reflect the character of their "father," "the Accuser" (Revelation 12:10, cf. John 8:44), than like Jesus, who reflects the loving character of his Father and the character that all humans are supposed to reflect.[6]

6. Gregory A. Boyd, *Benefit of the Doubt: Breaking the Idol of Certainty*, (Grand Rapids, MI: Baker Publishing Group, 2013, Kindle Edition), 63.

To think we can make that ultimate discernment between what is good and evil in *someone else's* life is to play God, that first and greatest of sins. To judge rightly, you must be able to see into a person's heart and discern all their motives and understand every extenuating circumstance in order to judge between good and evil in their life. Jesus said, "Don't even try to do that."[7]

Collateral Damage

Ray and Juliana pushed their iPhones across our dining room table with the latest pictures of their grandson. Of course, all babies are cute, right? But I didn't have to be polite about little Ryan. He was one of the most handsome, lively-looking little guys I had ever seen.

He'd recently been adopted by Christopher and Edward, our guests' son and son-in-law. And no grandparents could be prouder, but their enthusiasm is seldom reciprocated at their church. Tight lips and blank stares are the polite responses when the subject of their son comes up, because "gay" does not describe happiness at the conservative church they've been attending for the last fifteen years.

Ray and Juliana always knew their oldest of three sons was a little different, but it was on a family trip that the possibility of fourteen-year-old Christopher being gay first crossed Ray's mind. Their middle son had broken his arm and couldn't come, so they ended up taking one of Christopher's best friends.

"Everyone else was sleeping in the car while I drove," recalls Ray. "When I looked in the rearview mirror, I noticed Christopher gazing at his friend with a look of total infatuation, and he continued

---

7. Jesus' instruction to not judge in the context of Matthew 7 does not prevent duly established authorities from rendering decisions or dispensing punishments for proven crimes. Jesus' focus is on accusing one another of sin and condemning one another with shame or other consequences according to our verdicts.

to stare for so long that it reminded me of an adolescent's first puppy love. Suddenly it struck me that he might be gay. But I let it go. Didn't even mention it to Juliana." Ray went on to explain that he hadn't grown up in a family where there was a lot of prejudice, so if his son was gay, that posed no crisis for him.

As Christopher went on through high school, he dated girls, though mostly in group settings, except for one very beautiful girl who used to hang around Christopher all the time. Juliana and Ray could see she was infatuated with him, but the relationship didn't seem to go anywhere. When their middle son asked, "What's with you two, anyway?" Christopher shrugged, "Well, you know she's got a boyfriend." Yes, there was another guy who was her supposed boyfriend, but the strange thing to Juliana and Ray was, Christopher hadn't noticed that this beautiful girl had eyes only for him.

"When he did go on dates, I tried to coach him," admits Juliana. "You know, 'How'd it go? You try to hold her hand?' Until I began to realize his relationships with girls never ended up going anywhere. But he had good friendships with girls, so I just thought he was a late bloomer. It never dawned on me that he might be gay."

"Christopher was never flamboyant or effeminate," added Ray. "In fact, he was our most conservative, proper kid."

It wasn't until Christopher was twenty-two that he actually came out as gay to his family. He was going to college, living on his own, and working full time when he developed a relationship with a young man from Ohio and wanted his parents to meet him. So Christopher sat his parents down and told them the whole story. At that point, they weren't involved with a church that had a very conservative theology, so they accepted Christopher as he was, concerned only about some risky dating behaviors he was going through at the time—though those behaviors were not nearly as worrisome as the dating patterns of their heterosexual middle son. Looking back on Christopher's growing up years, Juliana considers him their least "problem" child.

But by that time, they were becoming more interested in evangelical Christianity. At the invitation of their next-door neighbor, Juliana got involved with a Bible study, and Ray's mother kept praying for and encouraging both of them. The big change for Ray occurred when he attended the 1997 Promise Keepers conference in Chicago's Soldiers Field. After that, he says his spiritual life caught on fire. When their neighbors invited them to visit their local Bible church, they did so, and it seemed that was exactly where God wanted them. "It was so rich," recalls Ray. "We were being fed regularly from the Word and growing in the Lord."

For several years, nothing came up about Christopher being gay. He was on his own, and seldom went to church with his parents, so all their church friends knew about him was that Christopher, like their other two sons, needed salvation. Small group members prayed for all three young men, and especially for their middle son who was fighting drug addiction.

As Juliana and Ray got more involved, they both found new ways to serve. Ray's technical skills led to his becoming the production manager for the sound and lighting, a major responsibility that put him in close relationship with the pastors on a regular basis. Juliana headed up the café, was involved in children's and women's ministries, served as a small group leader, and went on three mission trips to Ethiopia. The church and their Bible study groups became a major relational focus for Ray and Juliana.

When Christopher finally met Edward and realized he was the man he wanted to marry, Ray and Juliana were happy. But when they let their Christian friends know the "good news," some relationships turned sour. "What surprised me," says Ray, "is that the people I thought might not accept it, proved to be so loving and understanding, while others who I thought were more tolerant and gracious, couldn't handle it at all."

Ray and Juliana sought help from their pastors, who were very patient in meeting with them and explaining the church's basically neo-traditional position that identified homosexuality as the result of sin and sinful if acted upon, whether or not it was within the bounds of marriage, which, of course, they did not recognize as legitimate.

The church even went so far as to bring in an outside speaker to orient the staff concerning homosexuality and how to relate to gay people. There were many helpful elements that included not

using offensive language and being more loving, but in the end it was mostly a "kinder, gentler" expression of the claim that gay relationships were sinful, even if they involved marriage and family.

Ray and Juliana appreciated the conversations with the pastors and the seminar, but they had also been doing their own study of the Scripture. With the help of an on-line support group for moms of gay people and a number of books by gay Christians, they were not convinced that the traditional interpretations of the Scriptures were necessarily valid.

As the wedding approached, Juliana began to sense she was being excluded from various activities, and some of the women in the church seemed aloof. When she finally confronted them, they gave the excuse that it was because they wanted to be *sensitive*. "Even those who tried to reach out to me weren't doing so with empathy or as an ally but out of pity, as if they were saying, 'Oh, we're so sorry you have such a cross to bear.'"

Ray added, "When we refused to join them in condemning our son, it sometimes got tense, and we heard things like, 'How can you go to their wedding? Don't you want to see your kids in heaven? Do you want to see your son go to hell for eternity?'"

In the fall of 2012, Christopher and Edward finally got married. Juliana recalls it as a magical day for their formal wedding held at Pazzo's on Wacker Drive in Chicago's Loop. She and Ray felt God's presence and blessing as the minister—not from their church, of course—conducted the ceremony. Back at their own church in the following Sundays, they sensed a quiet disdain among many members who knew of the wedding.

In 2013, when the Supreme Court took up overturning DOMA, the Defense of Marriage Act, Ray was on duty as the production manager when the pastor took him aside in the green room before the service started. "I just want to tell you that what I'm going to say today is not an attack on you or your family, and I don't want you to take it personally."

Ray knew they were in a non-affirming church. He knew their position was very conservative, and he knew it was going to take a very long time before the church changed. But the pastor's speech—before his main sermon—was very strong about how

everyone should pray that the sanctity of marriage woulu preserved. Ray thought about that afterward. The pastor h. been thoughtful enough to warn him, but how could he not takᵗ it personally? Of course, the pastor was addressing policy, and he hadn't singled out Ray and Juliana by name, but many members knew. And how could any gay person or their family not take the message personally? It condemned anyone who was "affirming" as a threat to the sanctity of marriage.

Two years later, in 2015, as the Supreme Court's marriage equality decision approached, the comments from the pulpit again increased. The Sunday after the decision, Juliana and Ray were afraid of what might happen at church so they approached cautiously. They needed to pick up a gift for a friend's baby, so they figured they could at least stop in at the church gift shop . . . and test the mood.

"There was gloom and doom everywhere," recalls Juliana, "as if the world was going to end. And I felt like I was wearing a scarlet letter as we walked in. When I saw that the news media had been invited and was interviewing people in the café, I turned to Ray and said, 'We gotta get outta here!'" She explained that they had just been interacting with their son and son-in-law, "two of the kindest, nicest people on the planet," in Juliana's opinion, and she believed their decision to get married had actually been a compliment to the institution of marriage, not a blow to it.

Had they stayed that morning, Juliana and Ray would have heard the pastor begin his sermon by saying, "This is a time to lament . . . a time to be sad, to express sorrow—the blues, if you will."[8] What followed was a great message in terms of the principles for dealing with despair and grief, but the *specific* "tragedy" the pastor was leading the whole congregation in lamenting was the national legalization of marriage equality, something that brought such relief and joy to so many gay people and many—like Ray and Juliana—who loved them.

Three months later, a baby boy was born and put up for adoption, and Christopher and Edward were privileged to bring

---

8. According to the pastor's online recorded message for June 28, 2015.

him home when he was just three weeks old. Ray and Juliana were so delighted they could not help sharing the news with people at church. But the silence was like a blanket of new snow. No congratulations, only the whisper of quiet disapproval. When one woman frowned deeply at the news, Juliana couldn't help herself. She took the woman's face between both her hands and said, "No frowning! It's a beautiful thing!" And then she walked away to hide her hurt.

It's hard to stay in an environment like that, Ray acknowledges. "We know our sons will probably never attend a service at that church again, and yet . . . there's a way I feel called to stay because they get so much right. Also, I'm willing to be an advocate for gay people and refuse to let various church members pretend that their prejudice does not impact real flesh and blood people."

Juliana isn't so sure. "Christopher and Edward chose to buy a house not far from us so we can be grandma and grandpa to Ryan. It won't be long until I'll want to take him to Sunday school and then church. But I'm certainly not going to expose him to attitudes that undercut and disrespect his parents. I don't know what we should do."

Chapter 16
Disputable Matters

My hope is built on nothing less
Than Jesus' blood and righteousness.
I dare not trust the sweetest frame,
But wholly trust in Jesus' Name.

"The Solid Rock"
Edward Mote, 1834, verse 1

O F THE HUNDREDS OF STORIES NETA AND I RESEARCHED over the years about Christian heroes,[1] the most tragic were those involving Christians persecuting other Christians. When Jesus said, "Blessed are you when people insult you, persecute you and falsely say all kinds of evil against you because of me" (Matthew 5:11), he was presumably warning us about how unbelievers were likely to treat us. Among believers, however, he prayed for unity (John 17). So it became agonizing to study the transcripts and court records from the sixteenth and seventeenth centuries where, again and again, Christians put hundreds of other Christians on trial because they thought their convictions were heretical. And it wasn't just between Catholics and Protestants. There were plenty of Protestants who tried, imprisoned, tortured, and executed other Protestants. These disputes degenerated into the Thirty Years' War, which took the lives of millions of people, amounting to as much as 20 percent of the region's population when the accompanying famines and disease are calculated.

---

1. Resulting in five Hero Tales books, forty Trailblazer Books, *On Fire for Christ*, and *Fear Not*.

However, now that we are in the third millennium, I never expected to see Christians again putting other Christians on trial over theological disputes, as is described in the Collateral Damage report following this chapter. Of course, no one has been put on the rack or burnt at the stake, and no literal armies are ravaging the strongholds of opposing views, but if we could smell the spiritual stench of death, it might wake us up to the destruction caused by renouncing fellow believers, dividing churches, denominations, and ministries.

And yet, that's what's happening. As the Supreme Court decision regarding marriage equality approached, Al Mohler, president of the Southern Baptist Theological Seminary, warned, "This issue will eventually break relationships—personally, congregationally, and institutionally. This is the sad reality and there is simply no way around it."[2] His statement came the same week Tony Campolo, a long-time evangelical leader, announced his full acceptance of Christian gay couples into the church while David Neff, the former editor of *Christianity Today* cheered him on with, "God bless Tony Campolo. He is acting in good faith and is, I think, on the right track."[3] At the same time numerous denominations, Christian institutions, and ministries were facing the prospect of dividing over same-sex marriage or had already split.

Mohler may lament the broken relationships, but he has not been willing to seek unity with Christians with whom he disagrees. He had earlier drawn a line in the sand when he condemned World Vision for deciding to allow married gay people to serve on its staff, their reason being, with fifty denominations represented among staff, they felt the challenging theological and pastoral issue of gay marriage was best handled by each person's own church.[4] But Mohler disagreed: "No organization can serve

2. Albert Mohler, "Which Way, Evangelicals? There Is Nowhere to Hide," AlbertMohler.com, June 10, 2015, http://www.albertmohler.com/2015/06/10/which-way-evangelicals-there-is-nowhere-to-hide/.

3. Mark D. Tooley, "Tony Campolo and David Neff: From Evangelicals Left to Post Evangelical?" *Christian Post*, June 11, 2015, http://www.christianpost.com/news/tony-campolo-and-david-neff-from-evangelical-left-to-post-evangelical-140288/#8TVBb4FSBI8hYFvt.99.

4. See the "Collateral Damage" story about World Vision following Chapter 14.

on behalf of churches across the vast theological and moral spectrum that would include clearly evangelical denominations, on the one hand, and liberal denominations . . . on the other." His reason was, "Willingly recognizing same-sex marriage and validating openly homosexual[s] . . . in their homosexuality is a grave and tragic act that confirms sinners in their sin—and that is an act that violates the gospel of Christ."[5]

In other words, he thinks there is no way Christians with different convictions on how to relate to and love gay people can work together unless they agree with his interpretation of Scripture. And that's always been the *kind* of line that has divided Christians.

But is he right? Is there no way to stay together in the middle of differing convictions? The saddest part of Mohler's prediction is the inevitable damage his attitude can have. In the World Vision instance alone, his input and that of other leaders who agreed with him, caused donors to cancel support for 10,000 orphans. Real people—many people—will be hurt if we can't figure out how to get along together respectfully. And the cause of Christ will suffer as potential seekers sicken over our bitter infighting. Jesus declared, "By this everyone will know that you are my disciples, if you love one another" (John 13:35), but many of us don't consider the significance of that little word, *if*, because the opposite is just as true. If it is possible for the world to know we are Christians by our love, it is equally possible for the world to dismiss the Gospel because of our lack of love for one another and inability to respect one another.

Jesus' prayer in John 17 presupposed that we *can* be one, but the very need for that prayer—Jesus' longest recorded prayer—acknowledges that there is a danger our unity can easily be shattered, as has happened so many times over the centuries.

The challenge of accepting those with different views

For three reasons I have not given the same amount of space in this book to the arguments for traditional and neo-traditional

---

5. Albert Mohler, "Pointing to Disaster—The Flawed Moral Vision of World Vision," AlbertMohler.com, March 25, 2014, http://www.albertmohler.com/2014/03/25/pointing-to-disaster-the-flawed-moral-vision-of-world-vision/.

perspectives as I have to the inclusive position. (1) For those of us who are straight, it's the gay point of view with which *we* are least familiar. (2) In our evangelical circles there are plenty of apologists for the more traditional perspective. (3) I am admittedly more convinced by the inclusive perspective as a path to right a terrible wrong within our evangelical Christian family of condemning, rejecting, and driving away our brothers and sisters, sons and daughters, who are gay. And my change of heart is not based so much on the alternative interpretations of the prohibitive texts as on the larger example of how Jesus related to people, the primacy of his commands to love and not judge, and the example of the early church in resolving major disputes.[6]

However, one characteristic of the inclusive point of view is that while it calls for those of us who are straight to more lovingly include and respect gay people, it also calls gay people to include and respect people with traditional or neo-traditional views. This is why I have not used the common term, "affirming." To some, that term presumes a one-way street: everyone must affirm marriage equality. But some people (straight and gay) with sincere convictions don't believe gay marriage is right. However, that doesn't mean they can't respect and fellowship with (i.e., *include*) people who do accept gay marriage, and vice versa. Each one can accept the other while letting God be the judge. As Paul said, "Accept one another . . . just as Christ accepted you, in order to bring praise to God" (Romans 15:7). The term "inclusive" fulfills that biblical expectation when each person is willing to include and respect the other. But it's not easy.

The comfort of like-minded people

In his book, *Benefit of the Doubt*, pastor and theologian Greg Boyd points out how strongly we humans desire the comfort of certainty that we are *right*, and nothing reinforces certainty more than surrounding ourselves with like-minded people and insulat-

---

6. I chose three terms to describe different perspectives on relating to gay people: the "traditional" view, the "neo-traditional" view, and the "inclusive" view. Please refer to the introduction to this book for a description of each.

ing ourselves from people who might challenge us, either verbally or by their mere presence. Throughout the history of the church, we Christians have tended to separate ourselves from those we considered wrong on issues as small as which mode of baptism is valid or whether musical instruments are acceptable in worship to such weighty matters as who is the head of the church or whether an earthly head is even legitimate, plus all kinds of doctrinal issues in between. Today, even though we may not go to war over those differences, there are many among us—and whole denominations—who still will not fellowship with those holding differing convictions.

If it's legitimate to ignore Jesus' prayer for our unity and divide over such issues, it is no wonder many believe the morality of same-sex marriage is an issue worth separating over. But is it justifiable to break relationship over a difference of conviction? Some might say we can separate while still remaining friends. But anyone who has tried it knows that even among the best of friends, it is hard to maintain a relationship if you cannot affirm what is most important to each of you . . . not the other person's view but the other person's membership in the Body of Christ. If we do not recognize our brother or sister as valid members with whom we can share communion and serve Christ together as equals, we break relationship to a degree that cannot be overcome without repentance.

God's antidote to division

The remarkable thing is that God, in his wisdom, anticipated this problem and provided a way to handle those issues that so commonly divide us. In Romans 14, Paul wrote:

Accept the one whose faith is weak, without quarreling over disputable matters. One person's faith allows them to eat anything, but another, whose faith is weak, eats only vegetables. The one who eats everything must not treat with contempt the one who does not, and the one who does not eat everything must not judge the one who does, for God has accepted them. Who are you to judge someone else's servant? To their own master, servants stand or fall.

218

And they will stand, for the Lord is able to make them stand (vv. 1-4).

On the surface the "disputable matters" dividing the church in Rome may appear trivial to modern readers. They involved eating meat, observing holy days, and drinking wine. Most of us get along fine with vegetarians and vegans and omnivores. Drinking a glass of wine is no longer considered the sign of carnality it once was fifty years ago. And as for "holy days," we evangelicals seldom use that term. Somewhere along the way, blue laws evaporated and many faithful Christians shop, watch football, catch up on a little work, or even head for the lake on Sundays. Of course, some people still disagree with these liberties, but we usually manage to get along with one another because those issues aren't our core values. Even the British theologian N.T. Wright appears to trivialize the significance of the disputes in Rome by relegating them to what he calls "morally neutral" expressions of "ethnic boundary lines." He says:

> If you want to know why Paul insisted on tolerating some differences of opinion and practice within the people of God, and on not tolerating others, the answer is that the ones that were to be tolerated were the ones that carried the connotations of ethnic boundary lines, and the ones that were not to be tolerated were the ones that marked the difference between genuine, living, renewed humanity and false, corruptible, destructive humanity. . . . We need to make a clear distinction between the aspects of a culture which Paul regards as morally neutral and those which he regards as morally, or immorally, loaded.[7]

Wright is correct in saying Paul's primary concern was that the church not split along ethnic lines. But by characterizing these is-

---

7. N.T. Wright, "Communion and Koinonia: Pauline Reflections on Tolerance and Boundaries," a paper given at the Future of Anglicanism Conference, Oxford, 2002. http://ntwrightpage.com/Wright_Communion_Koinonia.htm.

DISPUTABLE MATTERS

sues as morally neutral, he seems to overlook what theological heavyweights they actually were for the ethnic groups involved. I'm not sure the Jewish and Gentile believers in Rome would have accepted Wright's declaration that their differences were "morally neutral." In fact, for the Jewish believers, failing to keep the Sabbath violated the fourth commandment—a huge moral issue. Eating meat that may have been offered to idols was paramount to breaking the second and third commandments.

Reinforcing the seriousness of these issues was the consequences Paul foresaw if they didn't learn to get along. It was not just a matter of a few hurt feelings. The divisions he was helping the Roman believers avoid were so serious they could "destroy your brother" (v. 15), "destroy the work of God" (v. 20), "cause your brother to fall" (v. 21)—the same bad fruit we've seen hurt gay people, divide churches over how to relate to them, and in too many cases drive both gay and straight people away from following Jesus.

I am highly indebted to Ken Wilson who explained how serious the divisions in the Roman church were in his book, *A Letter to My Congregation*. He points out that if they were insignificant, "the heritage of church splits that followed in the wake of the Protestant Reformation [were] inevitable. . . . [But] if Romans 14-15 applies to the very hotly contested differences today . . . it would actually help us maintain a unity in the spirit."[8]

In other words, if N.T. Wright's understanding that the disputable matters in the Roman church were really nothing more than cultural differences, then Romans 14 doesn't offer us any real help in how we are to handle our most deeply held differing convictions regarding gay marriage or any other difficult matter. But if Wilson is correct and the differences Paul was addressing involved profound moral disagreements, then this passage may be God's word to the church through the ages and to us today.

8. Ken Wilson, *A Letter to My Congregation: An Evangelical Pastor's path to embracing people who are gay, lesbian and transgender in the company of Jesus*, (Canton, MI: David Crumm Media: 2014, Kindle Edition), Kindle location 1584.

So how weighty were the disputes in Rome?

The congregation included both Jewish and Gentile believers, which might at first glance suggest they were dealing with merely cultural differences, and indeed the divisions probably did break down along ethnic lines. But from the beginning, it was not easy for Jewish believers to accept the validity of Gentile conversions unless they were willing to fully follow the Law, including circumcision. These were core convictions of the faith!

For centuries these requirements had been the only way Gentiles were admitted into the "family of God." Therefore, it had taken a major conclave a few years earlier at what became known as the Jerusalem Council (described in Acts 15) for the apostles to agree on *new* terms for accepting Gentile believers into the church. At that time, they sent a letter to the Gentiles saying, "It seemed good to the Holy Spirit and to us not to burden you with anything beyond the following requirements: You are to abstain from food sacrificed to idols, from blood, from the meat of strangled animals and from sexual immorality. You will do well to avoid these things" (vv. 28-29).

The crisis that arose in Rome a few years later was that some believers were not only offending their Jewish brothers and sisters by eating meat presumably offered to idols, but they were also *violating that sacred agreement* reached on their behalf years before by the Jerusalem Council.

If that doesn't demonstrate how morally weighty the "disputable matters" plaguing the Roman church were, the question of eating food offered to idols came up again later. John reported in his Revelation that Jesus himself indicted the churches in Pergamum and Thyatira for "eating food sacrificed to idols" (2:14, 20).

One does not have to read between the lines in Romans 14 or 1 Corinthians 8 to see that Paul didn't *personally* think eating this meat was so wrong, and as time passed, it ceased to be an issue in the church (an example of the legitimacy of prayerfully adjusting standards). But Paul was extremely concerned with helping the believers to respect and include one another *in spite of* their differing moral convictions. His tone sounds almost scolding as he wrote with urgency, "Who are you to judge someone else's servant? To their own master, servants stand or fall. And they will stand, for the Lord is able to make them stand" (v. 4). "Therefore let us stop passing judgment on one another" (v. 13). "So whatever you believe about these things keep between yourself and God" (v. 22).

But are there no boundaries?

If we are supposed to keep our opinions to ourselves, does that mean there are no boundaries concerning right belief and right behavior within the church? No, there *are* boundaries. Paul exhorted the Ephesians to "Make every effort to keep the unity of the Spirit through the bond of peace. There is one body and one Spirit, just as you were called to one hope when you were called; one Lord, one faith, one baptism; one God and Father of all, who is over all and through all and in all" (Ephesians 4:3-6). This is just one of several summary statements in the New Testament identifying parameters for right belief. The apostles and leaders of the New Testament church were not hesitant to denounce heresy that denied the central doctrines of the faith.

It wasn't long until leaders from the geographically expanding church found it useful to draft precise statements such as the Apostles' Creed and the Nicene Creed to clarify what was essential for orthodox Christianity and to counteract any heresies to those basics. Unfortunately, throughout the centuries, we have allowed lesser theological differences to divide the church innumerable times. For instance, the nature and meaning of the Eucharist/ Communion, eschatology (end times), church government, etc. However, you will notice that none of the issues plaguing the Roman believers—major as they were—involved the basic tenets of Christian faith later collected in those early creeds. Their disputes were about behaviors, behaviors that had theological significance, but behaviors, nonetheless.

So, since the disputes among the Roman believers focused on behavior, and Paul considered them "disputable matters," does that make all behaviors disputable? Again, no. There are biblical boundaries regarding right behavior. The numerous vice lists[9] found in the New Testament demonstrate bold teaching about what is right and wrong behavior. Additionally, several of the vice lists include a warning along the lines of "those who live like this will not inherit the kingdom of God" (Galatians 5:21). But the Roman example proves that some behaviors *are* disputable and should be handled as Paul prescribes.

Like the core beliefs represented by the major creeds, many vices raise no dispute among faithful Christians—murder, robbery, idolatry, adultery, fornication, lying, drunkenness, etc. Most Christians don't debate the wrongness of these behaviors ... except, perhaps, for those Christians from peace churches who consider war to be murder. Then you have a dispute certainly as volatile as what Paul describes in Romans 14. Modern believers would include the vice of slave trading among the indisputably wrong behaviors, but two hundred years ago, this also was broadly disputed!

In addition, there are several vices where disagreements commonly arise, not so much over the named vices but over *when the line of wrong doing* is actually crossed—greed, envy, covetousness, craftiness, gossip, quarreling, jealousy, selfishness, slander, licentiousness, conceit, bitterness, cowardice, faithlessness, etc. Do we believe these behaviors—most of us are guilty of some of these at one point or another—disqualify us from the kingdom of God? And not because of one little slip into sin, but because we justify our level of participation? After all, when is ambition, which we often admire, actually an expression of greed, envy, jealousy, or covetousness? How are we in the United States not defending gluttony (one of the sins of Sodom identified in Ezekiel 16:49) when 20 percent of us are obese[10] and we throw away 200,000 tons of edible food *daily* while as many as a billion people don't get enough food to support normal daily activities?[11] If we fellowshipped with believers with Amish or Old Mennonite standards, they might say

---

9. "Vice lists" can be found in Matthew 15:19; Mark 7:21-22; Romans 1:29-31; 13:13; 1 Corinthians 5:10-11; 6:9-10; 2 Corinthians 12:20-21; Galatians 5:19-21; Ephesians 4:31; 5:3-5; Colossians 3:5, 8; 1 Timothy 1:9-10; 2 Timothy 3:2-5; Titus 3:3; 1 Peter 2:1; 4:3, 15; Revelation 9:21; 21:8; 22:15.

10. http://stateofobesity.org/adult-obesity/.

11. http://public.wsu.edu/~mreed/380American%20Consumption.htm.

most of our clothing styles were licentious or at least prideful. And does the vehemence many Christians express toward gay people qualify as the vice of bitterness and wrath?

The point is, while each of these vices are real, *when* they have been committed—when we have crossed the line—involves at least a disputable definition. And for the subject of this book, while sexual immorality is unquestionably a vice, whether it includes faithful, monogamous marriage between gay people is what's in question.

We earlier noted that the Old Testament Law included 613 rules in an attempt to regulate right and wrong behavior at every turn. But even that didn't provide enough detail to cover all the disputable circumstances. The Talmud, a 6,200-page commentary, was added, but still the rabbis debate.

Some might consider New Testament vice lists an extension of Old Testament rules, but the New Testament lists are more in the tone of teachings, encouragements, and advice toward righteous living. And the general nature of many of them requires wise discernment so we don't judge one another, as was happening in the church in Rome.

When is something legitimately a disputable matter?

The thing that makes any doctrine or behavior disputable is that faithful Christians, making reasonable appeals to Scripture, come up with different interpretations. And it is probable that we face such a dilemma whenever we start saying, "My scholars are better than your scholars," or "You're being selective and I'm not," as so much of the current debate now involves as demonstrated by titles like, *What the Bible Really Says about Homosexuality* by Daniel A. Helminiak and *What Does the Bible Really Teach about Homosexuality?* by Kevin DeYoung, which take opposing views.[12] In time, and by God's grace, we may resolve this issue, but until we do, tolerating our differences for the sake of unity makes sense.

---

12. While the two titles illustrate how we are "shouting" at one another, the books are not of equal value. Helminiak seems to dismiss Scriptures with which he disagrees. I do not support that approach. While interpretations may differ, I accept and believe "All Scripture is God-breathed and is useful for teaching, rebuking, correcting and training in righteousness" (2 Timothy 3:16).

Ken Wilson actually offers three criteria that include more helpful detail for determining when something qualifies as disputable. A subject may be disputable . . .

1. When it doesn't involve a matter of basic Christian dogma such as we find in the great ecumenical creeds (Apostles, Nicene, Chalcedonian, etc.).

2. When the debate brings two or more biblical truths into dynamic tension (e.g. mercy-judgment, law-grace, free will-predestination) so that both parties make reasonable appeals to Scripture.

3. When faithful Christians take different views on the issue.[13]

Whether or not gay Christians can be allowed to marry one another does not challenge basic Christian dogma as collected in the historic creeds; therefore the issue can be considered disputable according to Wilson's first principle.

His second principle suggests we should tolerate a disputable matter if it invokes biblical themes that have long been recognized as appearing in tension with one another. For instance, two Christians can disagree over paradoxes involving free will and predestination without judging the other as a sinner or a non-Christian. And most differing views about how we relate to gay people qualify as disputable under this criterion. However, those who claim someone *can't* be gay and Christian are saying grace alone through faith is not sufficient to save someone who is gay. He or she must also exhibit the "works" (whether belief or behavior) of renouncing their sexual orientation or at least gay marriage. While this invokes the historic tension between works and grace, its result breaks fellowship by rejecting the other person as a brother or sister. It's a deal-breaking position.

---

13. Ken Wilson, *A Letter to My Congregation: An evangelical pastor's path to embracing people who are gay, lesbian and transgender in the company of Jesus*, (Ann Arbor, MI: David Crumm Media, LLC, 2014, Kindle Edition). Kindle location 1756.

Wilson's third principle is fairly self-explanatory. "When faithful Christians take different views on the issue" we can accept it as a disputable matter. Remember, on this issue we are not talking about endorsing the sexual immorality of a promiscuous lifestyle for either gay or straight people—people shacking up with one another or cycling through serial marriages, etc. We are talking about a certain group of people, who from whatever cause are not attracted to the opposite sex but would like to enter into a monogamous, life-long covenant with someone of their same gender. You may not agree that this is right, but if we can recognize that they are genuine believers, faithful and sincere Christians, we ought to be able to tolerate our differences within the same fellowship.

If we can get that far, we won't have to break relationships as Mohler predicted. Instead, we can genuinely "Accept one another . . . just as Christ accepted you, in order to bring praise to God" (Romans 15:7).

Collateral Damage

A heresy trial in this century, in this millennium? I could hardly believe it until I read the transcripts.

In 2003, Rev. Lee Irons, who had been ordained by the Orthodox Presbyterian Church and installed as the pastor of Redeemer Chapel of San Fernando Valley, California, was brought up on trial for heresy by the Presbytery of Southern California. The trial was complete with a jury (the Presbytery), prosecutor, the defendant (Rev. Irons), a defense attorney, multiple charges and stipulations, the plea, objections, witnesses, opening arguments, cross-examination, and on and on, leading to a verdict, an appeal, and censure.

There were four charges. Supposedly . . .

1. He publicly promoted and encouraged the practice of homosexuality in violation of the seventh commandment.

2. In violation of the ninth commandment, he distributed a letter slandering the church as well as several individuals.

3. He violated his ordination vow by teaching that the Ten Commandments are no longer binding on believers as the standards of holy living.

4. He violated his ordination vow by teaching that civil government must be religiously neutral and therefore not subject to the binding authority of God's special revelation in Scripture (including the moral law).

The second charge that he had slandered the church in a letter he'd written was dropped rather quickly after he apologized.[14]

If the other charges seem rather esoteric, it may be because the Presbytery's real complaint against Lee Irons was that he had posted on his own website a copy of an article written by his wife, Misty, titled, "A Conservative Christian Case for Civil Same-Sex Marriage," that she had previously posted on her website. Calvinists, of all people, she reasoned, ought to recognize homosexuality as a condition antecedent to choice (referencing the whole predestination/free will controversy). Additionally, Christians have always been adamant supporters of civil liberties when it comes to freedom of religion. After an extended survey summing up her research, she concluded by saying,

> We often think being a witness for Christ means doing some extraordinary thing. But sometimes the best witness to the gospel is as simple as being civil enough to respect people's legitimate freedoms, and being decent enough to put aside the name-calling and treat people like human beings. Supporting the civil liberties of homosexual American citizens is decent, civil and, yes, loving. Loving

---

14. After the second charge was dropped, the remaining charges were renumbered 1, 2, 3 in the trial transcripts.

at least in a way that gays and lesbians are more likely to understand.[15]

The article was initially posted on Misty's website and later on Lee's in a section reserved for discussing controversial subjects. There was ample pushback as dissenters published their objections to her ideas on several denominational discussion groups. So it's not obvious why posting it and expressing her opinion generated such wrath among the church hierarchy. The truth, as they understood it, was well represented.

Initially, the Presbytery intended to bring Misty up on charges, but when her husband stepped in and said it was his decision to post it on his website, they initiated charges against him while still considering charges against Misty. He agreed to post a disclaimer on his website that Misty's views did not represent the views of the church. But then they demanded she shut down her website and implied she would face discipline if she didn't.

The first charge against Lee—that he promoted and encouraged the practice of homosexuality—was dropped (without prejudice, meaning it could be reintroduced later) when he drafted a paper titled, "What I Believe about Homosexuality," in which he took a fairly conservative position, which made it difficult for the Presbytery to prove that he was guilty of publicly promoting homosexuality. They then began pressuring him to force his wife to remove the article from her website.

He tried to cooperate with them as much as he could by taking the article down from his own website. Misty was willing to make small wording changes, but she wasn't willing to take down the article, let alone shut down her whole website, and Lee wasn't about to force her. It then appears the Presbytery became focused on disciplining Lee through the other charges based more on things he had written and taught. Technically, the charge of heresy (at this point renumbered as Charge #2) involved whether Rev. Irons believed the Mosaic Decalogue given to Israel at Mount Sinai

---

15. Misty S. Irons, "A Conservative Christian Case for Civil Same-Sex Marriage," posted on November 19, 2000, http://www.musingson.com/ccCase.html.

(the Ten Commandments) is equivalent to God's eternal moral law, and whether the Mosaic Law was rightly divided into three categories—ceremonial, judicial, and moral commands—and to what degree believers and unbelievers were bound by that Law.

The verdict on Charge #2, involving Lee's views concerning whether the Mosaic Decalogue is the same as the moral law that binds all Christians today, was *guilty* by a 17 to 16 vote, and Rev. Irons was suspended from office for an indefinite period of time. Charge #3 failed by a vote of 17 to 17. But they had him. In spite of a strong protest signed by six members of the Presbytery concerning improper procedures during the trial, Rev. Irons' conviction was sustained on appeal, and therefore . . .

He was suspended from ministry.

Chapter 17
Jesus Shows Us
How to Apply God's Laws

Free from the law, O happy condition,
Jesus has bled and there is remission,
Cursed by the law and bruised by the fall,
Grace hath redeemed us once for all.

"Christ Hath Redeemed"
Philip P. Bliss, 1873, verse 1

I REALIZE THAT EVEN IF WE CAN LEARN how to manage a disputable matter within a congregation, we've not resolved everything. It's more of a stopgap so we don't explode the body, disgrace Christ, and drive people away from him. But there is still the question of God's perspective on a matter. For instance, the crisis around whether the believers in Rome should or shouldn't eat meat was averted by Paul's strong words to quit judging one another. But I wondered . . . did the congregation ever come to agree with Paul that abstaining wasn't necessary (see 1 Corinthians 8)? And if so, how did they get to that new understanding?

In our homes and churches, we're facing a similar juncture regarding gay marriage. Most of us come from a background where same-sex marriage was unthinkable. We not only had our intuition, admittedly arising from our own orientation, but there were, and still remain, strongly-held arguments claiming it is against God's laws. And the last thing I want to do is oppose God or encourage others to disobey him, even if that would keep the peace.

Finding my way out of this dilemma drove me back to studying how Jesus handled situations where old rules came into question.

God is for us

When Jesus said, "The Sabbath was made for man, not man for the Sabbath" (Mark 2:27), he was explaining that God's laws are not capricious. They have purpose, and that purpose is for our well-being. Jesus made his statement to justify why his disciples were breaking the Sabbath law . . . at least according to the Pharisees' interpretation. Confrontations where the Pharisees accused Jesus of breaking the Law occurred repeatedly. And yet, it was actually the Pharisees who broke the Law by twisting it to their own ends. Jesus told them:

> You have a fine way of setting aside the commands of God in order to observe your own traditions! For Moses said, "Honor your father and mother," and, "Anyone who curses their father or mother is to be put to death." But you say that if anyone declares that what might have been used to help their father or mother is Corban (that is, devoted to God)—then you no longer let them do anything for their father or mother. Thus you nullify the word of God by your tradition that you have handed down. And you do many things like that (Mark 7:9-13).

Again we see the purpose of God's laws is for our well-being, in this case, a command to help aging parents. So what are we to do when the *traditional* understanding of a law does not serve God's purpose of advancing our well-being? It appears Jesus would have broken at least the Pharisees' interpretation of the law.

Some people claim Jesus could never have *actually* broken the Law of Moses based on such passages as, "He committed no sin" (2 Peter 2:22), "God made him who had no sin to be sin for us" (2 Corinthians 5:21), and "We have [a high priest—Jesus] who has been tempted in every way, just as we are—yet he did not sin" (Hebrews 4:15). But that presumes violating Moses' Law is *always* sin. But is it? Is there no flexibility?

231

The more I thought about it, I realized that question became moot by the end of the New Testament. By then, several Old Testament laws had been explicitly nullified, whole categories rendered obsolete, because the overall purpose of the Law had been fulfilled by Christ's death and resurrection, thereby introducing the New Covenant: "By calling this covenant 'new,' [the Lord] has made the first one obsolete; and what is obsolete and outdated will soon disappear" (Hebrews 8:13).

Consequently, not all Old Testament commands apply equally to us today. In fact, several laws were *explicitly* rescinded. For example, the "law of retribution" (an eye for an eye) was overturned by Jesus (Matthew 5:38), God told Peter the Old Testament dietary restrictions no longer applied (Acts 10:9-16), circumcision ceased being required (Acts 15), animal sacrifices for sin ended (Hebrews 9:11-15), and a Levitical priest was no longer necessary to represent us to God (Hebrews 4:14-16). But numerous other Old Testament laws were not explicitly canceled or reinstated in the New Testament. So do they apply or not? Certainly not in the same old way, but under the New Covenant there remain distinctions between right and wrong belief and right and wrong behavior. So how do we sort out when, where, and how they apply?

Sorting it out

Some of my Bible professors divided the Law into categories (usually moral law, ceremonial law, and civil law) with more or less rational explanations for which laws fit into which categories and therefore which ones were abolished by the New Covenant. Those categories are helpful, especially where the Bible mentions certain laws specifically, as noted above. But *they aren't biblically defined categories.* James tells us that Jesus' commandment to love our neighbor as ourselves is supreme—he calls it the "royal law"—reminding us that if we are going to invoke Moses' Law (in the old way), then we have to deal with the *whole* Law. We can't invoke it piecemeal.

If you really keep the royal law found in Scripture, "Love your neighbor as yourself," you are doing right. But if you show favoritism, you sin and are convicted by the law as lawbreakers. For whoever keeps the whole law and yet stumbles at just one point is guilty of breaking all of it. For he who said, "Do not commit adultery," also said, "Do not murder." If you do not commit adultery but do commit murder, you have become a lawbreaker" (James 2:8-11).

In other words, we can't divide up the laws and say that one is ceremonial from which we are exempt while another is moral and still binding. Under the New Covenant, we relate to the Law in a different way. James says, "Speak and act as those who are going to be judged by the law that gives freedom, because judgment without mercy will be shown to anyone who has not been merciful. Mercy triumphs over judgment!" (v. 13).

I went back to Jesus to discover how "the law that gives freedom" works in sorting out when, where, and how to apply any other commandments. The answer came from another instance where the Pharisees were trying to trap Jesus, this time asking, "Teacher, which is the greatest commandment in the Law?"

Jesus replied: "'Love the Lord your God with all your heart and with all your soul and with all your mind.' This is the first and greatest commandment. And the second is like it: 'Love your neighbor as yourself.' All the Law and the Prophets hang on these two commandments" (Matthew 22:36-40).

By saying *all* the law hangs on these two important commandments, Jesus showed that *all* the other commandments were intended to serve one of those two goals: "To love God with all our heart, soul, and mind,"[1] and "To love our neighbors as ourselves." Are there times and places and ways in which some biblical rules

---

1. This first command was part of the Shema, the daily prayer in Jewish tradition. The second command also comes from the Hebrew Scriptures in Leviticus 19:18, but it was buried in a list of sometimes obscure rules until Jesus brought it forward and explained how it summarized all other interpersonal laws.

do not serve those goals? The answer is most certainly yes. Though God had a purpose in issuing a law against wearing clothing made of two materials when he initially gave it (see Leviticus 19:19), who would claim it advances our love for God or our neighbor today? But by explaining the two objectives *behind* all the Law and the Prophets, Jesus fulfilled the Law by offering a far superior means of evaluating when, where, and how to interpret and apply any biblical Law . . . or any contemporary rule *we* might propose (such as anti-slavery laws).

In contrast, when we rely on our subjective presumptions (as N.T. Wright did by dismissing the disputes discussed in Romans 14 as merely cultural) or when we devise categories such as "moral law," "ceremonial law," and "civil law," we appeal to human constructs without objective foundation. The futility of these approaches is evident in that they did not provide enough moral wisdom to rule out slavery for over eighteen hundred years! To me, that's not a very good method of discerning right from wrong.

St. Augustine (354-430), whom many consider the most significant Christian theologian of the first millennium, described the preeminence of love this way:

> Whoever, then, thinks that he understands the Holy Scriptures, or any part of them, but puts such an interpretation upon them as does not tend to build up this twofold love of God and our neighbor, does not yet understand them as he ought.[2]

The power of love for God and neighbor

Some people object to putting so much emphasis on love, as though that is the weak side of the Gospel, while enforcing the Law is the more muscular side. But that's not true. Enforcing the Law could be done by a computer, but as Justin Lee points out, "No one would want to be tried in court by a computer, because we know

---

2. Augustine, *De Doctrina Christiana* 1.35, ed. Philip Schaff, trans. J.F. Shaw, under the title *On Christian Doctrine*, Nicene and Post-Nicene Fathers, vol. 2 (Buffalo, NY: Christian Literature, 1887; reprint, Peabody: Hendrickson Publishers, 2004), 532.

that only a human being has the reasoning ability to look at a situation and see all the nuances and extenuating circumstances that need to be taken into account."[3] It's actually a *weak* religion that creates a rule for everything so you don't have to do the hard work of discerning what love looks like in various situations. Why else would the New Testament writers have emphasized love so much?

In his letters, John virtually hammered on Jesus' command to "love one another" (1 John 3:11, 23; 4:7, 12; 2 John 1:5). Peter cheers us on: "Now that you have purified yourselves by obeying the truth[4] so that you have sincere love for your brothers, love one another deeply, from the heart" (1 Peter 1:22). James calls it the "royal law," saying, "If you really keep the royal law found in Scripture, 'Love your neighbor as yourself,' you are doing right" (James 2:8). Paul echoes Jesus' explanation, ". . . whatever other commandment[s] there may be, are summed up in this one rule: 'Love your neighbor as yourself.' Love does no harm to its neighbor. *Therefore love is the fulfillment of the law*" (Romans 13:9, 10, emphasis added). If that isn't clear enough, he says it again to the Galatians. "The entire law is summed up in a single command: 'Love your neighbor as yourself'" (Galatians 5:14).

Keep the first commandment, first

As I meditated on Jesus' summation of the Law, the importance of his answer hit me at a deeper level. Whenever we engage in the discernment process of applying any biblical law—whether it is as big as keeping the Sabbath or as specific as not having tattoos (Leviticus 19:28)—the first commandment must be considered *first* for a reason. We must check and reaffirm our love for the Lord with all our heart, soul, and mind *by embracing God's heart for the matter*. And we can know God's heart most completely in Jesus' life and ministry. Colossians 2:9 says, "In Christ *all* the fullness of the Deity lives in bodily form" (emphasis added). That is why in this

---

3. Justin Lee, "Justin's View," https://www.gaychristian.net/justins_view.php, "The Purpose of Rules."
4. The "truth" to which these believers were obedient and by which they were purified was not the keeping of the Law—"the empty way of life handed down to you from your forefathers" (v. 18)—but the Gospel itself. See verses 3-5.

book I began by reviewing the life and ministry of Jesus, his embodiment of grace and truth, and the fact that it is *only* by his grace and sacrifice that any of us has access to the Father. And that's why I begin every chapter with a verse from an old hymn affirming the truth that grace alone saves us. Keeping rules—old or new, great or small—will never earn our salvation. We must clearly focus on the "First Commandment" by asking whether our approach to any rule ends up subtly replacing *faith* with *works*, a switch we humans are so prone to make because we can so easily take pride in our works.

Only after we have checked whether any rule, law, guideline, or interpretation advances our commitment to love the Lord our God with all our heart, soul, or mind, can we rightly move on to ask, is it loving toward our neighbor? And does it help *us* love one another, as Jesus commanded?

Audacious discernments

Okay. But to be honest, I still had questions. Do we have the authority to make such discernments? Is it appropriate in some instances to decide that a traditional rule doesn't apply in our specific situation? In Matthew 18:18 Jesus said, "Whatever you bind on earth will be bound in heaven, and whatever you loose on earth will be loosed in heaven." Whew. That's a heavy responsibility. But in John 16:13 he promised to send us the Holy Spirit, who "will guide [us] into all truth."

Since Jesus is our most complete revelation of God's heart, how did he deal with similar situations? Did he ever set aside the Law because enforcing it was not loving? Both Leviticus 20:10 and Deuteronomy 22:22 say that anyone caught in adultery *is* to be put to death, not just *can* be put to death. It wasn't an option allowed to appease an offended spouse if they were sufficiently outraged. The law actually *required* death; they "must die" says the Deuteronomy verse. And yet when the Pharisees brought the woman caught in adultery before Jesus in John 8:3-11, he said, "Let any one of you who is without sin be the first to throw a stone at her" (v. 7). In so doing, he took control of the situation in such a way that none of them could punish her. But he was without sin, leaving him as the only one qualified to condemn her. And yet, even though the Law *required* death, he made a discernment about when, where, and how to apply it and chose—out of concern for her wellbeing—not to obey it. Such discernment is actually how Jesus went about *fulfilling the law*.

In another situation we read:

> One Sabbath, when Jesus went to eat in the house of a prominent Pharisee, he was being carefully watched. There in front of him was a man suffering from abnormal swelling of his body. Jesus asked the Pharisees and experts in the law, "Is it lawful to heal on the Sabbath or not?" But they remained silent. So taking hold of the man, he healed him and sent him on his way. Then he asked them, "If one of you has a child or an ox that falls into a well on the Sabbath day, will you not immediately pull him out?" And they had nothing to say (Luke 14:1-6).

Notice that Jesus did not engage the Pharisees in a scholarly debate as to whether the Law prohibited work on the Sabbath. The fourth commandment is clear: "The seventh day is a Sabbath to the Lord your God. On it you shall not do any work . . ." (Deuteronomy 5:14).[5] What he did, however, was exercise discernment as to when, where, and how that law should be applied. And in this case—as in six other recorded instances where he did a miracle on the Sabbath—he chose to do the greater good even though his actions appeared to violate the Law.

The fact that Jesus exalted saving a child[6] above keeping the letter of the Law has powerful implications for whether we are willing to risk "breaking the law" so as not to drive our gay sons and daughters away from Jesus.

Following this model, the process of carefully discerning when, where, and how to apply the law was demonstrated by the Je-

---

5. It's as clear as Leviticus 18:22: "Do not lie with a man as one lies with a woman."

6. Some less reliable manuscripts use the Greek word, ὄνος (meaning donkey) rather than υἱός (meaning son), perhaps as a result of a scribal error. But even if Jesus only mentioned animals, certainly our sons and daughters are of far greater value.

rusalem Council's decision in Acts 15 to release Gentile converts from the requirement of circumcision. Later, for the Philippian Christians, Paul prayed that "love may abound more and more in knowledge and depth of insight, so that [they] may be able to *discern* what is best and may be pure and blameless until the day of Christ" (Philippians 1:9-10, emphasis added). Discernment is required *only* when the letter of the law as the Pharisees taught it isn't obviously the "best" thing to enforce.

This is not a new set of rules nor a "slippery slope"

Jesus' solution isn't a means of creating a new set of rules by which we can decide who is in and who is out of the kingdom. But I'm convinced it does allow for a dynamic application of Jesus' new commandment to "love one another." Similarly, it doesn't unleash anarchy because it doesn't take much discernment to demonstrate how lying, cheating, greed, adultery, usury, slander, prostitution, incest (like the man in Corinth), murder, fighting, gossip, fornication, and most other things on biblical vice lists literally harm people. Think about any one of those sins, and it won't take you long to discern *and explain why* we legitimately oppose those behaviors, not simply because there's a rule against them but because they can easily be shown to hurt people. Even divorce usually hurts people, but there are times when people are hurt worse if it is absolutely forbidden.

This discernment approach also allows us to look at things that aren't explicitly forbidden in the Bible—such as slavery or segregation or misogyny—and determine they aren't acceptable Christian behaviors either. And finally, it gives room to discern that even though there are biblical passages that condemn certain kinds of homosexual behavior, like pederasty and prostitution and rape—all for good reasons—those condemnations might not apply to faithful same-sex marriages.

That's a big step, but I believe that's the reason Jesus said the first and second commandments were the linchpins upon which all the other Law and Prophets hang. They provide the guidelines for when, where, and how to interpret and apply any specific law.

There will be those who claim I've just come up with some kind of a loophole mechanism for changing God's Word. But I don't believe that's the case. The writer of the Book of Hebrews seemed to envision such an ongoing process of discernment by saying, "Solid food is for the mature, who by constant use have trained themselves to distinguish between good and evil" (Hebrews 5:14). If the Christian life could be reduced to a list of rules (as we have often tried to do), there would be no need for the mature ability to discern between good and evil behavior. The immature can look up answers. And even if the process of testing new ideas by Jesus' first and second commandment was not explicitly articulated, the practical outworking of change according to the law of love began in New Testament times and has continued throughout the ages.

How does this work?

I am not suggesting scholarly efforts to determine the original intent of a biblical passage are unprofitable or that we can't identify general categories within the Old Testament Law such as moral, ceremonial, and civil law that can assist our *general* discernment. But we need to remember those are human constructs, and when we end up with no consensus or it becomes obvious that harm is resulting from a questioned interpretation, Jesus has provided us with a superior way out of the maze. And the church has used that superior way to great benefit throughout the ages, though often the transition has been difficult.

Let me offer three examples of applying Jesus' criteria in post-New Testament contexts. The first cancels a New Testament rule. The second affirms one. And the third adds a rule—all demonstrating the dynamic, living wisdom of Jesus.

Canceling a New Testament rule. Prior to the 1960s and '70s, short hair for men had been traditional for over half a century in this country. Then suddenly, many of us started letting it grow, admittedly as a symbol of opposition to what we saw as a corrupt "establishment."

Many church leaders, parents, and others over thirty trotted out 1 Corinthians 11 (a New Testament passage, you will notice) in which Paul says, "Does not the very nature of things teach you that if a man has long hair, it is a disgrace to him . . .? If anyone wants to be contentious about this, we have no other practice—nor do the churches of God" (1 Corinthians 11:14-16). That's a pretty clear and inflexible rule. And some tried to argue it from that perspective. But as time went on and it became obvious that some young men with long hair were faithful followers of Jesus—more radically "Jesus freaks" than some old timers—the controversy ultimately fizzled, and it's been decades since I've heard anyone object to men's hairstyles *based on Scripture* whether long, short, shaved, dreadlocks, or green and spiked.

Affirming a New Testament rule. Adultery and fornication were unequivocally outlawed in the Old Testament (Exodus 20:14) with examples of the disastrous consequences such as David's adultery with Bathsheba (2 Samuel 11). And Jesus reiterated this prohibition even more clearly: "But I tell you that anyone who looks at a woman lustfully has already committed adultery with her in his heart" (Mathew 5:28). In 1 Corinthians 5, Paul commanded the Corinthian church to expel the young man who was sleeping with his father's wife (at least until he fully repented). The King James Version of the Bible translates the Greek word, *porneia*, as "fornication" all twenty-six times it appears in the New Testament. Clearly, adultery and fornication were not approved in the New Testament. They are the "sexual immorality" the Bible condemns.

But now people wonder, why? In today's culture, among consenting adults, with effective birth control, why not? Some consider extramarital sex as recreation, a form of release, a diversion. For others, it fills a gaping emotional hole, an escape from a dry and boring or even bitter marriage.

Is the church's clarity on the issue weakened by submitting it to the tests of Jesus' first and second commandants? I don't think so. First of all, this isn't an issue over which faithful Christians (or even biblical scholars) are divided as to what the Bible actually says. But any Christian leader who can't explain *why* extramarital sex inevitably hurts or threatens to hurt people is just plain lazy. In fact, the majority of secular stories or movies involving extramarital affairs, even if they are sympathetically portrayed, reveals the profound hurt to *someone* if the stories are honest and played out to the end. It may be the cheated spouse, the children, or the couple themselves. But people get hurt! That's why the cheated spouse is so angry and why the cheater tries to avoid getting caught. It's why the girl feels used and is so devastated when the guy doesn't follow through with marriage after all his beguiling promises.

And so as a church in the twenty-first century, we can continue to say, as Jesus did to the woman taken in adultery, "go and sin no more." Do we tell people they are going to hell if they disobey? No. But we have a clear rule of wise and holy conduct that we can teach boldly, supported by reasons revealed with Jesus' second commandment.

Adding a new rule. As society changes and as we become more aware of people's needs and points of pain, we sometimes have to come up with a new rule for right behavior that was never explicitly expressed in Scripture. The abolition of slavery is a prime example. You can arrive at that rule with solid biblical principles of how we are to treat other people, but it's not specifically stated in the Word.

However, let me suggest an even more recent addition of a rule for a God-pleasing life. For generations, many Christians in the South saw no problem with raising tobacco or using it. Lottie Moon, the Southern Baptist's "patron saint of missions" grew up on her strong Baptist family's 1,500-acre tobacco plantation called Viewmont. Though some Christians considered tobacco use a rather nasty habit, others indulged with aplomb, including such notables as C. S. Lewis, J. R. R. Tolkien, C. H. Spurgeon, and Dietrich Bonhoeffer. But as the health risks became more obvious, sincere believers—applying Jesus' second commandment to love our neighbor—came more and more to the conclusion that tobacco growing, profitable though it was, was not something a Christian should do.

In fact, in 1984, the Southern Baptist Convention passed a resolution discouraging its members from using or growing tobacco. It even called for the government to end tobacco subsidies. It was the right thing to do even though many members had relied on growing tobacco as a livelihood for generations.

The point is, Jesus gave us the authority and the means to reevaluate our guidelines for holy living, not apart from the Bible but in sync with biblical principles as we discern whether an old interpretation is to be affirmed, adjusted, or even if a new "law" should be added.

Problems looking for solutions

Some traditionalists criticize this process by saying I'm beginning with a problem and then looking for justifications to revise the traditional solutions. Instead, they say, we should begin with the Bible (as though it exists in a vacuum) and apply its laws regardless of how they affect people. We should conform to God rather than expect God's laws to accommodate our circumstances: "He's God, and we're not!"

Put that way, yes, but sound bites seldom convey the whole picture. And such inflexibility does not often characterize how things were done in the New Testament. Issues arose *first* and *then* policy decisions were made to resolve them. Consider the following examples.

- The Greek widows in the first church not receiving their fair share.
- The Gentile believers desiring full acceptance without circumcision.
- Church fathers formulating the historic Creeds to combat heresy.
- The Reformers counteracting corruption that had invaded the church.
- Scientific evidence challenging the theories of a geocentric universe.
- Abolitionists seeking the end of slavery.
- Suffragettes seeking rights for women.
- Civil rights advocates opposing segregation and Jim Crow laws.
- Pacifists opposing war.
- Opposition to an absolute prohibition of divorce in all circumstances.
- Acceptance of women in all positions of church leadership.

- Scientific evidence challenging the theories of a young-earth and six-day creation.
- Gay Christians seeking church approval to marry one another.

Each of these examples began as a "problem looking for a solution" while those in authority often resisted on the grounds that the status quo was the "biblical position" to which all others should conform. I deliberately included examples you may still feel go against the biblical position. But try to see them in comparison to the other examples that show the status quo needed to conform to a new biblical understanding or a new application of biblical freedom.

Consider the example of the disciples' experience of Jesus crucifixion. Based on the Scriptures, they (and most other Jews) expected the Messiah to come in triumph. That was their "begin with the Bible" point. And had they stuck to it, Jesus' crucifixion completely disqualified him as the Messiah. But on the road to Emmaus, they allowed the *problem* of their experiences over the previous three years to be their new starting point so Jesus could *reinterpret* those passages and open their eyes to the truth: "Did not the Messiah have to suffer these things and then enter his glory?" (Luke 24:26). Therefore, beginning with a problem is not necessarily wrong. It all depends on the process of discernment and yielding to the Holy Spirit.

The tenacity of our own point of view

We all tend to forget that our own agenda, whether pro or con on a matter, plays a larger part in our considerations than we realize. We who are straight have a great deal of momentum opposing marriage equality for gays. For a long time I thought I was objective, unaware of how strongly my ideas were propelled by the "ick factor," the unimaginable notion to me of anyone being sexually attracted to someone of the same gender. I felt that way until my love for my daughter forced me to try and set aside my bias and look at the question from her point of view. When it comes down to it, I'm not sure our bias is ever as much of a problem in discerning the right path as our denial of bias is. If we admit that we have an agenda, whether we are defending or challenging the long-standing tradition of the church, we might be able to proceed with more humility.

Pastor and author Greg Boyd recalls a man who in a theological discussion adamantly maintained, "I don't *interpret* the Bible. I just *read* it." But we all interpret the Bible. We strive to interpret it accurately, but our "map"—our understanding of reality—is not *the* "map," it's not the Bible itself, and it certainly is not the actual "territory," the whole mind of God.[7] "'For my thoughts are not your thoughts, neither are your ways my ways,' declares the Lord. 'As the heavens are higher than the earth, so are my ways higher than your ways and my thoughts than your thoughts'" (Isaiah 55:8-9). It's as true for us as it was for Israel.

This is why we should always test any "law" regarding Christian behavior by Jesus' first and second commandments in order to discern when, where, and how we can love our gay family and friends like Jesus.

Collateral Damage

Roger Cunningham has served as an associate minister in his Southern Baptist church for twenty years. He loves the Lord. He loves the Word. He loves his church and the other pastors on staff. But he also loves his gay son. I'll let him tell his story in his own words.

* * * *

I was raised in a very traditional Southern Baptist home, went to a Baptist college and a Southern Baptist seminary, and I spent two years as a missionary, so I'm about as well steeped in Southern Baptist tradition and theology as anyone could get.

---

7. Gregory A. Boyd, *Benefit of the Doubt: Breaking the Idol of Certainty*, (Grand Rapids, MI: Baker Publishing Group, 2013, Kindle Edition), 148.

I hadn't studied homosexuality that deeply, but I didn't think it was God's design, and I certainly considered homosexual activity sinful. The idea of same-sex marriage, in my opinion, was an assault on society. But I'm not one to be highly dogmatic, so those assumptions were where my head was my entire life even though my ministry through music and drama brought me into contact with numerous gay people outside the church. I was not repulsed by them, outwardly judgmental of them, nor did I feel any need to keep myself away from them. In fact, I loved many of them. So my heart was in a different place than my head.

My wife Gail and I began noticing that our son, Robert, was having difficulties with interpersonal relationships when he was in high school. He's highly intelligent—graduated as valedictorian of his class—and was always a thinker, not willing to swallow anything without asking questions. But he could also be rather opinionated and rigid concerning his conclusions. It wasn't unusual for his ideas to get him into some kind of tension with other people.

At one point in high school, Robert was dating a young lady—a truly beautiful, sweet, kind, pastor's daughter—and Gail and I noticed that his relationship with her seemed awkward. He just didn't seem to know how to navigate it in a way that appeared comfortable. One night as Gail and I lay in bed, thinking about Robert, I said, "Do you think there is any possibility that he's struggling with homosexuality?" We didn't say much more, but later I brought the subject up with our youth minister, who had been in the church nearly as long as I had and deeply loved Robert. He kind of brushed it off. "Nah. He's just a different sort of kid, still finding his way."

After high school, Robert took a gap year to work in an inner-city mission. He's always had a heart for ministry, particularly for the most needy. Our denomination has a special needs retreat in this part of the state, and every year Robert has gone, often recruiting a bunch of friends to go with him.

After his gap year, he got a full scholarship to a top university, and now, four years later is getting ready to graduate. But one October he called me and broke the news: "Dad, I have same-sex attraction." He then began to share with me that since he was twelve or thirteen he had struggled with attraction to boys. For a long time he tried to deny it and hoped he would grow out of it. When he didn't, he devoted himself to praying that God would deliver him from it. But what broke my heart was that he had to go through the struggle alone and without our support.

Maybe he anticipated how stunned I'd be . . . and was. In spite of thinking I wasn't prejudiced, this news was one of the hardest things I could've ever heard from my son. It blew away all my expectations for his life, and I spent a good amount of time just crying over this situation.

Robert had been talking to a counselor who recommended he read Wesley Hill's book, *Washed and Waiting*, which Robert said represented his intention to commit himself to a life of celibacy. We read it too, in an attempt to understand. But it wasn't long before Robert's beliefs progressed to where he considered same-sex marriage something God could bless. We read several other books, including Justin Lee's book, *Torn*, which helped us understand the difference between Side A (those who believe God blesses same-sex marriage) and Side B (who believe God calls gay Christians to celibacy). It was a stretch for us, but we were just grateful Robert was still turning to God.

In other settings, however, he'd been taking some heavy hits. While at college, he had started working in the youth ministry of a large church. That's where his heart was. He was up-front from the start with the leadership about his homosexuality, and they basically said as long as he kept it quiet, he could serve. But when he progressed to the opinion that gay marriage was possible and shared that with them too, they asked him to step down from leadership. That really broke his heart.

He made a few attempts to find a good affirming church, but he finally gave up.

On the heels of all this, he'd worked every summer as a counselor at an area Christian summer camp. He was very close to the leadership and had been asked to serve that summer as well. After meeting with the staffing director to share his journey, he was told he couldn't serve. He came home and cried for two days.

About six months ago, a very talented musician, a young guy in his twenties in our praise band, came out. The staff decided to ask him to step down from that leadership role. So I asked if I could be the one to talk to him because I thought I could at least do it with empathy and sympathy. I suggested he needed to find another church where he could serve and use his God-given gifts. But when I told Robert about our conversation, he was so angry with me. "How could you do that, dad?" According to him there are other gay kids hiding in church, which stands to reason with a youth group of over a hundred, so I understand why he thinks I let them down.

During all this Gail and I had kept everything about Robert's orientation away from members of my side of the family. I knew they were very traditional and rigid, and I just didn't want to risk what their response might be. My mother lives very near my sister. They have a house church where my sister's husband and their two sons do all the preaching and teaching. There came a point when Robert shared with my mother that he was gay. Boy, that's when it really hit the fan. Soon after, my nephew—my sister's son—wrote Robert a long text saying he was no longer welcome at family gatherings and he couldn't have any association with his children until he repented.

I had a number of long conversations with my sister and mother basically explaining to them that I have some priorities in my relationships. Number one is my relationship with Christ, and I'm not going to let my other relationships interfere with that. Secondarily, my wife and then my children. I said, "Mom, you're in the top five, but my children come before you. And I'm not going to abandon them."

Prior to that, we had shared every Thanksgiving and Christmas together as an extended family. But there was no way I was going to leave my son alone at home. At least, I had to stand up for him.

But due in part to all this rejection from people who strongly claim to represent Christ, Robert told us he's lost his faith and no longer believes.

That's our biggest heartbreak of all!

I struggle with what to do as a minister in my church. I've been open with my senior pastors and other pastors on staff and, although they have been loving and personally supportive, they have shown little openness to addressing the issue in any other less traditional way than hoping it will go away. That's probably one of the reasons Robert felt so alone and like he had to hide.

But this last January, Robert and I attended the Gay Christian Network conference together. I was so grateful because for once he was with hundreds of gay people who truly love the Lord. I had to leave early to get back to the church for Sunday morning, but Robert asked if he could change his plane reservations and stay for the rest of the conference, which we managed to do. And he's kept up with some of the friends that he made there. So maybe God *is* working all things together . . .

Chapter 18
The "Ick Factor," Myths, and Lingering Fears

For nothing good have I
Whereby Thy grace to claim,
I'll wash my garments white
In the blood of Calv'ry's Lamb.

"Jesus Paid It All"
Elvina M. Hall, 1865, verse 3

THE OTHER NIGHT NETA AND I WERE WATCHING an episode of *Last Tango in Halifax*. It's a BBC series about Alan and Celia, both widowed and in their seventies, who met again after fifty years of separation, fell in love, and got married. That heartwarming story opened the series. But soon the many crises in their dysfunctional extended families provided the main fodder for the ongoing series . . . and pretty much ruined the quaint charm of an older couple finding love again. In some ways, Celia's adult daughter, Caroline, was one of the more balanced characters. She's a lesbian, married to Kate. But a prolonged scene of them deep kissing made us squirm. It felt like the last straw, and we gave up on the series.

Afterward, I got to thinking about it. I've come to respect gay people as made in God's image just as I am, and for whom "it is not good . . . to be alone," and whose search for a "suitable" partner is just as legitimate as Adam's (Genesis 2:18-20). But "suitable"—as most biblical love stories demonstrate—includes attraction. Therefore, suitable partners for gay people must take into account their innate attractions. I understand that. So why does the sight of two people of the same sex kissing still trigger such a strong "Ick Factor" in me?

What's with the Ick Factor?

There are those who might say I am repelled because it's so *unnatural*, it goes against nature, and my reaction is the last remnants of my conscience telling me it's wrong. But hold on a moment. That line of thinking strings together several things that don't necessarily follow. Yes, it's unnatural for *me*, but that doesn't mean it goes against *their* nature, and my reaction certainly doesn't establish an objective measure of right and wrong.

A dish with wild mushrooms may look enticing even though some could make you violently ill or kill you. On the other hand, you may gag at the idea of eating grubs and insects, even though many are highly nutritious and eaten by 80 percent of the world's population. So the Ick Factor may be a flag, but it's certainly not an objective standard.

Still, where does it come from?

I realized I'd heard it before in regard to intimate relationships. I don't recall our kids ever saying it, but I've heard other small children express disgust when their parents kissed or embraced too intensely. "Come on, you guys. That's icky!" Personally, I can even recall my first understandings of procreation translating into the shocking realization that my parents must have "done it" at least twice since we had two children in our family. And I was appalled that my friend's parents must have done it at least seven times since he came from a large family.

But at some point around adolescence, most kids begin considering sex more positively. I'm not talking about lust or an Oedipus complex, but merely the internal recognition of the personal appeal sex holds, and romantic kisses and embraces or even the idea of sex itself lose their Ick Factor. So innate desire can cancel "ick."

None of us who are straight should be surprised if we continue to experience a degree of "ick" when it comes to same-sex behavior even if we have acknowledged that gay marriage can be legitimate when it follows the same biblical standards as straight marriage.

We are like children who understand something of what mommy and daddy did "to have a baby" but still find the idea "icky" because it doesn't stir any positive archetypal resonance within us.

If lack of innate desire contributes to the Ick Factor, then do gay people experience the same reaction when confronted by a steamy *straight* love scene in a movie? Some don't, but many do, according to any thread you Google on the subject. As one gay man put it, "Tell you what, you don't think about our sex lives, and we won't think about yours. There. Everything is better now."

Pretty good advice for us Christians who probably don't want other people imagining our sex life, either. Right? When we think about our married friends and family, we should be focusing on and appreciating the love and support, the commitment and sacrifice, the servanthood and cooperation, the long-term care and companionship, the fun and richness evident in their relationship, not what goes on in their bedrooms.

Myths we haven't clearly renounced

The Ick Factor as a reliable measure of right and wrong is only one of many myths affecting our attitudes toward gay people. I've directly or indirectly addressed several other myths already. But if you're like me, sometimes when I'm wrestling with a difficult subject, I will walk through the process of looking at its components without clearly committing myself along the way. In my head I say, "Okay, let's *suppose* that's true. Where will it take us?" In the end I may agree with the conclusion, but on shaky grounds because I failed to explicitly vet the underlying premises.

So, walk with me through the following myths. I've offered some additional comments following each one, but even before you read those comments, stop for a moment and ask yourself, "Is this what I think? Why or why not? How does that affect the way I regard and relate to gay people?"

- *Most gay people have chosen to be gay and therefore could choose to change.*

Many gay people will tell you that if they could have changed, they would have. We all make choices about our sexual *behavior*—

whether we will have sex, go to bars or other places to hook up, view pornography, indulge in extended fantasizing, flirt, etc.— but none of those are choices about orientation. So, do you still presume people have a choice regarding their underlying sexual orientation?

- *"Reparative therapy" (prayer, counseling, and commitment) is an effective way to overcome same-sex attraction.*

If same-sex orientation were a sin, then the power of Christ's blood should be able to break it. But as Alan Chambers, who for ten years served as the president of Exodus International, an umbrella organization over 250 "ex-gay" ministries, says, "The majority of people whom I have met, and I would say the majority meaning 99.9 percent of them, have not experienced a change in their orientation." Later he explained, "In the years that have followed [since making that statement], even though oh-so-many people would love to discredit me, not one person has come forward to disagree with me. Not one has said my statement was untrue."[1]

Being a gay person himself, having known thousands of gay people, and through the umbrella of Exodus having been in a position to receive news concerning many thousands more, Alan's conclusions are well informed and agree with most scientific studies. His whole ministry could have survived had there been genuine evidence of orientation change. But while there continue to be *rumors* of "success," when the stories are tracked down, they prove untrue or—as in the case of my friend, Ed Hurst, whom I helped write *Overcoming Homosexuality*—the definitions change.

It's been over forty years that Ed has been trying to "overcome" homosexuality. After undergoing reparative therapy himself and working in a Christian "ex-gay" ministry for ten years, he admitted in his book that he still had same-sex attractions, but he believed, "Homosexuality is a learned condition and can therefore be unlearned."[2] Now Ed has redefined "overcoming" to mean

---

1. Alan Chambers, *My Exodus from Fear to Grace*, (Grand Rapids, MI: Zondervan, 2015), 196.
2. Ed Hurst with Dave and Neta Jackson, *Overcoming Homosexuality* (Elgin, IL: David C. Cook Publishing Co., 1987), 7.

avoiding *acting* on his same-sex impulses, for which I genuinely respect him. But I am just as sure this was not what Ed envisioned forty years ago, and it's not the obvious meaning of the title of his book or the hope he held out to readers.

Some make the argument that under the right circumstances, any of us could face temptation to *any* sin, and that's all that's happening to "ex-gay" people who still experience same-sex attraction, they say. But there's a difference. Yes, *under the right circumstances* any of us could succumb to any sin. That's why I avoid circumstances that would give power to any temptation to commit adultery—being alone for an extended time with an attractive woman who is not my wife, for instance. And I pray that God will keep me from such desperate straits that I would be tempted to steal just to survive.

But realizing that we *could* commit a sin does not mean we are perpetually inclined to do so. In fact, I know of no sin from which Christ's blood cannot deliver a person from its persistent intrusion into his or her life. Some will ask, "What about alcohol and drug addictions? Don't some people struggle with them their entire life?" Yes, for a variety of underlying psychological reasons. But it's the inverse that proves my point. There are many who have experienced a true change in terms of substance abuse, meaning the temptation to abuse those substances no longer looms over their lives. They are free from the addiction. But this cannot be said for most "ex-gay" people.

Even Paul's treatise in Romans 6—8 on the struggle within us regarding sin includes the constant promise of new life in Christ where there is freedom from sin and death—not "sinless perfection" but basic and genuine freedom from its domination. Again and again in Romans and 1 Corinthians, Paul uses language similar to Romans 6:17-18: "But thanks be to God that, though you used to be slaves to sin, you have come to *obey from your heart* the pattern of teaching that has now claimed your allegiance. *You have been set free* from sin and have become slaves to righteousness" (emphasis added).

This truth is well put in the old hymn, "O for a Thousand Tongues to Sing," by Charles Wesley (1739). Verse 4 says,

He breaks the power of canceled sin,
He sets the prisoner free;
His blood can make the foulest clean,
His blood availed for me.

Christ's blood not only cancels our sin—gives us a "not guilty" verdict—it releases us from sin's looming power that would otherwise follow us the rest of our life. If same-sex attraction is sin, then Christ's blood not only declares the gay person "not guilty," it should also free him or her from its haunting presence. It is only by faith that we believe we are justified before God, but the absence of that haunting presence should be observable in the thousands of gay Christians who have anguished and prayed for deliverance. The fact that same-sex attraction lingers, and in some cases is not even diminished in the vast majority—over 99 percent, according to Alan Chambers—should tell us something. And I do not believe it tells us the power of Christ is inadequate to change people, nor does it impugn the sincerity of all those believers. The only alternative seems to be that they (we) were trying to change something God never intended or promised to change.

So, what do you now think about same-sex orientation? If you still think it is a sinful condition, how do you understand the fact that sincere believers attempting every form of deliverance over any length of time have been unable to alter their orientation from gay to straight? If, on the other hand, you accept that *being* gay is not a sinful condition, what are the implications for how you consider and relate to gay people?

* *A gay person could respond to the opposite sex if he or she chose to.*
Bisexual people can respond to people of either sex, and there are innumerable points on the sexual orientation spectrum—from gay to straight. But many gay people are exclusively attracted to people of the same gender. They may even find the idea of having sex with someone of the opposite sex repulsive and unnatural. While it is possible that some can learn to respond in time, that does not end their same-sex attraction. Alan Chambers, who was mentioned earlier, acknowledges he was born gay and reports that

while he is now deeply in love with and physically attracted to his wife, it took him nearly nine months to consummate his marriage to her.[3] I'm glad Alan and Leslie Chambers are making it, and I pray they always will, but the challenges they have faced have been too great for many cross-orientation couples.

Think about it—my wife knows I can be physically attracted to other women, but she also knows she is my chosen fulfillment of my basic orientation. That is so different than if my orientation were toward something she could never fulfill.

What do these realities say to you about your expectations for how gay people should live?

- *AIDS is God's judgment on gay people.*

In 2013, 24 percent of white evangelicals believed this might be true (10 percent higher than the general population).[4] But while all sickness, from the common cold to cancer, is part of the curse of sin and death in this world, you probably know far more people who have had cancer than AIDS, and you probably wouldn't declare their cancer to be God's judgment. Promiscuity among *both* gay and straight people can have numerous tragic consequences, and HIV can be one of them. But children and other innocent people also contract the disease. Jesus warned us in Luke 13:4 not to presume any tragedy is the result of God's judgment.

Have you clearly renounced the presumption that AIDS is God's blanket judgment on gay people?

- *Homosexuals are more likely than heterosexuals to abuse children.*

Back in 1977, when Anita Bryant campaigned successfully to repeal a Dade County, Florida, ordinance prohibiting anti-gay discrimination, she named her organization "Save Our Children" and warned that "a particularly deviant-minded [gay] teacher

3. Alan Chambers, *My Exodus from Fear to Grace*, (Grand Rapids, MI: Zondervan, 2015), 144.

4. Antonia Blumberg, "Fourteen Percent of Americans Believe AIDS might be God's Punishment: Survey," Huff Post Religion, 02/28/2014. http://www.huffingtonpost.com/2014/02/28/aids-hiv-gods-punishment_n_4876381.html. The chart within the article pinned the number at 24 percent for white evangelicals.

could sexually molest children."[5] Far more recently, the Family Research Council produced an article claiming "homosexual men molest boys at rates grossly disproportionate to the rates at which heterosexual men molest girls."[6]

However, extensive peer reviews conclude the FRC's research simply doesn't hold up. Professor Gregory Herek of the University of California points out, "Most of the studies they referenced did not even assess the sexual orientation of abusers."[7] He points to many other studies that show gay people are *not* more inclined to molest children than straight people. For example, among 175 adult males who were convicted in Massachusetts of sexual assault against a child, none of them had an adult homosexual orientation. Instead of gender—either the same or opposite—their sexual attraction was fixated on children.[8]

In conclusion, Herek says, "The empirical research does *not* show that gay or bisexual men are any more likely than heterosexual men to molest children. This is not to argue that homosexual and bisexual men never molest children. But there is no scientific basis for asserting that they are more likely than heterosexual men to do so."[9]

Nevertheless, the presumption that molesters abuse children of their same gender receives a lot of media attention when Catholic priests are accused of abuse or someone voices fears about the Boy Scouts accepting gay scoutmasters. But abuse occurs tragically more often with children of the opposite gender, often within families or by close friends. *Pedophilia is real!* Children should always be taught and empowered to report anyone suggesting or attempting inappropriate touch. And *anyone* working with

5. Anita Bryant, *The Anita Bryant story: The survival of our nation's families and the threat of militant homosexuality*, (Old Tappan, NJ: Fleming H. Revell, 1977), 114.

6. Timothy Dailey, "Homosexuality and Child Sexual Abuse," Family Research Council 07/02/2002, http://www.frc.org/get.cfm?i=IS02E3.

7. Gregory Herek, "Facts About Homosexuality and Child Molestation," http://psychology.ucdavis.edu/rainbow/html/facts_molestation.html.

8. A.N. Groth and H.J. Birnbaum, "Adult sexual orientation and attraction to underage persons," *Archives of Sexual Behavior*, 7 (1978, 3), 177.

9. Gregory Herek, "Facts About Homosexuality and Child Molestation," http://psychology.ucdavis.edu/rainbow/html/facts_molestation.html.

children should be required to pass a thorough background check and remain accountable for their conduct with children.

So, even if you aren't in a position to evaluate the competing claims of researchers, are you willing to set aside suspecting all gay people of endangering children in exchange for requiring appropriate safeguards for everyone working with children?

Fears that tend to linger

Not unlike various myths regarding homosexuality, many of us carry around vestiges of fears regarding homosexuality that end up influencing how we regard and relate to gay people. Some of those fears may be based on myths or misunderstandings, but often they simply involve concepts we haven't thought through. So, do the same thing with these fears. Read each one and ask yourself what you really think, or what did you once think and now know differently, but haven't truly allowed your new understanding to change your behavior and attitudes regarding gay people.

- *If we don't oppose homosexuality, will it expand in our church and society?*

What feels like an increase in the percentage of gay people around us most likely results from two things—honesty and backlash. As civil rights have been secured for gay people and as discrimination (even within the church) has decreased, more gay people have been willing to "come out," to publicly acknowledge they are gay. In reaction, those who are strongly opposed to gay people have become more vocal, so it becomes a far more frequent issue of public dispute.

Based partially on the flawed research of Alfred Kinsey in his 1948 and 1953 books, it was commonly claimed that 10 percent of the population was gay. But more accurate research shows that rather than increasing, the estimate has actually come down. The Williams Institute at UCLA School of Law, a sexual orientation law think tank, released a study in April 2011 which says, "Drawing on information from four recent national and two state-level population-based surveys, the analyses suggest that there are more than 8 million adults in the US who are lesbian, gay, or bisexual, comprising 3.5 percent of the adult population."[10]

- *Maybe I caused this "condition" in my loved one.*

Our parents profoundly affected most of us as we grew up, hopefully for the good. But abuse, neglect, or simply a lack of wise guidance can definitely harm children. Such children can grow up with deep resentments, twisted ideas about life and God, and numerous social handicaps. When those injuries happen to a gay child, it is easy to think parental deficiencies and abuse caused him or her to become gay. For decades, many social scientists made this presumption and concocted elaborate theories to support the connection[11] . . . to the consternation and deep anguish of thousands of decent parents. Neta and I struggled with guilt when our daughter, Leah, came out, largely because we had studied many of those theoreticians as I helped Ed Hurst write his book. Fortunately, those theories have been broadly discredited, freeing parents like us from a cloud of guilt. But from the beginning, Leah tried to reassure us that it was not our fault. "That's just not the way it works," she'd say.

Of course, we weren't perfect parents, but as far as we knew—even after combing back through the years—we were good parents. Our friends, many who knew us on a day-to-day basis, under every circumstance, day or night, assured us we were *good parents*. It was only after we discovered these theories had been debunked, and after hearing the testimonies of numerous gay Christians that they, too, had grown up in *good* Christian homes, that we began to believe what our daughter had tried to tell us.

This is not to say there aren't many gay people who have been damaged by their parents' mistakes in the same way straight kids have been. Those mistakes may underlie the kids' anger, rebellion, depression, or self-destructive behavior. And it's conceivable that

---

10.   http://williamsinstitute.law.ucla.edu/research/census-lgbt-demographics-studies/how-many-people-are-lesbian-gay-bisexual-and-transgender/#sthash.clQ60FoJ.dpuf.

11. These theoreticians include Paul Cameron, Robert Kronemeyer, Elizabeth R. Moberly, Joseph Nicolosi, Leanne Payne, George A. Rekers, Walter Schumm, John White, and Frank Worthen.

abuse or trauma during childhood could drive someone to seek solace with someone of the same gender as the only safe place to have sex, but does that make them truly gay in their baseline orientation? I actually know a woman who fits that profile. From a childhood of abuse, she ended up a prostitute and heroin addict, spending several years in prison. She felt safe only with other women and considered herself a lesbian. But after release, she became a Christian, met a Christian man who truly loved her, and risked marriage. They have now been happily married for many years. She comes the closest I've ever known to someone who says their orientation "changed." So you might say her childhood experiences "made her gay," but only God knows. And her experience certainly does not represent the many gay people who testify they grew up in good and loving homes, yet always knew they were "different."

- *If I become too tolerant, I might develop a same-sex attraction myself.*

If one could become gay, then it would follow that breaking down whatever barriers have "kept you straight" could result in an apparent orientation change. But that line of thinking fails. Just as there is no evidence gay people can become straight, you can be sure your straight orientation won't go the other way, either.

Of course, as we've noted earlier, human sexual orientation occurs on a spectrum, and so you might discover that you aren't as purely "straight" as you thought you were. Perhaps you are a little bit toward the bisexual middle. But discovering that—as frightening as it might seem—doesn't mean you've changed. And if you should make such a discovery, that doesn't give you freedom to act on it. And here's why—I don't know much about bisexuality, but I do believe a bisexual person must make a choice—*the same kind of a choice* any straight or gay person must make—to be chaste as a single person and sexually faithful in marriage to only one person. Being straight, I might be attracted to lots of women, but as the marriage vows say, "forsaking all others," I have chosen only one to marry. A bisexual person must make the same choice and cannot excuse his or her "wandering eye" any more than I can, simply because he or she *can* be attracted to people of either sex.

Know who you are. Don't be frightened of who you are. And be faithful to God's call on your life, which in the area of sexual behavior is chastity before marriage and monogamy after marriage . . . with very good reasons in accord with Jesus' second commandment.

- *If I look too deeply into this issue, secrets from my childhood curiosity and experimentation may be exposed.*

They might. Mine might. Somebody else's might. But that fear is no excuse for not doing the right thing now.

Or, if you were molested or inappropriately touched as a child, those memories may seem too painful to face, but rather than avoid the past, perhaps this is the time God intends for you to seek counseling and healing.

- *If I allow my gay family member to bring home his or her partner, will it encourage their relationship?*

First, ask yourself how you would respond to a straight couple visiting, and do the same with the gay couple. That doesn't make the question easy. It could be very delicate, but if you are honest in treating the gay couple no differently than a straight couple, you'll have a chance of being understood. We accepted Leah and Jane sleeping in the same room once they were married even though it wasn't yet legal in Illinois. They had set up a permanent family, they had bought a home together, and they had formalized their covenant to one another in a public wedding ceremony. Asking them to sleep apart would have been pointless even though God had not yet fully changed our minds.

- *If I attend a gay wedding, will I be endorsing it?*

That was one of our big questions concerning Leah and Jane's wedding. Albert Mohler, President of the Southern Baptist Theological Seminary, says you should boycott gay weddings because a wedding involves an endorsement of the union. He cites the language of traditional ceremonies where the guests are asked, "If

anyone knows of any cause that should prevent the marriage—
'speak now, or forever hold your peace.'"[12]

Another pastor disagrees, even though he does not support the concept of gay marriage. He said, "I've gone to a lot of weddings that I didn't think were a good idea. But my presence was an expression of my love and support for the participants as people, whether or not I thought the match was right."

I would agree. And once a couple is married, most of us would nonetheless do what we could to encourage that relationship to be healthy. Jesus never presumed his association with people was an endorsement for what they did, whether they were prostitutes, drunkards, or tax collectors. (I'm not comparing those practices to gay people getting married.) I'm glad we attended Leah and Jane's wedding. At the time, they received our attendance as evidence of our love for them even more because they knew we didn't approve. The Holy Spirit had already told us, "Don't burn any bridges," and I'm glad we didn't add the level of rejection and hurt that boycotting their wedding would have created.

God's prescription for our mistakes

Whether you have actively or passively opposed gay people, whether you have marched against them with hateful signs or merely kept quiet when policies that drive gay people away have been enacted in your church or ministry, whether the source of your response or lack thereof was the Ick Factor or an unresolved myth or fear, God has a prescription for reconciliation with those we've hurt.

One of the things I've learned over the years about racial reconciliation is the value of asking for forgiveness. Asking for forgiveness is often hindered by fear, fear of owning our responsibility and fear of absorbing the other person's anger. It's hard for me to admit that I've been wrong and that I've contributed to and (particularly in the case of racism) benefited from other people's wrong actions and attitudes.

---

12. Albert Mohler, *We Cannot Be Silent*, (Nashville, TN: Thomas Nelson, 2015), 164.

But it's the truth in this case as well, especially for me having helped write the book, *Overcoming Homosexuality*. And it's not the degree of our wrong (that book didn't have a very large circulation). Instead, it's like sin. How much of it does it take to make us sinners? I'm truly sorry for having hurt gay people, especially my daughter. And I'm sorry for how the church—my corner of the church, the church I love, the church that has nurtured me—has hurt gay people.

So please forgive me. Please forgive us. Whether you are gay or straight, if you have fled because you couldn't take it any longer, please don't turn your back on Jesus. He is the Good Shepherd, who is leaving the ninety-nine to come and rescue you.

Collateral Damage

By Matthew Williams[13]

© 2016, Matthew Williams. Used by permission.

My earliest recollection of being attracted to the same sex was when I was eleven years old. I had a crush on a boy in my sixth grade class. At the time, I didn't realize it was a crush. I thought, "I really like this guy, and I want to be his friend." There was nothing more than that. But it was only a few months later that I realized I might be different from others.

During the next few years, I hid this part of me. Deep inside. I didn't dare tell anyone about these feelings. I grew up hearing boys like girls . . . end of story. There was so much shame attached to being different, especially during a time in my life where kids can be incredibly mean and hurtful. (Heck, adults can be mean and hurtful.) There was no one I knew in middle school who was openly gay, and I didn't want to be the first. On top of not wanting to be different through my immensely awkward puberty years,

---

13. "The Real Matthew," Matthew David Williams blog, Feb. 24, 2016, http://matthewdavidwilliams.org.

I had heard things from the Catholic school I was going to that being gay was a sin. This further cemented the idea that I would not accept this part of me, and with enough prayer, I could change. God could change me.

My high school days were a blur. I didn't date or have any interest in girls. I mostly kept to myself and did safe activities (photography, yearbook, honor societies). I didn't want to do anything that would draw too much attention. What if someone suspected something and asked me? What if they already knew? What if they started spreading rumors? I didn't want to give anyone ammunition to say something about me, although that happened several times.

I have some painful memories from those teenage years. One day a kid wrote the word "fag" on the back of my shirt in middle school without me knowing. I was so embarrassed when I got home that I washed it out before my mom could see it. In high school, there was a girl that would constantly call me faggot in class and in the hall between classes, and I couldn't shake her. It bothered me that as much as I wanted to fit in, I still got picked on for something I thought others couldn't see. I prided myself on hiding any sign that I was different, but I think some people saw past that and wanted to expose me.

Fast forward to college where I knew I still liked guys, and if anything, it had intensified. I didn't know what to do though. I craved a relationship (anyone that knows me well, knows that I absolutely love relationships), but I only dated girls to cover up my feelings. I was adamant that being gay was a sin and sometime soon God would change me. The church continued to reinforce these expectations by how it interpreted Scripture to say homosexuality was a sin. So, with that, I further suppressed this part of me. I tried to "pray the gay away" for almost all of my teens and twenties. I saw counselors, pastors, went through programs, and prayed every night for God to take this away from me. I have stacks of journals that recount the painful feelings of wanting God to change me and take this away. Nothing happened though, and I feared nothing would.

It's hard to articulate how frustrating and demeaning it is to have others tell you to pray something away so God will accept you. They'd say "If you just *prayed harder* or *believed more*, you wouldn't be gay." I felt like such a failure as a Christian. I was trying so hard, but had no fruit to show for it. I never asked to be gay and no one seemed to understand that. Why would I ask to be gay if it meant more hardships in my life? If you've ever questioned if it's a choice, it most certainly is not. It wasn't until after finishing a stint in mission work and being in the real world for a while, that I learned a lot more about myself.

I went to Atlanta for a wedding and stayed with a friend while I was there. He is one of my closest friends, like an older brother to me. We've always had great conversations and shared deep parts of our lives with each other. This time though, I wasn't prepared for what we ended up talking about. He told me he was gay, and he's still a Christian. I just stared at him. I didn't know what to say. He had known I struggled with my sexuality for a while, but I never thought he would fully come out. Not surprisingly, I had lots of questions . . . about Scripture, about God's design, and about which churches were accepting of him. It was a very hard weekend to process. Lots of tears and confusion. As you can imagine, I went back to Charleston with a lot on my mind.

For the next five months I was very depressed. I didn't know what to do. I had a decision in front of me: accept who I am or continue to suppress my feelings and hope that one day they would work themselves out. It seems simple looking at it now, but it was one of the hardest and lowest points of my life. I had panic attacks weekly, I cried almost every day, and life just seemed to be falling apart. To give you an idea of what I was going through, here's a journal excerpt several months into my depression:

> I don't recognize the Matthew I am right now. He doesn't laugh. He makes himself smile when he doesn't want to. He is more emotional and depressed than ever, and is tired from all the swirling questions. He isn't pleasant to be around and just wants to be left alone. Who is this guy, and what has he done with the man that just loved life? Where

is the guy that loved to talk about travel, wanting to see his friends in far away places, and explore new things? That guy seems dead right now. He seems distant. This Matthew right now . . . he's just ok. Always messy, often conflicted, and constantly sad.

After what seemed like years, I finally woke up one sunny November morning in 2014 and realized God had made me this way. It's hard to articulate how I knew that, but I knew God knew me before I was born. He knew the things I would face. He knew ME. He knows ME. He made me fearfully and wonderfully, and His works are wonderful (Psalm 139). The best and most beautiful part is that as soon as I accepted myself as gay, all my depression and anxiety lifted. For the very first time, I felt like the Matthew that God had intentionally made.

The process of "coming out" is something I was never prepared to go through. You don't know how anyone is going to react or openly reject you. Thankfully, my experience with friends and family was incredible. I am surrounded by the most amazing people (tearing up writing this now). My sister and parents were great. They accept me as me, and as simple as that sounds, there are more heartbreaking stories from many of my friends about parents rejecting their gay sons and daughters. Don't get me wrong, I had a handful of bad experiences, but I realized most people wanted to love me unconditionally. They didn't care that I was gay. They loved me. Plain and simple.

The journey has been an interesting one, and I'm sure there will be more thoughts and musings along the way. All I know right now is that I'm Matthew, I love Jesus, and I'm gay. And I wouldn't have it any other way.

Chapter 19
Jesus, Help Us Live in Peace

His love has no limits, His grace has no measure,
His power no boundary known unto men;
For out of His infinite riches in Jesus
He giveth, and giveth, and giveth again.

"He Giveth More Grace"
Annie J. Flint, "Casterline
Card" series, circa 1910

RECENTLY, OUR CHURCH WAS WORKING on racial reconciliation, an ongoing effort to build up the community life among our members from over fifty different countries. In telling her life story, one woman explained the impact of coming from a shame-based society. Hers happened to be Asian, but I was appalled to hear how often and in how many small ways the threat of shame manipulated her into doing what others wanted her to do.

Except among ethnic minorities like this woman, the fear of shame no longer exercises as much control over most Americans as it once did. Think of how easily young people deflect shaming pressure with the gesture or words of "F___ you!" But shame was a major element in Jewish culture, demonstrated most dramatically against women who were declared "unclean" for seven days after every menstrual cycle—not because of some wrong deed for which they needed to repent, but simply because of *who they were*. But the threat of shame affected everyone. Forty-two times in the Psalms, we read verses such as, "I trust in you; do not let me be put to shame, nor let my enemies triumph over me. No one who hopes in you will ever be put to shame, but shame will come on those who are treacherous without cause" (Psalm 25:2-3). Proverbs 13:18 says, "Whoever disregards discipline comes to poverty and shame, but whoever heeds correction is honored." If we were to write the same proverb, we'd probably just skip the warning about shame, thinking the fear of poverty is the only relevant motivator these days.

New Testament writers occasionally bring forward the concept of shame, but usually to emphasize our *release* from it[1]. Speaking of the Messiah, both Peter and Paul quote Isaiah 28:16: "The one who trusts in him will never be put to shame."[2] That is because Jesus, the "suffering Servant," bore our suffering, being despised, rejected, "like one from whom people hide their faces" and held "in low esteem"—all synonyms for shame. (See Isaiah 53.)

But because of Jesus, "There is now no condemnation [or shame] for those who are in Christ Jesus" (Romans 8:1). In addition to these theological truths, there was the social reality that early Christians became outsiders to both the Jewish and Roman worlds and could not allow any shame heaped on them to stifle their life or mission. They learned how to stand tall, as it were, in the face of rejection and ridicule.

In contemporary culture, we are more inclined to speak of responsibility or even guilt in response to specific wrongdoing, but shame is far more sweeping. It puts the recipient perpetually off-balance by producing within them negative, degrading judgments and emotions about *who they are*. Applied long enough, the person is likely to begin believing any social stress around them is their fault, and they become willing to do anything to restore equilibrium and get back in the good graces of those around them.

This is why shame can be such a powerful tool to manipulate and control people in any culture, particularly if it is as tight-knit as family or church. Sadly, too many of us have found the tool of

---

1. In one instance, Paul does invoke shame. In 2 Thessalonians 3:14 he says not to associate with those who refuse to obey his instructions "in order that they may feel ashamed." But note that the shame is over a *specific* action, not because of *who* the people innately are.
2. See Romans 9:33; 10:11; 1 Peter 2:6.

shame irresistible in attempting to control gay people. Keep them out or keep them hidden, but for sure, discourage their "coming out," because that is the first sign that they are rejecting the power of shame over their lives.

The opposite of shame

One might say the opposite of shame is pride, but I'm not sure that's correct. The dictionary defines pride as "a feeling of deep pleasure or satisfaction derived from one's own achievements, the achievements of those with whom one is closely associated, or from qualities or possessions that are widely admired." And indeed, gay pride parades have been one means by which gay people have attempted to counter the shame heaped on them in our society. And perhaps pride does help reduce the sting of shame for some wounded people.

However, peace is a better antidote for shame. Perhaps that's why "peace" is such a prominent salutation in the Bible. From the many passages that could be cited, consider these examples:

"The Lord bless you and keep you; the Lord make his face shine on you and be gracious to you; the Lord turn his face toward you and give you peace" (Numbers 6:24-26).

"Go in peace. Your journey has the Lord's approval" (Judges 18:6).

"On David and his descendants, his house and his throne, may there be the Lord's peace forever" (1 Kings 2:33).

"Glory to God in the highest heaven, and on earth peace to those on whom his favor rests" (Luke 1:79).

"Go in peace and be freed from your suffering" (Mark 5:34).

"Peace I leave with you; my peace I give to you" (John 14:27).

Again Jesus said, "Peace be with you!" (John 20:21).

Grace and peace to you from God our Father and the Lord Jesus Christ (1 Corinthians 1:3).

These examples could go on and on, with each one demonstrating the opposite of shame. Declaring the ancient Christian greeting (usually before communion in liturgical churches), "Peace be with you," and the response, "And also with you," communicates acceptance, no hostility, and a prayer for the other person's well-being. Similar to the ancient Hebrew greeting, "Shalom," there is no shame held over brothers and sisters when the peace of Christ is genuinely exchanged. Consequently, people do not feel the need to hide or flee. This should be our goal in relating to anyone.

Concern for the scattered "sheep"

A poll taken by USA TODAY in April 2015 found that 46 percent of Americans had a gay or lesbian family member or close friend who is already *in a gay marriage*.[3] And yet very few evangelical churches have thought through what they will do when people in gay marriages come through their doors. Will the message those people hear communicate shame? Does the church use the threat of shame to keep gay singles celibate? Does our approach invite gay people to Jesus or drive them away?

In Chapter 6, "What Can Separate Gay People from the Love of God?" we saw how our behavior toward gay people *can* drive them away from experiencing the love of God. And brothers and sisters, we have done just that to thousands and thousands of gay people who were—and some who still are—in our evangelical churches. We've broadcast such animosity toward them by radio, the Internet, in books and articles, and from our pulpits that many gay people who once were seekers or might become seekers of God won't dare darken the doors of our churches. If there is still a place for shame, it is we who need to fall on our knees and repent!

Why do you think Jesus was so angry that he could say, "It would be better for [such a] person to have a large millstone tied round his neck and be drowned in the deep sea" than to cause a child or vulnerable person to lose their faith (Matthew 18:6-7)?

---

3. "Poll: U.S. has turned the corner on gay marriage," USA TODAY—Chicago Sun-Times, April 20, 2015, p. 29. Source: USA TODAY/Suffolk University Pol of 1,000 people, taken April 8-13. Margin of error +/- 3 percentage points.

This behavior was at the core of Jesus' outrage toward the Pharisees: "You load people down with burdens they can hardly carry, and you yourselves will not lift one finger to help them" (Luke 11:46). "Woe to you . . .! You shut the door of the kingdom of heaven in people's faces. You . . . [won't] let those enter who are trying to" (Matthew 23:13).

In contrast, our Jesus is the Good Shepherd, who leaves the ninety-nine to go out and find that *one* lost sheep (Luke 15:3-8). To carry Jesus' analogy a little further, do you think this made the ninety-nine happy? Might they have preferred he stay behind to affirm what good sheep they were by telling them "what their itching ears want to hear" (2 Timothy 4:3)?

But this problem did not begin with the Pharisees of Jesus' day. Speaking through the Prophet Ezekiel, God had the same complaint about the religious leaders in Ezekiel's day:

> "Woe to you shepherds of Israel . . . ! You have not strengthened the weak or healed the sick or bound up the injured. You have not brought back the strays or searched for the lost. You have ruled them harshly and brutally. So they were scattered . . . over the whole earth, and no one searched or looked for them. . . . I am against the shepherds and will hold them accountable for my flock" (Ezekiel 34:2-6, 10).

And it's not just the shepherds that the Lord holds accountable:

> "As for you, my flock . . . Because you shove with flank and shoulder, butting all the weak sheep with your horns until you have driven them away, I will save my flock, and they will no longer be plundered" (Ezekiel 34:17, 21-22).

This prophecy to Israel concludes with God's promise to rescue his scattered sheep and to "place over them one shepherd, my servant David," a clear messianic prophecy referring to Jesus. "You are my sheep, the sheep of my pasture, and I am your God, declares the Sovereign Lord" (Ezekiel 34:31). Ezekiel's address to

Israel clearly demonstrates God's heart for *anyone* who has been scattered and lost.

No wonder when Jesus came he had such harsh words for the Pharisees, words that should echo a warning in our ears today—to love like Jesus loves, we must begin by not projecting shame that discourages and scatters his sheep, especially the weak ones who are barely hanging onto their faith by their fingernails.

If you are a pastor of a church of 200 people and have not chased away those who are gay, then statistically, six or seven members of your flock are gay, sitting right there in front of you, hearing everything you preach. Do you know who they are? Have you lifted the shame so they are not afraid to come out? Or is what you say likely to discourage them so much they will ultimately leave? If you pastor 1,500, you are responsible for the welfare of as many as fifty gay people.[4] Do you need to go out and bring the lost ones back? Would you *and your congregation* rejoice with the angels over the return of each one . . . or only if they could become straight like the rest of you?

A truly seeker-friendly church

To the degree that "seeker-friendly churches" have relied on an entertainment/consumer-based business model for growth, they deserve criticism. But authentic efforts to renounce shame as a way to hold and control people and a desire to love those on the margins can help make a church as friendly as Jesus was in person and for entirely different motives.

Turning away from hurtful approaches requires more than putting a line in your Sunday bulletin saying, "Everyone welcome," or adding that to the sign outside your church. It requires more than using kinder, gentler language while still heaping shame on people. Effective change must be intentional, and since the old toxic positions were so widely disseminated, they need to be addressed by public repentance and public education to instruct

---

4. These numbers are based on research finding 3.5 percent of the adult population is LGBT. http://williamsinstitute.law.ucla.edu/research/census-lgbt-demographics-studies/how-many-people-are-lesbian-gay-bisexual-and-transgender/#sthash.clQ60FoJ.dpuf.

the congregation why and how the traditional approaches were failures and did not represent Jesus.

And it all needs to be accompanied by *listening* to gay people and what they have experienced.

Our daughter's painful experience occurred in an essentially neo-traditional church. In fact, the two pastors had "agreed to disagree" over their views regarding people with same-sex orientation—one believing marriage equality was something God might allow and the other maintaining it was wrong. That compromise might even sound like an "inclusive" approach. But it was not. During the years prior to our daughter's family moving to their city, I'd become quite familiar with the pastors, having met with them periodically as their church wanted to implement elements of Christian community that were strong in our church while we wanted to learn from important strengths in their church. So, after Leah came out and moved to the same city, I felt hopeful when she started attending their church. Apart from a few brief exchanges when we visited, I kept my nose out of how they were pastoring her, trusting that if anyone could lovingly bring "correction," it would be them. However, as described earlier, the relationship ultimately crashed and burned—largely, I believe, because they had never worked through *how* to live with and respect one another in the midst of disputable matters. In fact, given what happened to Leah and Jane, the church hadn't even figured out how to be lovingly neo-traditional.

To be a family or church gay people find friendly, the very first step is to *be intentional* about being friendly. If you realize that is not how you have been in the past, then the second step is to repent. In many cases, it is helpful to communicate this directly. However, it will be received best when it is accompanied by concrete ways you intend to change. Adopting the following habits can help us. Some are for people with a neo-traditional conviction, some apply more to those of an inclusive persuasion, and some apply to both.

- If your child trusts you enough to come out to you, assure them from the get-go that you love them no matter what!
- Listen to their stories.

272

- If your gay friend or family member has a relationship with God, never make statements that make them feel they have to choose between their sexual orientation and their faith.
- Thank God for the privilege of knowing gay people and for what God will teach you through them.
- Don't be afraid of gay people.
- Oppose any policies or views that spread fear of gay people.
- Accept and do not penalize gay people who "come out." God always prefers truth.
- Be careful with your language. Calling gay people "sodomites" is unbiblical. And even the label "homosexual" can be used with very pejorative intent.
- Do not presume that because someone comes out as gay that he or she is sexually active.
- What does God seem to be doing in the life of your gay family member or friend?
- Celebrate abstinence among *both* gay and straight singles as *equally* important.
- Recognize anyone's genuine calling to a life of celibacy. (A genuine call will not be driven by fear or shame.)
- Affirm the fruit of the Spirit in the life of gay Christians.
- There is no greater compliment than to need someone. Express your need for your gay family and friends, including your appreciation for their friendship, wisdom, and areas of expertise.
- Celibacy is challenging. Celibate gays need relationships they can count on to be there for them—in sickness, in health, in old age, and in death. If you are family, *be family* throughout all life's stages. If you are their church, encourage close friendships and small group fellowship for gay people.
- In your church, come up with a redemptive response to gay couples, especially those with children. You may disagree with the choices they have made, but there are still many ways to love, respect, and support them.
- Do not be dogmatic. As rare as genuine orientation change may be, we worship a God of miracles who raises the dead.

So don't deny a person's claim to have changed unless you *know* it to be untrue.

- Be respectful of straight or gay people who aren't "inclusive."
- Do not confuse support for marriage equality with sexual permissiveness outside marriage.
- Be sure to provide gay couples the same support straight couples need—parenting training and help, financial and relational counsel, etc.
- Ask gay people to assist in ministry outreaches. Ask for their wisdom.

Pastor Tim Otto[5] is one of the most relaxed celibate gay people I've met, perhaps because he does not believe it would be sinful for him to enter a gay marriage, thereby relieving him of the fear and threat of shame. And yet he has chosen to remain celibate for the sake of his current ministry, which he enjoys with a grateful heart. But inclusive friends (or churches) can wrongly presume all gay people want to be sexually active. It becomes "the issue" that sets them apart from traditional and neo-traditional people. But that's not always the case. In fact, many married gay people would like to turn down the temperature on the subject of sex. Their lives aren't necessarily focused on sex any more than the lives of married straight people. They have money problems, relational problems, parenting problems, and scheduling problems just like everyone else and would like to be supported in those ways too.

Recently when we were asked to share our story at a church that was adopting an inclusive position, one of the leaders approached us afterward to say, "You know, the 'marginalized people' we must now endeavor to include are those who personally hold a neo-traditional point of view. They're the ones in the minority and most likely to feel looked down upon." If we're going to be inclusive, it has to go both ways.

We need to learn how to live in peace, as expressed in this song by J.D. Martin:

---

5. Tim Otto is a pastor of the Church of the Sojourners in San Francisco and author of *Oriented to Faith, Transforming the Conflict over Gay Relationships*, (Eugene, OR: Cascade Books, 2014).

Jesus, help us live in peace
from our blindness set us free.
Fill us with Your healing love
help us live in unity.

Many times we don't agree
on what's right or wrong to do.
It's so hard to really see
from the other's point of view.

And how we long for power and fame
Seeking every earthly thing.
We forget the one who came
As a servant not a king.

Jesus, help us live in peace
From our blindness set us free.
Fill us with Your healing love
Help us live in unity.[6]

Collateral Damage

By Amber Cantorna

© 2015, Amber Cantorna. Used by permission.

I was twenty-seven when I finally mustered every last bit of courage to have "the talk" with my family. I had been pondering, planning, and praying for months. My heart weighed heavy and anxiety took my mind down every possible outcome. I knew, as the daughter of a Focus on the Family executive, the results of my truth could be devastating. But I had reached the point where living a lie was worse than whatever lay on the other side of truth. After much counsel, preparation, and prayer, I felt the time had

---

6. "Unity (Jesus Help Us Live in Peace)," Words & Music by M. Gerald Derstine (J.D. Martin), © 1971, 2003. Used by permission.

come to tell my truth. So on April 14, 2012, I invited my parents and brother over and told them the journey I'd been on the past several years. Then I spoke the three short words that would forever alter my future . . .

* * * *

Though I was born in Kalispell, Montana, by my third birthday we moved to Glendora, California, where my dad accepted a job with Focus on the Family. When the company relocated to Colorado Springs in 1991, my family did as well, and that's the town where I grew up.

With the values and teachings of Dr. James Dobson at the core of our family's foundation, my parents decided to homeschool my brother and me from start to finish. They made daily devotions and cultivating a relationship with God a priority from a very young age. With programs like AWANA, we memorized Scripture both in the program and as a family. A typical girl, I grew up playing with American Girl dolls and having frequent tea parties. I believed my knight in shining armor would come for me, if only I would wait for him. At my thirteenth birthday, I even had a "Purity Ceremony" in which I signed a vow to stay chaste until marriage and was given a ring to be worn until it was someday replaced by a wedding band. I embraced all these characteristics of what love and traditional marriage should look like.

My mom came from a musical family, so almost from the womb she trained us as well, investing a lot of time in fostering our musical talents. We frequently sang at retirement homes and Christian schools. We did full concerts at small churches and were always ready to perform for visiting family and guests. I was blessed to be given thirteen years of classical piano training, and by the time I was fourteen, I was touring Europe with a youth choir and soon after, with the Young Continentals. Performing was a huge part of my life, and I thrived on it. As a high-achieving perfectionist, I constantly put pressure on myself to rise to the top.

However, not all of that pressure came from within. As I moved into my teen years, I began to feel the outside pressure to uphold my family's reputation. As the daughter of a man who held a high-profile position at Focus, I felt the weight to maintain the appearance of that "perfect Focus family." Friends would often comment on how lucky I was. But behind the mask of perfection, I found myself struggling with depression and anxiety.

By the time I reached my early twenties, I still had never dated a guy. At times I thought maybe there was something wrong with me, but mostly I just believed what I had been taught: If you prepare yourself spiritually and wait sexually, the right man will come along at the right time. The fact that I might be gay never really crossed my radar. I truly believed God was just shielding me from the heartache of the high school romances my friends were having. I believed the first man I would seriously date would just magically be "the one."

But at age twenty-three, things took a drastic turn when I suddenly found myself falling in love with my roommate . . . a woman! What started as a simple friendship, morphed into something more. I was so aghast the first time we kissed! I wasn't even sure what was happening. My head spun! I tried to figure out this mysterious attraction. Though I didn't know it at the time, that experience ended up being the beginning of a deeper wrestling, the beginning of searching and eventually, the beginning of coming out.

I knew I couldn't just sweep this "problem" under the rug, but I was terrified. On the one hand, I feared that in studying and digging deeper into God's Word, I might find what I'd been taught all my life was true: God disapproved of homosexuality, and therefore he disapproved of me. On the other hand, because Focus on the Family teaches that marriage is strictly between one man and one woman, I was equally terrified that if I discovered the Bible didn't support their view and God indeed had made me as I was, then I would become part of the stigmatized minority in my Christian circles. So either way, my life would never be the same.

But, as I sat one night with my journal in hand, heartbroken over the loss of my first love and altogether confused as to how and why it all happened to begin with, I gathered my courage and told God I was ready to start walking the difficult road ahead. I prayed, studied and researched for months, offering up to him everything to be re-examined. I talked to people on similar journeys and, in doing so, found those who were both completely in love with their same-sex spouse and also completely in love with God, without any conflict between the two. That was when I began to realize there didn't have to be a dichotomy between my faith and my sexuality as I had been led to believe. Finally, after a long and difficult climb, the Scriptures in question settled in my heart. I found the answers I needed and knew that, in God's eyes, I was not only accepted but also loved for exactly how he had made me.

The odds were high, however, that my family would not agree. Anxiety, panic attacks, and nightmares swelled as I approached the day where telling them my truth would disappoint and break the illusion of that "perfect Focus family." As I mustered every ounce of strength I had on that chilly April day, I looked my family in the eyes, and said those three small, but life-altering words, "I am gay."

With my exposed heart hanging in the air, I waited.

"I have nothing to say to you right now." My dad got up and walked out the door.

From that moment on, things went from bad to worse. In a follow-up conversation weeks later, my parents compared me to murderers and pedophiles, told me I was selfish for doing this to the family, and asked me to turn in my keys to their house, my childhood home. Over time, because of their unwavering belief in Focus on the Family's teaching and interpretation of the Scriptures, I was quietly pushed aside and shunned by the family. Only in my worst nightmares were the consequences as drastic as what they proved to be in real life. I lost not only my immediate family, but also my relatives, my church, many of my friends, and essentially, even my hometown.

Because of the toxicity I felt in a city where it seemed my every move was watched, I ended up moving to Denver. Even though almost four years have passed, I still feel anxiety every time I drive to Colorado Springs. Unfortunately, though many of my loved ones claimed to have unconditional love, what I discovered is their love actually came with strings attached.

My world felt as if it were spiraling out of control. I felt lost, alone, and experienced consistent nightmares. The prospect of self-injury reared its ugly head as a distraction to the pain within. And for the first time, I truly could not see the light at the end of the tunnel. Suicide teased as a viable out.

Over the coming months, several key people invested in me, slowly adding value to my life and rescuing me from that dark pit. I don't remember an exact turning point, but I finally decided I wanted to live . . . some ten months after coming out. Once the tide had truly turned, I shared my life story during community hour at the Denver church I was attending. Though I didn't know it at the time, that was the day I met the woman who would become my wife.

I didn't pay her much attention at first, but Carla noticed me from the start. After several months of intentional pursuit on her part, we started dating. We both quickly knew that each other was "the one," and about a year and a half later, we were married.

But as my relationship with Carla solidified, my relationship with my parents became even bleaker. When we got engaged, they realized this wasn't just a phase that would pass, and the gavel came down as they cut all ties.

Not having any family at my wedding was one of the hardest things I've ever had to go through, and yet it was still the best day of my life. In front of the people who stood by me when it mattered the most, I got to consecrate my love to my wife in a sacred covenant before God. In that moment, all the labels washed away, and I was able to be fully myself, completely in love with Carla and also completely in love with God.

We've been married a year and a half now, and our journey continues forward. There are still bumps in the road and hard days where I miss my family. The truth is, I still cherish my family values just as much today as I ever did, but I've just had to learn to re-focus my family. I truly have so much to be grateful for. God has given me beauty for ashes and is continuing to be true to his promise and make all things new and beautiful in his time.

Chapter 20
The Cost of Risking Grace

May Thy rich grace impart
Strength to my fainting heart, my zeal inspire!
As Thou hast died for me, O may my love to Thee,
Pure warm, and changeless be, a living fire!

"My Faith Looks up to Thee"
Ray Palmer, 1830, verse 2

WOW! READ THE WORDS OF THAT OLD HYMN AGAIN. Better yet, sing it if you can. If you're anything like me, that's what I need—an infusion of God's grace to strengthen my fainting heart with zeal, a living fire, a willingness to follow in the steps of my Lord and Savior, who died for me. Am I willing to put it all on the line no matter what the cost?

I am convinced that accepting gay people "just as Christ accepted [me]" (Romans 15:7), without adding additional requirements to the Gospel, represents God's heart toward gay people. But I'm not so naive as to disregard the many Christians who disagree. And challenging their views will no doubt result in disapproval, hostility, and possibly even pressure for me to recant.

In spite of the fact that no one wants to be a people-pleaser, only the arrogant are untouched by the disapproval and disrespect of others they esteem. And it's not enough to be sincere. I could be sincerely wrong. So how dare I challenge what has been the church's traditional teaching for nearly two thousand years?[1]

---

1. Historically, the church's opposition to homosexual liaisons did not take into account the people with same-sex orientation who could enter

The Apostle James wrote, "My brothers and sisters, if one of you should wander from the truth and someone should bring that person back, remember this: Whoever turns a sinner from the error of their way will save them from death and cover over a multitude of sins" (James 5:19-20). There are certainly some who would like to "bring me back" to my old position. But I believe it's the church (or large portions of it) that has wandered from the truth of God's grace and needs to be brought back. Might bringing our evangelical church back to Jesus' approach be the thing that will "save them from death and cover over a multitude of sins" (James 5:20)?

Self-examination

It is a somber matter to challenge recognized church leaders. After all, what is the value of the spiritual gifts of apostle, pastor, and teacher if we will not listen to them? But there is also the role of prophet. In the Bible we see prophets as those who speak the word of God usually to encourage and build up, but also to correct. When the people or even the leaders got off track, God nudged someone to stand up and represent (re-present) his word. They were sometimes rather unassuming people. For instance, the evangelist Philip "had four unmarried daughters who prophesied" (Acts 21:9). On other occasions, prophecy was bolder as when the apostles confronted the established and recognized religious leaders of Israel: "We must obey God rather than human beings!" (Acts 5:29). In so doing, they were just . . . obeying God.

But the question remains, are *we* obeying God? Am *I* obeying God? Is he pleased with my change of mind?

I can't count the number of times while writing this book that doubts washed over me, and I hope similar doubts have troubled you as well. That's the only honest path to truth. But I can also say

---

permanent same-sex commitments parallel to heterosexual marriage. Though those people have always existed (usually undercover), the phenomenon they represent only began to be understood in the latter half of the twentieth century as gay people "came out," but the church hesitated to see them differently than the idolatrous, promiscuous, exploitive, or abusive expressions of homosexuality (and heterosexuality) the Bible clearly condemns. Slowly, however, that myopia is starting to change.

that every time I took my questions to the Lord as the Psalmist did and cried out, "Search me, O God, and know my heart; test me and know my anxious thoughts. See if there is an offensive way in me, and lead me in the way everlasting" (Psalm 139:23-24), God answered me.

His response was often to point me to Scripture passages that applied precisely to the next subject I needed to address. These insights were unbidden in the sense that they came up in my scheduled Bible reading or were texts mentioned in a Sunday sermon on a completely different topic but clarified what I was to say in my next chapter. I would take out my iPhone and send myself a quick text message to look up those verses before proceeding.

Other times the reassurance came via someone hearing what I was doing and encouraging me by saying this book was desperately needed to help them or someone else.

Of course, such subjective affirmations prove nothing to the person demanding proof that God was leading me. Perhaps the Scriptures I found were simply the result of my subconscious mind casting about and noticing verses or implications I hadn't previously considered. Perhaps the people who supported my work were not so much conveying encouragement from God as approval according to their own needs. But *proving* that God was speaking to me is not the point. I'm just being transparent here about my writing process, because it may have relevance to your reading process and how you digest what I've written. Hopefully, you too, have consistently been asking, "Am I following you, Jesus? What pleases you, Jesus?"

I hope you've been mulling over the ideas in this book with the same uncertainty I've embraced because, in the end, we must "walk by faith, not by sight" (2 Corinthians 5:7). "Sight" refers to what can be proven. What comes by faith cannot be proven. After all, "Faith is the substance of things hoped for, the evidence of things not seen" (Hebrews 11:1 NKJV). While true faith is not without *supports*, its truth is confirmed in our spirit because of a living relationship with God in which the Holy Spirit responds to us when we sincerely ask for God's guidance. This approach echoes Paul's confidence in Christ: "The Spirit himself testifies with our spirit that we are God's children" (Romans 8:16). And as Jesus promised, the Holy Spirit "will guide you into all truth" (John 16:13).

This relationship-based faith with Jesus is the only faith I've found worth clinging to when life gets tough. It is the same kind of relationship Jesus had with his Father, the kind that sustained him through death on the cross and raised him from the dead.

The example of Jesus' life

There is a kind of religion that tries to decipher God's will like diagraming a sentence. And while there's much to be learned from critical exegesis, it often leads to prideful disputes. On the other hand, there is a faith that is based on relationship. Jesus said, "[My] sheep follow [me] because they know [my] voice. But they will never follow a stranger; in fact, they will run away from him because they do not recognize a stranger's voice. . . . My sheep listen to my voice; I know them, and they follow me" (John 10:4-5, 27).

If you know Jesus, if you've studied the Word in order to get to know the *character* of the main character, if you've walked with Jesus for years, then you know his voice, and you know how he loves people, especially the marginalized and abused. Follow him. Do as Jesus would do. It's not such an indecipherable plot. And when faced with a dilemma, use the two guidelines he gave us for figuring out what you should do: "Love the Lord your God with all your heart and with all your soul and with all your mind. . . . [and] Love your neighbor as yourself" (Matthew 22:37-40). Don't make preserving your "rightness" the top priority. Risk grace. Put your money on grace. That's what Jesus did, even though it led him to the cross.

That is why I am so grateful the Bible is more than a list of precepts and facts that can be used or misused like political sound bites. Instead, it includes a narrative in which God is most profoundly revealed in the life and heart of Jesus. At the beginning of this book, I mentioned one of the things that started me on this quest was the fact that as an author, I saw a grave disconnect between the *character* of Jesus as revealed in the Bible and the way we Christians have been treating gay people. This disconnect was not so obvious if I only looked at the isolated "prohibitive texts," because I had been accustomed to viewing them through a traditional, unquestioning "lens" that supported our traditional response to gay people. But when I looked at Jesus' life and how he related to people and reflected on how I have been saved by grace and not by my works of righteousness (right-ness), then something terribly inconsistent began to emerge. And the inconsistencies kept coming up.

Any disconnect between the character of Jesus and how we behave as a church body or as individuals who call ourselves Christian indicates something is wrong with the story we're telling—as well as living—and that brings "dis-grace" (an absence of grace) to the Gospel.

It's always important to come back to Jesus. WWJD may seem like a trite slogan, but it has always challenged me: What *would* Jesus do? And that must be what we try to do in order to *love our gay family and friends like Jesus*!

Sacrificial love is not sentimental

My search for the reasons behind the disconnect between the character qualities of Jesus and how we as a church have treated gay people started with my daughter. It had to start there. God used the most tender place in my heart to get my attention. I was not enticed by tangled theories or a grandiose desire to jump into the latest controversy.

But I have a daughter!

All the arguments we've briefly touched on in this book are worth considering. But they are more or less background chatter that constitutes the "What about . . .?" questions you have to clean up before you can fully embrace a new perspective. None of them, however, is as important as the people we affect. That's how Jesus lived, and it was Jesus' love for my daughter, for every gay person, every marginalized person, that compelled me to reconsider my perspective and the limits I'd placed on my love. Did I love like Jesus loves?

Glenn Stanton of Focus on the Family dismisses this approach to heart change as mere sentimentality:

There is no theologian who comes to the conclusion that the Bible embraces homosexuality, that either he himself or she herself is not gay or lesbian, or have a gay or lesbian loved one. There is no theologian that I know of that makes that case and has written about it and argues about it, that has come to that conclusion solely by their honest and objective look at Scripture. There's an inherent conflict of interest that must exist in order to come to that conclusion. . . . There is a personal motivation due to my sexuality or because somebody I love very dearly, typically a family member or a child, oftentimes, has come out as same-sex attracted. They adjust their theology based on sentimentality, if you will.[2]

Is that what we're supposed to do, close our eyes to hurting people so we can be "objective" in seeking God's direction? Perhaps that kind of hard-heartedness played a part in Amber Cantorna's parents cutting her off as she described in the previous Collateral Damage story since her father was a long-time executive with Focus on the Family.

Back in Chapter 17, we discussed whether "problems looking for solutions" is a valid way God guides us, noting that many pillars of our Christian faith were established in just such a manner. That's because Christ-like love responds to real, human problems and actually looks to bring relief to hurting people, whether they are Greek widows, Gentile converts, slaves, or gay people. While Stanton impugns the very motives of anyone who loves a gay person enough to reject the status quo, should we let his criticism deter us?

Having someone accuse you of acting out of nothing more than sentimentality is a small price compared to the price Jesus paid to love us. And true Christ-like love is never sentimental! If there's any sentimentality left in us, it will get purged as the price of love goes up. "God so loved the world that he gave his one and only son" (John 3:16). It cost God, it is likely to cost me, and it could cost you as well.

---

2. Warren Cole Smith, "Glenn Stanton on loving your LGBT neighbor," World News Group, Nov. 17, 2015. http://www.worldmag.com/2015/11/glenn_stanton_on_loving_your_lgbt_neighbor/page2.

Loving your gay family and friends is risky

According to 1 Corinthians 3:10-15, if I am wrong and merely building with wood, hay, or stubble, my efforts will be burned up even though—because of my faith in Jesus—I "will be saved, but only as one escaping through the flames." The greater risk is whether I am displeasing my Lord, and I do not want to do that. On the other hand, remaining silent could displease him even more.

In the end, I have to pray, search the Scriptures and live as faithfully as I am able according to the character of Jesus those Scriptures portray . . . and then be ready to pay whatever price may come.

I no longer believe gay Christians desiring a life-long, monogamous marriage with the only person to whom they are attracted are choosing a sinful path. Rather, gays who marry are affirming the very qualities God-ordained marriage is supposed to develop in us: losing one's self-interest in sacrificial love to another, learning the virtues of grace, forgiveness, patience, fidelity, commitment, and discipline that come with the vulnerability of sharing life with another. But even if I am making a mistake in supporting my gay brothers and sisters in their honestly-held belief, even if I am making an even bigger mistake in suggesting God's grace will forgive them, did Jesus tell us anything about taking such risks?

In Matthew 25:14-30 he told the "Parable of the Talents" in which the master entrusted one servant with five talents (or bags of gold), one with two, and the third servant with one talent. And then he went on a long trip. When he returned and asked for an accounting, the one to whom he had entrusted five talents had multiplied them into ten. The one he'd given two, turned them into four. To each of them, the master said, "Well done, good and faithful servant!"

It's the commendation we all hope to hear from Jesus, our master. But as for the third servant . . .

Then the man who had received one bag of gold came. "Master," he said, "I knew that you are a hard man . . . So I was afraid and went out and hid your gold in the ground. See, here is what belongs to you." His master replied, 'You wicked, lazy servant! . . . Take the bag of gold from him and give it to the one who has ten bags. . . . And throw that worthless servant outside, into the darkness, where there will be weeping and gnashing of teeth'" (vv. 24-30).

I'm not sure I previously considered what a great risk the first two servants took, especially if this master was "a hard man." They might have been wrong in how they invested his gold and lost it all. They might have forfeited that coveted commendation, "Well done, good and faithful servant!" The master might even have been angry with them. But in the end, the servant the master threw out was the one who was afraid to take the risk.

If we're going to love like Jesus, this is what *Jesus* taught us about taking or avoiding risks!

We must throw ourselves on God's mercy, risking that his grace will cover us. Doing so reminds me of the words to Rich Mullins' song, "If I Stand." He was confident God would help him stand on the promises he'd received, but he also admitted, "And if I can't, let me fall on the grace that first brought me to You."[3]

Thankfully, we have a God who is "good, and ready to] forgive, and abundant in mercy to all those who call upon [him]" (Psalm 86:5, NKJV). Being humbly aware that we might not be right need not paralyze us. This is what "risking grace" is all about, a recognition that we cannot rely on our own righteousness (right-ness), our own intellect, our own academic degrees or scholarship, but must step out in integrity, honest belief, and faith to love like we see Jesus love.

If you are worried about risk, then count the cost that is already mounting up higher than we can imagine from the traditional approach. In our evangelical churches, our lack of love toward our gay children and brothers and sisters in Christ has driven far too many away from the church and even from the root of their faith

---

3. "If I Stand," by Rich Mullins and Steven Cudworth, © Universal Music Publishing Group.

THE COST OF RISKING GRACE

in Jesus. We can no longer shut our eyes and ears to this spiritual tragedy or sit by helplessly wringing our hands when reports leak through. We must allow our hearts to be broken like God's heart in order to be inspired by Jesus' love and life and ministry. Why he came to earth. How he related to people. Why he took on the religious theologians of his day. And what he ultimately sacrificed . . . his very life!

Accept the moral mandate

If you have a gay friend or family member, why do you think God allowed that relationship—that "complication"—to enter your life? Might it be that God considers *you* the very best person to love your gay family member or friend? What a privilege! What a mandate, a moral mandate to make a change! And for what God assigns, he will equip you and sustain you if you follow Jesus' example.

There are so many ways to volunteer for this moral task force. Show and speak love directly to gay people. Pray for them. "Come out" by acknowledging you too have a gay loved one (if he or she has already "come out"). Traditionalists and reactionaries—those who incite fear and cast shame (even those using genteel language)—capitalize on our silence by claiming *they* represent "the Christian position" or "the biblical position." Don't let such hubris go unchallenged. *You* are a Christian with hopefully a different position. By "looking unto Jesus, the author and finisher of our faith" (Hebrews 12:2, NKJV), *you* too represent a biblical position. Speak up when others malign gays. People expect younger folk to be outspoken—and sometimes dismiss them because of it. But if you are more "senior," perhaps it's time to step up and use what respect you've earned to write or speak to those in authority in your church, on radio, in your alma mater, or the Christian ministries you support. Put your money where you believe God's heart is.

We are not alone. God is on the side of love, and an increasing number of committed believers and courageous evangelical leaders are realizing that, as a church, we've gone astray and must repent for how we've treated gay people. In some cases, repenting requires asking for forgiveness, but at the very least it means changing our minds: Gay people are first of all loved by God, worthy of our care and respect, an essential part of the family of God. Within every church, we *need* gay people who don't have to hide or feel ashamed.

That's why your gay friend or family member is worth "risking grace."

Cities of Refuge

We were attending the Gay Christian Network conference January 7-10, 2016, when Neta's daily Bible reading described the "cities of refuge" God instructed Moses to set up in the Promised Land—three on the east side of the River Jordan and three on the west. Anyone accused of manslaughter could flee to those cities and live safely until the high priest died and then return to their home exempt from prosecution. (See Numbers 35:6-15.) From the sixth to the seventeenth century, many churches were legally recognized as places of asylum for anyone accused of a crime, fleeing a mob, or needing safety from someone wanting to harm them. In fact, many churches claim to be "sanctuary" for refugees, even today.

This was the twelfth annual conference of the organization Justin Lee started to support Christians who are gay. And it was truly a "city of refuge" for most of the 1,500 attendees and for many of the 20,000 people who followed the general sessions online. In fact, over 30,000 people worldwide have signed up with the GCN.

Why gay people need a city of refuge was profoundly demonstrated in the testimonies of scores of attendees as they shared at an open mike the last night of the conference. Here are a few samples.

* * * *

I GREW UP IN AN EVANGELICAL DENOMINATION where there was a lot of emphasis on intercessory prayer. But prayer can be used as a way to point at other people's sins. I'd been out as a gay guy since before high school, so almost every week someone laid hands on me and prayed that God would take away the gay and wrap me in righteousness. It happened so often, I felt like I had religious PTSD. In our first worship service here at the conference, when we began singing, "I Exalt Thee," I started to panic that someone would lay hands on me again. But almost immediately God's peace washed over me, and I realized that no one here would ever do that to me.

I GO TO A CHURCH THAT IS WELCOMING but not affirming. Gays can come to church but cannot be who they are. My minister says all gays are going to hell, and for a long time I felt like I was the only one. But last September I fully came out on my blog and discovered other gay Christians. And here at GCN I don't have to feel like a freak. However, God has called me to stay in my church because there are other gay people there, and he wants me to help advance the conversation so things won't be so hard for them. I walked into this conference with a lot of anger, but God said, "Are you done being angry with the people who have hurt you? Because I love them too." So, that's what I'm walking away with from this weekend. And I'm not tired anymore, and I don't feel angry anymore.

I GREW UP IN A MISSIONARY COMMUNITY and didn't know what gay was until middle school. I came here with internalized homophobia, but I've learned so much in the workshops I've gone to. Someone suggested I invite my parents, and there's my dad, sitting in the front row. I love him very much.

THIS IS MY SEVENTH CONFERENCE. I live in the northern woods of Wisconsin. I do not attend church anymore because when I was in a church, they gave me an ultimatum: Be in church or be gay. Since I couldn't change who I am and had to be authentic, I left and will never set foot in there again. This is my one time per year to go to church.

The number one question I've asked everyone in one way or another is, am I good enough? I asked God if I was straight, would I be good enough?

This is my first conference. My son came out two years ago. For me, one of the most profound events of the conference happened a few hours ago. I'd lost my room key, and I was sitting on a couch in the hall near my room waiting for someone to come and let me in. From another room, I overheard a most painful conversation as a girl came out to her mother over the phone. It took everything in me not to pound on the door and beg her to let me come and be her mother in that moment. But what was really needed was to come alongside her mother and help her through this. When my son came out, I found a support group with 150 moms, but every day more mothers are being added, and now there are 850 supportive moms. That's why we wear these "Free Mom Hugs" buttons.

At my Southern Baptist college, I often felt cheated out of what all the straight couples have since I couldn't dance with my girlfriend without making a huge political statement and offending hundreds of people. So last night, at the Mary Lambert concert when I got to dance with the woman I love, it was the reassurance that God has not forgotten us and that our love is truly valid and normal.

I've known I was gay from the time I was fourteen, but last year I ended up in a mental hospital after writing a suicide note and tying a noose around my neck in my closet. My past was so dark that I didn't have any hope and was thinking what it would be like to end it all. Then I found the GCN, and it has really saved my life. I feel like taking off my shoes because we are standing on holy ground.

I grew up in a Pentecostal COGIC church and then headed off to Liberty University where I went through an exorcism and was sent to an ex-gay program. It was devastating. I finally did a Google search where I found the Gay Christian Network.

I GRADUATED FROM AN EVANGELICAL COLLEGE a year and a half ago. While there, I spent three years struggling with my faith because I had such a hard time believing that God loved me. Then I went on a mission trip, and that trip opened my mind to the power of God's grace—so much so that I could believe God's grace was enough to give me the courage to come out as who I am. But I didn't feel safe at church anymore and stopped going. Then six months ago, I decided to go back because I knew there were people in the church who felt like I did, and I can't leave them there alone.

I'VE BEEN HIDING SO LONG, even from myself. But this weekend I made the decision to come out as a lesbian to my family and my church.

I'M AN ASSEMBLY OF GOD PASTOR'S SON and also an ex-gay survivor. That means I tried reparative therapy and it didn't work, but I'm still alive. I had said I would never come out to my mom. But this is the first conference where I'm returning to you finally as an out gay man, and I'm here with my mom's full blessing. In fact, she would have been here herself, but she's afraid to get on an airplane.

GOD HAS CALLED ME TO THE MINISTRY, and I now serve as a United Methodist pastor. It's a wonderful thing, and I love being a pastor. Unfortunately, my denomination is not affirming, so I've remained in the closet as I serve the three hundred people in my congregation every Sunday. I'm pretty sure most of them don't know I'm gay. But in May, I'm going to walk down the aisle and marry the man I love. I haven't told my church because I'm not fully ordained yet. I may lose my ministry, but the reason I'm sharing this is because God has reminded me why he wants me to be brave. I don't know what is going to happen for the rest of my life. I don't know if I'll ever be ordained, but I know God is here and God is with me, and that's all I need.

I'M A LUMBERJACK BY TRADE. And last year my wife came with me to the conference. I thought everything was fine between us, but then she told me she wanted a divorce, and I had to realize that the mixed orientation marriage we'd had for thirty-three years was nothing but a house of cards. So about six months ago, I decided to come out to more people and to my church. My biggest problem was to get them to believe me. Being a Paul-Bunyan-like man, it was easy to cover my gayness. But I'm out of the closet now, and I will speak with a strong voice in favor of all LGBT people. However, we've got to be sure we don't take up the same mantle of hate our detractors have worn. Love will win out. Love won out at Calvary when they drove the nails into Jesus' hands and he said, "Father forgive them, for they know not what they do."

I COME FROM A FAMILY OF TWO PASTORS. So in my family it has always been either be a lesbian or be a Christian. I didn't even know you could be a gay Christian. My own mother told me to hide it. But yesterday, one of the moms here at the conference came up to me in the hallway and said, "You look lost, can I help you?" Then she embraced me as I fell apart. God has given me hope, so much hope.

SHORTLY BEFORE LAST YEAR'S CONFERENCE, I wrote a letter to my church in which I came out. For that, I was excommunicated, but I returned to the church of my youth, which is also not a fully affirming church, but at least they don't excommunicate people. And now some other gay couples have started coming, along with some people who are allies. It's amazing to me. If you are serving Christ, he is the boss, and not necessarily the church institution. I don't have to worry about what happens in the future. That's his business.

MY JOURNEY HAS BEEN MOMENTS OF TRAUMA and moments of growth. But God is answering my prayers of twelve years ago to be there for the women who are now going through what I've gone through. I went to Liberty University where I struggled so hard to repress my lesbian orientation that I turned to alcohol. Then a pastor sexually abused me, and the people who found out were sure the sexual abuse led to me being gay, but that's not true. I was a closeted lesbian long before that. Their ideas were so confusing that I had to be away from the church for a while in order to discover God again. I thank him that I'm now seven years sober. I've finally finished my

MSW and have a new job in an agency for women with substance abuse. I even disclosed my sexual orientation before I was hired, and they had no problem with that. It was revolutionary.

I WAS A WORSHIP LEADER IN OUR CHURCH. But that ended when I came out. It's been so long, I want to sing my heart out here with the others, but I end up choking back the tears a couple verses in.

I'M A FORMER MISSIONARY AND PASTOR'S KID. One day my parents asked me if I thought I was in love with my best friend, who happened to be a girl. I told them I didn't know, but I thought so. My mother said she would rather have cancer than for me to be gay. Now I'm here with my beautiful girlfriend. One of the moms here told me to be patient with my parents because it takes time. I hope she's right.

I WAS A MUSIC LEADER IN MY AFRICAN AMERICAN CHURCH. One day, even before I actually came out, one of the leaders pulled me to the side and said, "Sister, some people are predestined to walk the Christian life, but I don't believe you are one of them." I took her cue and got out of there and drifted away from my Christian faith. But coming here is like entering a room full of unicorns. You guys aren't supposed to even exist—gay *and* Christian—but here you are. Maybe, maybe God hasn't forgotten me.

FOR YEARS I'VE BEEN AN EVANGELICAL PASTOR in a welcoming church. But I've come up here to say I'm sorry because we have not been kind. Three years ago God gave me an incredible gift when my seventeen-year-old shared with me that he is gay. It rocked my world. It changed my world, and since then I've been trying desperately to help my congregation live in the tension and listen to and treat people as people and not an issue. But religious people don't like tension, so unfortunately, the day before I came here, I had to resign my pastorate. But you have been here and have surrounded me with love and support and encouragement. Thank you for that. I long for the day when the church is no longer just "welcoming" but also affirming and loving and inclusive.

I'm a pastor's son, and when I let it be known that I liked a boy, I had a major conflict with the church. It was so painful I could no longer pray in church. I left and ended up getting into drugs, renounced my faith, and joined anything that would accept me because I couldn't accept myself. My parents confronted me and told me I was sick, my compass was broken, and I needed to see a counselor to get fixed. In fact, they sent me away. A few years later, they realized my being gay wasn't going to change. But God used it for good, and a couple of months ago, I said, "Hey God." And a couple of minutes ago, I said, "Hey Jesus." And I know he accepted me even when I couldn't accept myself.

What God has done for me here as a woman is to give me a family of fifteen hundred people, and though I thought I'd lost my mom, now I might have hundreds.

I grew up in a very conservative home. My dad was the youth pastor of our church, and my mom was the children's pastor. But I couldn't fulfill their expectations for me. A little over a year ago, I was in my room, crying myself to sleep. I was terrified that if I stopped fighting my natural orientation, I would lose my relationship with God. I was just so scared all the time. But last year at this conference, things began to change. I listened to the speakers, and my tears became tears of joy because I didn't have to fear God was rejecting me. And every day since then, God has shown me the happiness of trusting him. I came out to my family, and God has brought us closer together. My mom is even here with me this year. God has shown me that following him and being genuine can go together. I've never felt more loved by my family. I've never felt more loved by God.

For several years I was angry with myself for who I was and with God for abandoning me. But recently I've realized God hasn't abandoned me, even when I was pushing him away. He's still there for me.

Two years ago when I went home for Christmas, I had a conversation with my grandfather in which he told me he hated all gay people, and if I was a lesbian, he hated me too. I haven't seen him since, but last month he was rushed to the hospital, and a week later, he passed. I've been dealing with so much pain and guilt. In the workshop we had the other day, we were invited to pray and ask Jesus for what healing we needed. I thank God for providing this place of healing for so many people because it is so important.

I GREW UP IN WEST TEXAS where it's not easy being a gay Christian, so even though I knew I was gay, I put it on the shelf to deal with later. About five years ago when I was in my first year of seminary, I decided it was time to deal with my orientation. I thank God; his answer was the word *grace*. A week from now, I'll be preaching in a church in California, and they will be voting on whether to make me their first gay pastor. So please pray for me.

* * * *

Testimonies like these went on for two and a half hours. I've never been around so many gay people, let alone so many gay Christians. It was humbling to see how much they prized the safe place where their faith could be revived.

Though the age of the conference attendees ranged from late teens to seniors, you may have noticed that many of those who shared sounded young, having just found a safe place after painful rejections by family, college, or church. The older folks seemed more settled, many having found lasting peace in the Lord and Christian fellowship in affirming churches. But there's a reason the feelings of the young are so raw. Lesbian, gay, and bisexual youth are 4 times more likely to attempt suicide than their straight peers.[4] Those who reported high levels of family rejection during adolescence were 8.4 times more likely to have attempted suicide, 5.9 times more likely to report high levels of depression, 3.4 times more likely to use illegal drugs, and 3.4 times more likely to have engaged in unprotected sexual intercourse compared with

---

4. CDC. (2011). "Sexual Identity, Sex of Sexual Contacts, and Health-Risk Behaviors Among Students in Grades 9-12: Youth Risk Behavior Surveillance." Atlanta, GA: U.S. Department of Health and Human Services.

peers from families with no or low levels of family rejection.[5] Each episode of LGBT victimization, such as physical or verbal harassment or abuse, increases the likelihood of self-harming behavior by 2.5 times on average.[6]

Even though not every conference attendee was that wounded, far too many had gone through utter despair. These are our children, the children we've rejected, kicked out, or offered only conditional love.

Something has to change!

I'm reminded of what happened after the conversion of Cornelius and the other Gentiles with him in Acts 10:

> The apostles and the believers throughout Judea heard that the Gentiles also had received the word of God. So when Peter went up to Jerusalem, the circumcised believers criticized him and said, "You went into the house of uncircumcised men and ate with them." Starting from the beginning, Peter told them the whole story (Acts 11:1-4).

We need to tell the whole story. I join the many witnesses reporting that there are tens of thousands of gay believers who deserve our honor, respect, and full acceptance as brothers and sisters in Christ. No more rejection! No more fear! No more shame! No more conditional love! And while this host of believers is by no means confined to those who associate with the Gay Christian Network, that's a good place to start if you wish to check them out for yourself. Of course, among them you will find wounded people who are barely hanging onto their faith by their fingernails. But many others are mature, faithful followers of Jesus who have recovered their spiritual equilibrium and are bold in their witness for Christ, evangelical in their faith, and filled with the Holy Spirit

---

5. Family Acceptance Project™. (2009). "Family Rejection as a Predictor of Negative Health Outcomes in White and Latino Lesbian, Gay, and Bisexual Young Adults," *Pediatrics*. January 2009, Vol. 123(1), 346.

6. IMPACT. (2010). "Mental Health Disorders, Psychological Distress, and Suicidality in a Diverse Sample of Lesbian, Gay, Bisexual, and Transgender Youths." *American Journal of Public Health*. 100(12), 2426-32.

so that they can say with all sincerity that "Jesus is Lord" as Paul described in 1 Corinthians 12:3.

Whatever their situation, they all need "cities of refuge," and the tragedy is, they have not found that refuge in most of *our* churches and in too many of *our* homes. Let's turn that around, and as we used to say back in the day, "Extend the right hand of fellowship to these brothers and sisters." For we know, "In fact God has placed the parts of the body, *every one of them*, just as he wanted them to be. . . ." [And we must not say to any part,] "I don't need you!" (1 Corinthians 12:18, 21, emphasis added).

Annotated Bibliography

Barr, Adam T., and Ron Citlau. *Compassion Without Compromise.* Bloomington, MN: Bethany House Publishers, 2014. Its description reads: "How the Gospel Frees Us to Love Our Gay Friends Without Losing the Truth." The authors are pastors who say they regularly relate to people "struggling with homosexuality." Citlau tells his personal story of sexual abuse, same-sex and heterosexual chaos, and drug-use. In 1997, he met Jesus and experienced forgiveness, sexual purity, and finally "began to see the reordering of my sexual desires." He is now a Christian, husband, father of four boys, and pastor, yet he still admits, "I have had gay feelings for most of my life." While Citlau is no longer living in sexual chaos, the authors are careful not to promise orientation change. Instead they use phrases like, "transformed in their sexuality," focusing more on behavior and relief from compulsions. For the gay Christian who is not "struggling with homosexuality" but with the church's rejection of them, the authors don't compromise their message. They just urge more "sensitivity and winsomeness" in presenting it.

Brown, Michael L. *Can You Be Gay and Christian? Responding with Love and Truth to Questions About Homosexuality.* Lake Mary, FL: Frontline, an imprint of Charisma House, 2014. Promising to give biblical answers to "the great moral and spiritual issue of this generation," Brown poses questions. "How do we respond to gay people who tell us how much they love the Lord and experience God's power? How do we answer them when they say that the greatest law is the law of love, and that love requires us to embrace them as they are? What do we do with the argument that the Old Testament laws (such as the prohibition against homosexuality and the dietary laws) no longer apply?" Ultimately, Brown's answer is, "If you say [you are] a practicing homosexual . . . and following Jesus at the same time, I say, no. According to the scriptures, the two are mutually incompatible."

Brownson, James V. *Bible Gender Sexuality: Reframing the Church's Debate on Same-Sex Relationships.* Grand Rapids, MI: Eerdmans Publishing Company, 2013. Though academic in its approach, this book presents a biblical case in favor of allowing marriage equality. Brownson embarked on the project after his eighteen-year-old son came out as gay. He is the professor of New Testament at Western Theological Seminary, Holland, Michigan, so his work is very scholarly, and much of his book focuses on the nature and meaning of marriage in the Bible.

Cottrell, Susan. *"Mom, I'm Gay."* Louisville, KY: Westminster John Knox Press, revised and expanded edition, 2016. The book's description says, "When your child reveals that he or she is attracted to the same sex, how you respond may have a lot to do with your faith. Doesn't the Bible say that's wrong? Will we have to leave our church? Worst of all, you may wonder, 'Do I have to choose between my Christian faith and my child?' Susan Cottrell is a mom who has been there and wants you to know that loving and accepting your gay child does not mean abandoning or even compromising your faith." She is the founder of FreedHearts, a ministry for families of LGBTQ individuals.

DeYoung, Kevin. *What Does the Bible Really Teach about Homosexuality?* Wheaton, IL: Crossway, 2015. DeYoung is senior pastor at University Reformed Church in East Lansing, Michigan. He has authored or coauthored numerous well-known books such as Just Do Something and The Hole in Our Holiness, as well as the award-winning books Why We're Not Emergent and Why We Love the Church (with Ted Kluck). Homosexuality is described: "After examining key biblical passages in both the Old and New Testaments and the Bible's overarching teaching regarding sexuality, DeYoung responds to popular objections raised by Christians and non-Christians alike, making this an indispensable resource for thinking through one of the most pressing issues of our day." But DeYoung focuses on proving that homosexuality is sin with little attention to how one is to love and relate to gay people.

Gushee, David P. *Changing Our Mind.* Canton, MI: Read the Spirit Books, an imprint of David Crumm Media, LLC, 2014. As the Distinguished University Professor of Christian Ethics and Executive Director of the Center for Faith and Public Life at Mercer University, he received the Evangelical Press Association's Christian Journalism Award for 1991, 1992 and 1997 and has been a columnist for the Associated Baptist Press and Christianity Today, which awarded his book Kingdom Ethics: Following Jesus in Contemporary Context the Theology/Ethics Book of the Year award for 2004. In that book, which is a standard text in many evangelical seminaries, he presented a neo-traditional view of LGBT issues and opposed marriage equality. However, as he explains in Changing Our Mind, when his sister came out as a lesbian, he felt compelled to go back to the Scriptures for a closer look and has changed his mind to a more supportive perspective.

Harper, Brad, and Drew Harper. *Space at the Table: Conversations Between an Evangelical Theologian and His Gay Son.* Portland, OR: Zeal Books, 2016. If you love a gay family member, this book portrays in vulnerable, honest pathos the pain, misunderstandings, and hurts that transpired between a father, Brad, and his son Drew, who—because he was gay—grew up to defy the God of his father in the classic form of a Greek tragedy.

For a time, this rift destroyed their relationship and nearly killed Drew. It was only the underlying love they had for each other that finally brought reconciliation. The lifetime drama they recount back and forth is punctuated by warnings and advice to the reader—sometimes in the form of confessions—concerning the words and actions that damage gay people. All of this is good.

But over the years, Brad vacillated between admitting, "When all was said and done, there was a part of you I could never fully accept," to telling Drew, "It would be a struggle for us, but we would accept you, fully." In the end, healing came as

Brad truly did accept his son unconditionally, and that brought them back to the table together.

However, Brad never seemed able to clearly state that God accepted Drew unconditionally as a gay person. In fact, the father's insistence that while he loved his son, he had to remain true to his convictions about God's views of homosexuality, inevitably communicated God's profound disapproval. Even before Drew became sexually active, Brad sent him to reparative therapy, so it wasn't just behavior but who Drew actually was that needed "fixing." Brad never said, "Oh, so you're gay. That's great. Let's talk about how to live as a gay Christian." No, he wanted to "fix" the homosexuality, not merely influence how Drew behaved, though of course, his behavior ultimately became a big issue.

Because his dad was Drew's primary interpreter of what God thought, it's no wonder Drew considered himself "damaged and broken," filled with perpetual "self-loathing," and believed he needed to be "punished." Being unable to change the way God had made him, he was left with the inevitable choice: Deny who he knew himself to be or deny God.

Perhaps Brad agonized along the way over whether his religious convictions misrepresented God's heart, especially as revealed in the life of Jesus. But he never reports doing so. He repeatedly refers to his convictions as immutable. After all, he's a theology professor.

Would it have made a difference if from the beginning Brad had emphasized God's grace? What if the message had been as clear as: You're saved by grace alone, through faith, and not by the "works" of changing or renouncing who God made you to be? Would that have made a difference for Drew?

Who knows? There are thousands of gay Christians who maintain their faith in Jesus without needing to deny who God made them to be. But the tragedy in this story is that his father never seemed able to affirm that as an option for Drew.

Hill, Wesley. *Washed and Waiting*. Grand Rapids, MI: Zondervan, 2010. Wesley is a gay Anglican pastor who discovered at age thirteen he was interested in guys rather than girls. He grew up in a loving home, his family attending a Southern Baptist church where he accepted Christ and was baptized. He attended Wheaton College where he nervously wrote a paper on the Christian view of homosexuality. That and further study convinced him that homosexual behavior was sinful and same-sex attraction—while not sinful in itself—was the result of the fall. He is committed to being a faithful, celibate Christian, though he acknowledges his continuing same-sex attraction and longs for the deep inter-personal relationship marriage could provide even if sex plays no part.

Lee, Justin. *TORN: Rescuing the Gospel from the Gays-vs.-Christians Debate*. New York: Jericho Books, 2012. One of the most powerful books written by an evangelical (Southern Baptist) gay man who tells his story of discovering he was gay as an adolescent even though he came from a healthy Christian family, had good relationships with his parents, was not involved sexually, tried desperately for years to "not be gay," agonized in prayer that God would deliver him . . . until he finally accepted his orientation and later concluded that the Bible legitimately can be understood to allow gay marriage on the same basis as straight marriage. Nevertheless, he remains celibate, not having yet met the partner he believes God has for him. He is the founder of the Gay Christian Network, with some 30,000 members.

Marin, Andrew. *Love Is an Orientation: Elevating the Conversation with the Gay Community*. Downers Grove, IL: IVP Books, 2009. Marion works to build bridges between the LGBTQ community and conservatives through scientific research, biblical and social education, and diverse community gatherings. His book explores many of the ways we "miss" each other amid all the hot rhetoric, and he claims, "It is possible to disagree and yet still peacefully listen, learn and dialogue so that something significant can happen for the kingdom."

McDowell, Sean, and John Stonestreet. *Same-Sex Marriage*. Grand Rapids, MI: Baker Books, 2014. This makes the case for marriage being legitimate only between one man and one woman. It represents a neo-traditional perspective but endeavors to rally the readers to combat the trend toward marriage equality by providing answers to "the standard talking points for same-sex marriage."

Otto, Tim. *Oriented to Faith: Transforming the Conflict over Gay Relationships*. Eugene, OR: Cascade Books, an Imprint of Wipf and Stock Publishers, 2014. Otto is a gay evangelical pastor who grew up in a loving family on the mission field. He has not only accepted his same-sex orientation, but he has concluded the Bible allows gay marriage. However, he has remained celibate for the sake of his ministry—he ministers among a population that would not be able to understand a gay marriage. This is a very personal story of a boy who was not abused in any way, loved the Lord, but discovered in adolescence that he was looking at other guys while his friends were noticing girls. He invites readers to explore how God is at work in the world, even amidst the most difficult circumstances, redeeming and transforming the church through this difficult debate.

Paris, Jenell Williams. *The End of Sexual Identity*. Downers Grove, IL: IVP Books, 2011. Writing as an anthropologist, Paris says, "Sexual identity has become an idol in both the culture at large and in the Christian subculture. And yet concepts like 'gay' or 'straight' are relatively recent developments in human history. We let ourselves be defined by socially constructed notions of sexual identity and sexual orientation—even though these may not be the only or best ways to think about sexuality." She assesses problems with popular cultural and Christian understandings of heterosexuality and homosexuality alike.

Stanton, Glenn. *Loving My (LGBT) Neighbor: Being Friends in Grace and Truth*. Chicago: Moody Publishers, 2014. Stanton is the Director for Family Formation Studies at Focus on the Family and a research fellow at the Institute of Marriage and Family in Ottawa. He debates and lectures extensively on gender, sexuality, marriage, and parenting at universities and churches around the country. One might think he would be a harsh hard-liner, and he does stick to the "truth" as he interprets it, but his personal friendship with many gay people has given him respect and empathy for them.

Vander Wal-Gritter, Wendy. *Generous Spaciousness, Responding to Gay Christians in the Church*. Grand Rapids, MI: Brazos Press, a division of Baker Publishing Group, 2014. In the introduction she says, "Being the leader of a national organization [New Direction, part of the Exodus network in Canada] with the legacy of promoting and defending a clear and certain position (which is not only the traditional position that says sexual intimacy is reserved for marriage between one man and one woman but also the evangelical ex-gay position that says freedom and change are possible for the same-sex-attracted person), makes it particularly threatening to go to that honest and authentic place, where doubt and questions and uncertainty live, with an utterly childlike expectation that God compelled me to take, albeit with much fear and trembling on my part. And it is a journey that has allowed me and the organization I lead to emerge as a place of generous spaciousness." That compelled her to publicly ask forgiveness for herself and her ministry and ministries like it for hurting gay people. Her goal now is to encourage the church to respect different perspectives regarding homosexuality by avoiding three distractions: politics, fixating on orientation change, and preoccupation on the question of causation.

Vines, Matthew. *God and the Gay Christian*. New York: Convergent Books, 2014. Vines attended Harvard University from 2008 to 2010. He then took a leave of absence in order to research the Bible and homosexuality and work toward LGBT inclusion in the church. In March 2012, Matthew delivered a speech at a church in his hometown about the Bible and homosexuality, calling for acceptance of gay Christians and their marriage relationships. Since then, the video of the speech has been seen nearly a million times on YouTube, leading to a feature story in The New York Times. While he affirms marriage equality, he remains single and has founded the Reformation Project, a Bible-based, Christian non-profit organization that seeks to reform church teaching on sexual orientation and gender identity. He expresses an evangelical position in background and view of the Scriptures.

Wilson, Ken. *A Letter to My Congregation*. Canton, MI: Read the Spirit Books, an imprint of David Crumm Media, 2014. Described as, "An evangelical pastor's path to embracing people who are gay, lesbian, and transgender into the company of Jesus." Ken was the founding pastor of the Vineyard Church of Ann Arbor. He became concerned over how the church rejected gay people and undertook a journey of "rethinking what the fully authoritative and inspired Bible ought to be taken to mean in the life of the church today." While he deals with many scriptural passages, his insights constantly relate to real people and situations. The publication of this book was not welcomed by the Association of Vineyard Churches, and Wilson now pastors Blue Ocean Faith, an "all-people friendly" church in Ann Arbor.

Yuan, Christopher, and Angela Yuan. *Out of a Far Country*. Colorado Springs, CO: WaterBrook Press, 2014. Christopher Yuan, now an adjunct instructor at Moody Bible Institute in Chicago, discovered at a young age that he was gay. His story parallels old stereotypes concerning homosexual males—a cool and distant father, a smothering and manipulative mother, persistent rebellion and rejection of God, a lonely and socially awkward childhood (until he came out), involvement in gay clubs, the gay party circuit, gay orgies, short-term hook ups, and finally the drug scene . . . until he was infected with HIV and finally arrested for major drug trafficking. The story of his conversion to Christ and deliverance from his former life is powerful in its pathos, and there's no denying there are many gay people—as well as many straight people—who live similarly destructive and sinful lives and therefore need deliverance. However, his experience does not parallel that of many gay Christians (and non-Christians) who did not embark on such debauchery. Hence, many don't necessarily find his "solutions" germane.

Acknowledgments

Appreciation and admiration are first due to our daughter and daughter-in-law for allowing me to tell our family story. I am more convinced than ever that one should never "do theology" without paying attention to how it impacts real people. It is, after all, people for whom God gave his son, not a theory or even a principle.

For the same reason I'm indebted to all who shared your experiences for the "Collateral Damage" stories. Thanks for sitting down at our table, inviting us to yours, talking on the phone, enduring the interviews, or letting me adapt something you'd already written. You made this book real. The same goes for the scores of people at the Gay Christian Network conference who shared your testimonies, many of which I reported in the "Cities of Refuge" section.

Thank you, Neta, my life companion and lover for these last fifty years. You are the greatest in every way, including being my brainstorming partner, my challenger, encourager, and first editor.

I'm grateful to Anita Lustrea for the strong Foreword and to my endorsers, even though there was not room for all of them. Thanks to those who still have questions but found *Risking Grace* a valuable contribution to the conversation. I know I don't have all the answers.

To my prayer team—Bill D., Bill S., Charlotte, Cindy, Hilda, Jean, Janalee, Jim, Joan, Julia, Julian, Kristin, Mary, Nick, Shelly, Ted, Theda, Tim O., Tim N., and Virgil—I could not have done this without you. Whether you prayed often or occasionally, whether you challenged me or encouraged me, I needed it all. You cannot imagine the number of times God answered your prayers by guiding me to the next Scripture, the next question, the next person, the next resource so I could proceed with this journey and assignment.

Finally, much appreciation to my editor, Rogena Mitchell-Jones, and my team of proofreaders: Alison, Jayne, Jill, Laurie, and Michelle.

Want to Help
Other Families and Friends?

This book does not have the promotional muscle of a large publisher behind it, but circulation of any book is largely dependent on personal recommendations. Here are some ways you can help get the word out:

- Write a review on Amazon.com or BarnesandNoble.com.

- Mention *Risking Grace* on social media. How is it affecting you? Why?

- Review it on your personal blog. Make your review personal. Why does this matter to you? (Be sure to send people to www.riskinggrace.com for more information.)

- "Come out" yourself as an ally of a gay friend or family member. (However, don't out them if they are still in the closet.) In every group we've mentioned that our daughter is gay, other people have come up to us to share their experience—often one of feeling alone, having questions, and not knowing how to respond. There's your perfect opportunity to help them by suggesting *Risking Grace*.

- Encourage a study group to read and discuss *Risking Grace*.

- Buy a copy for a friend, a youth leader, a pastor, or a counselor.

- Give copies of *Risking Grace* to your extended family members to help them understand your love for your gay loved one.

Thanks for helping us get *Risking Grace* out there. Thanks for bringing a little peace to another family. Thanks for lifting imposed shame and fear off gay people.